MARK
TAYLOR

MARK TAYLOR

Time

to

Declare

WITH IAN HEADS

IRONBARK
Pan Macmillan Australia

First published 1999 in Ironbark by Pan Macmillan Australia Pty Limited
St Martins Tower, 31 Market Street, Sydney

Reprinted 1999

National Library of Australia.
Cataloguing-in-Publication data:

Taylor, Mark, 1964– .
Mark Taylor: time to declare

ISBN 0 330 36184 8.

1. Taylor, Mark, 1964– . 2. Cricket captains - Australia -
Biography. 3. Cricket players – Australia - Biography.
4. Cricket - Australia - Biography. I. Title.

796.358092

Typeset in 11½/15 Bembo by Midland Typesetters
Printed in Australia by McPherson's Printing Group

But sure as sure, the day will come too soon when . . . the cricketer hits a ball for the last time, bowls a ball for the last time, fields a ball for the last time, and for the last time walks home with his companions to the pavilion in the evening glow, his sweater flung across his shoulders.

Neville Cardus

Contents

Foreword

By The Hon. John Howard, MP

Mark Taylor came to the captaincy of the Australian Cricket Team in 1994 with the high demands of an expectant cricketing nation. It had been twenty years since Australia had been led by an opening batsman. Moreover, under Allan Border, and the watchful eye of the then coach Bobby Simpson, Australia had developed a strong team which enjoyed increasing success in both the Test and one-day international arenas.

From the earliest days, there could be no doubting Mark's abilities as a batsman and superb slips fieldsman. His first two Tests in 1989 against a rampant West Indies team, then at the very height of its dominance, had been encouraging. A triumphant first full series against England followed with Mark becoming the second highest Australian runs scorer in an Ashes series behind Sir Donald Bradman. Further successes with the bat at home and abroad followed so that, by the time of his appointment to the captaincy, Mark had scored centuries against each of the teams Australia encountered in Test matches. This is a feat that has been emulated by only one other Australian batsman since Australia began playing Tests against Sri Lanka in 1983.

Mark proved his leadership credentials at an early time. The agonisingly close one-wicket loss to Pakistan in 1994 heralded the start of a new era in Australian cricket. Leaving aside the one-off Test played in New Delhi against India in 1996, Australia was to lose only one other series during his tenure as captain, to India in 1998.

In his penultimate series as captain, Mark led Australia to an historic series victory on the subcontinent against Pakistan later in the same year. In between, Mark's record as captain will be long remembered—the West Indies was twice defeated, the Ashes were retained in England and South Africa was overcome at home and away. His success in leading Australia to the brink of victory in the 1996 World Cup was another highlight.

Mark deployed the resources available to him with great aplomb. While his attention to detail and analysis of opponents are well known, his ability to make bowling changes to secure wickets for Australia at crucial times and to press for the selection of players he thought would advance Australia's cause were renowned.

Similarly, the spirit and adventure with which Australia played under Mark's leadership recalled an earlier halcyon era in Australian cricket. Faced with defeat, Mark was always gracious and generous towards his victor—never churlish.

Perhaps the greatest victory for which Mark will be remembered will be the way in which he courageously responded to a lapse in personal form in the mid-1990s.

Despite the individual and team success which Mark had enjoyed up until that time, his 21 Test innings in 1995–97 without scoring 50 proved to be testing days for Mark personally and for Australian cricket as a whole. The incredible support which Mark received during this period from his wife Judi, parents and team-mates has been well documented. The fact that he emerged from the slump with a century against the 'old enemy' and went on to equal Sir Donald Bradman's highest score by an Australian batsman in Test cricket is an outstanding testimony, not only to his fighting qualities and inner strength, but to the confidence shown in him by the Australian selectors and the Australian public.

At the conclusion of the recent Ashes series, the Chairman of the Australian Cricket Board, Denis Rogers, spoke of the debt of gratitude which Australian cricket owed to Mark Taylor. Much is, of course, already on the public record. I am, nevertheless, looking forward very much to reading the autobiography to gain fresh insights into, and perspectives on, one who over the past decade has contributed enormously to the strength and stability of Australian cricket and been responsible for giving pleasure to so many who cherish the game around the world.

One of the greatest honours and pleasures, for me as Prime Minister has been the opportunity to not only follow the fortunes of the Australian Cricket Team, but to spend time with its members, particularly under the captaincy of Mark Taylor. Mark has been a credit to himself, his family, his team and his country and a worthy recipient of Australian of the Year in 1999. He has been a great representative of cricket and of Australia. I will always admire his strength of character, his ability to meet every challenge and to always maintain a love of the game in the greatest traditions of Australian cricket.

John Howard

MARKS *on* MARK

Neil Marks

*I*n smaller ways and larger, Neil Marks has been part of Mark Taylor's life in cricket ever since the day young Taylor first put a toe in the water of Sydney grade cricket, with Northern District back in 1981. Neil Marks played first-grade with Northern District at fifteen and Sheffield Shield for NSW at twenty. In his first game for the Blues he scored 180 not out and was acclaimed as a rising star of exceptional talent. But at twenty-two he was diagnosed as having a serious heart condition, requiring a series of operations in Australia and the USA. The health problem put an end to his ambitions in big-time cricket but he continued to play with his old club for many years and his involvement with the game has never ceased. Raconteur, author and all-round good fellow, Marks has been an official with Northern District for countless seasons and a NSW Sheffield Shield selector for the last thirteen years. Over the seasons since 1981 he has been friend, supporter, ally and advisor to Mark Taylor. Suggestions that he has been Taylor's 'mentor' are deflected by Marks, however. 'We're mates. We talk,' he says. Here he recalls aspects of the young man who came to Northern District's practice one day in the early spring of 1981—and went on to become one of Australia's most successful batsmen and famous captains.

I knew the kid was coming to a practice session. A bloke from Lindfield Shires Club had rung me, as Northern District's chairman of selectors. So he duly turned up. 'Mr Marks,' said the nuggetty youngster, 'I'm Mark Taylor and I was told to come and see you.' 'Okay, yes . . . that's fine,' I said, a little distracted. 'Now, you go over there and do some slips fielding, Matt.' 'It's *Mark*,' he said. 'Mark Taylor.'

I watched him for a while, catching and hitting some catches . . . that sort of thing—and something my father used to say came back to me. My dad, who had played interstate cricket and rugby, had a theory that he could see a kid take one catch or kick one ball—and he could tell whether the youngster was a good cricketer or good footballer. Not necessarily whether he was a potential champion, but whether he could play. He would say: 'I've only got to see them do it once.' I thought of that as I watched Mark Taylor for the first time that day. Austie Hughes, Northern District's president, sidled up as the practice session wore on. 'What do you think?' he asked. 'I think he's the best we've had since my brother Lynn,' I replied. Although they were both left-handers, Mark and Lynn in fact were pretty much different in style. Lynn, who played State cricket, was a thrashing player, but a fairly classical one too—though even back then Mark looked a better defensive player. His feet moved correctly.

When his turn in the nets came, I made sure that a good bowling attack was in operation against him. He looked just great. Already the little tuck around the corner was a highly refined weapon in his armament. I like to call it his 'bread-and-butter shot' or his 'Sunday suit shot'. Throughout his career, when that shot was functioning well, Mark Taylor was going well. I had a debate with News Limited journo Robert 'Crash' Craddock about it only a while ago. Crash's theory was that when Mark was hitting his cover drive well, then he was in touch. I agreed—to an extent. When he was middling his cover drive well, his toe or the ball of his foot would make first contact with the ground, his head well over the ball.

When he wasn't hitting the cover drive well, his heel would hit the ground first, his head back from the ball. But to me it was always that little bread-and-butter shot that was the key. When he wasn't hitting the ball well, it would be cracking him on the thigh pad.

Tayls has never been a classical player. But he's not what you'd call an ugly player either. When he's hitting it in the meat he can be darned good to watch. Take that square shot he plays where he pulls away and smashes it backward of point. In the main, toughness and grit were his staples. Even from those early days he never had the grace of a Sobers or an O'Neill, or a Mark Waugh or a Greenidge, but hell he could bat.

At the Districts, we picked him in third grade. I said right from the start that he was good enough for firsts—but that we should leave him for a time in thirds. I said the same thing the next year when he went up to firsts. My father Alec many years ago had become the youngest player ever picked for first-grade cricket in Sydney. He was thirteen years and ten months. In his first five innings he got five ducks. But they stuck with him—and at seventeen he was playing for NSW. That sort of faith in talent has always been important to me.

The story of Mark's late arrival for a third-grade match at Asquith on a day that I happened to be captain has been often repeated. I certainly tore strips off him that day. It hadn't been his fault; his sister Tina was having a driving lesson and Judy Taylor had got lost heading to the ground. Mark never offered that as an excuse. He just copped it sweet as I ripped into him. As he told me in later days: 'I thought you were a big-headed bastard!'

His progress through the ranks at Northern District had an absolute air of inevitability about it. He was a mature kid—without being adult, if you know what I mean. He related to kids of his age, but he was mature in the way he conducted himself, and he was always a great listener and watcher. Over the seasons, he never changed in that way. I've had numerous conversations with him in which he'd nod, and listen. Sometimes I'd walk away thinking: 'I don't reckon that got through.' But inevitably he'd be back later with a precise view on why he agreed with me, or one on why he didn't. He captained his teams that way. He never captained by consensus, but he would always listen to others and then make his decision. At Northern District he was never over-coached; identifying the talent that lived in him, we let him go.

But he always listened. After his first season in Sheffield Shield I spoke to him one day about what he had achieved, and what might lie ahead. 'Things will change now that you are a second-yearer,' I told him. 'By now they will have identified you as a predominantly leg-side player, and seen how much success that has brought you. The cricket telegraph is pretty efficient, I can tell you. Next year they'll bowl off-stump, or outside off-stump, to you.' Typical of Mark, he was ahead of me. 'That's interesting,' he said. 'I noticed that in the last couple of games this year.'

Of course, that's the way it is in cricket. Graeme Pollock was a great off-side player, so opposing attacks would bowl on his legs. Greg Chappell was the reverse—a great leg-side player, who was targeted on the off. After a season or so it doesn't matter. If the batsman is good enough, he adapts—and becomes a complete cricketer. And that's the way it became with Mark Taylor.

In one of my first seasons as a NSW selector, Mark's third in the NSW Shield team, he very nearly got dropped. He struggled for runs that year as opposing bowlers peppered what they figured might be a weakness—if he had one—on or outside off-stump. There were times when his continuing place in the team was precarious, as the claim of this player or that was pushed forward at selection meetings. For reasons of propriety I won't take you inside those meetings. Suffice to say that I feel comfortable and pleased in hindsight that my own support for Mark never wavered.

One of the great unknown stories about his career concerns the Sheffield Shield final of 1989–90. On the day before the final (against Queensland), skipper Geoff 'Henry' Lawson was struggling with a shoulder injury. There were five NSW selectors—the State has always had a panel of that size—and we ordered a fitness trial for the captain. He went okay, and the physio rated him about 85 to 90 per cent fit. 'He should get by,' we were told. That was pretty much where it stood—that the captain was less than fully fit, but we had a very good attack, and Henry, even at 85 per cent, was as good as most of the others.

However, I was uneasy with it—and especially so as I was the selector nominated to turn up early the next day when the match began to keep an eye on things. I said to Steve 'Brute' Bernard, the chairman of selectors: 'What if he's not okay in the morning? What then—if I'm the only selector here at ten o'clock tomorrow, and there's a problem?' Brute re-assured me: 'He's fit . . . it'll be okay.' I persevered: 'Mate, it's not good enough,' I said. 'I want the selectors called together.'

Now, for some stupid reason the NSW team had never had a vice-captain—and had almost always announced the 12th man the day before the game. It was tradition. 'We've always done it that way,' people would say. I said to Brute: 'I want us to pick a vice-captain in case Henry is a problem in the morning . . . and I'm the only one here.' The rest of the selectors were still hanging around the nets, so he summoned them back, and told them of my request. The others were Mark Clews, Terry Davies and Alan Campbell.

So Steve asked us who we thought should captain the team if Henry proved not to be fit. There were two nominations, Mark Taylor and Steve Waugh, though Mark Waugh's name came up too. A fair amount of discussion ensued, to-ing and fro-ing. Nevertheless, the good news was that whoever got the guernsey would do the job as well as anybody in the country. The Blues were blessed. I remember commenting: 'I reckon the Poms would swap us.' The voting was close, but eventually Mark got the nod.

The next morning Henry was bowling in the nets and he was struggling. I pulled him aside. 'Mate, you're having trouble, aren't you?' I asked. 'Don't worry,' he said. 'I'm about 75 to 80 per cent.'

'How about 55 to 60—and even that's optimistic?' I said. 'Yeah, I'm not too good,' he admitted. 'Well, Henry,' I told him, 'you can't play— we just can't go into a Shield final with ten players.' Henry was understandably disappointed. 'We'll get through,' he insisted. 'I'll go out and captain the side and see how I feel.' The coach, Steve 'Stumper' Rixon, was with me and he agreed with my view. To everyone's disappointment, the captain would have to step down.

The decision was made alongside the nets at SCG No. 2, twenty minutes or so before the game started. And so it was that Mark Taylor became captain of NSW. It was one of those seminal moments in sport. No doubt the decision had some—although not total—influence on the Australian selectors further down the track when the time came to announce Allan Border's replacement as Australian captain. I think 'Tugger' Waugh probably felt then that he was a bit unlucky—that he should have been captain. Personally, I thought (and think) the world of Steve Waugh. I have known him since he was a boy, when I was chairman of selectors for the State schoolboys. He is now, and will be, a great Australian captain. That day we voted as individuals for the player we believed was best for the job. With the benefit of hindsight, we would have been right whichever way we went.

History has long since recorded the punchline to that match— Mark's century in each innings, and a comprehensive win for NSW. To this day I feel sorry for Henry. He deserved to captain his state to a Shield victory.

At the end of the second day, with NSW hugely in the ascendancy, I had an interesting conversation with the new skipper. With stumps drawn and NSW beautifully placed—360 to Queensland's first innings of 103—I was in the bar with a group of pals, including Mark's parents Tony and Judy. Tayls popped in for a quick drink, wearing tracksuit and socks. 'What are you going to do?' I asked him. 'I'm undecided,' he answered. I replied: 'You can't lose if you bat now. The only way you could lose would be if they knocked you over for hardly any, then had a target to chase on the last day with someone like Border there. Don't put yourself in a position of having to bat last under pressure, even if you've only got to get 100.'

When the teams had come off the field that day I had spoken to Stumper Rixon—whose view was roughly: 'Put 'em in again while we've got them on the floor; let's put the slipper in!'—and Steve Waugh. Waugh's inclination was for NSW to bat again—and put the match right out of Queensland's reach. I said to Mark: 'Have a yarn to Tugger and see what he thinks.' 'Do you know what he thinks?' he asked me. 'Yeah, he wants to bat,' I said. 'That's interesting,' said Mark thoughtfully. Well, of course NSW did bat again, got about a million in front and Queensland couldn't have won if it had gone for ten weeks. NSW won the Shield.

I'm sure the experience gained then by a rookie State captain influenced decisions he made later on when he became Australian captain. Now and then Mark chose for Australia to bat again when the temptation was there to send the other mob back in. Occasionally he was criticised for it. Perhaps it stuck in his mind, although he became an increasingly creative captain—so shrewd at summing up the different situations that cricket can throw at you and then coming up with the right decision.

I have no doubt that Ross Turner, the Northern District captain, was a considerable influence on the way Mark approached captaincy. I know that Mark rates Turner above any other captain he played under. He learnt a lot from him, in the areas of man-management and being cool and clear-headed in tight situations. Ross was a wonderful captain and a great bloke. These days he holds an important job with the ICC at Lord's.

At Northern District we identified Mark's leadership qualities and added value to his CV for what lay ahead by making him club captain for a time after Ross Turner retired. That wasn't so easy— with Mark balancing State and then Test duties—but we felt it important that he had the experience of captaining at the grass roots, adding a tick alongside his name for what we believed might lie ahead.

A deep-down quality that stands out with Mark Taylor is that he's never really changed, even while growing magnificently in the roles handed to him. He always was, and is, unafraid of facing the truth, unworried by facing people who may disagree with him. He never backed away from admitting any actual personal faults or mistakes, or being prepared to discuss with others any faults they may have thought they saw in him. He always seemed able to see the viewpoint of others. At the start and the finish he was always just one of the boys. The give-and-take of the dressing room with its banter and ribbing never worried him. He would give as much as he took.

Stepping back occasionally into grade cricket was maybe one of the harder things he had to do. He often said to me that he would get more nervous playing a club game than he would, say, a Shield game—because in grade cricket he was on a hiding to nothing. If he scored 100, he was a bully—if he failed, then people would say he wasn't trying.

As Australia's captain he shouldered comfortably the range of responsibilities that come with that job. If there was a problem with an individual player, he would confront it and deal with it. He brought his teams together in the old-fashioned way for a beer or two at the bar to talk about things at the end of the day's play. And everyone would be included. As captain on NSW tours he would inevitably room himself with one of the newer, younger blokes, or maybe with a player who was struggling a bit. Letting the side break into cliques or sticking with some of his senior mates was never his way as captain.

I felt for him hugely during the bad time in 1997 when the runs had dried up. My wife Kay and I had a fair bit to do with Judi at that time. We used to provide what encouragement we could, get her over to home with the kids occasionally, play some cricket on the tennis court with the boys. It was a tough time, probably for Judi as much as Mark.

Batting slumps are a reality of almost all careers. Sometimes things seem so bad that you could have John the Baptist coaching you, and it wouldn't help. You just have to bat your way out of it. Somehow. And sometimes it can change in an instant, on a single moment. The catch Dean Jones dropped off Mark in the game before the First Test at Edgbaston was a great example of that. It was the turning point. If the catch had stuck . . . who knows what would have happened in the Mark Taylor story?

Percy (Peter) Philpott, the former NSW leg-spinner, tells the story of dropping a chance off Bill Lawry in a Shield match in Sydney, just before they picked a Test team in 1961. Lawry was on single figures at the time. He went on to make 266, got picked to tour England, won the Test on the Lord's ridge—and finished up captain of Australia. Ian Redpath was dropped on 0 in his first Test by Colin Bland of South Africa, one of the greatest fieldsman of all time, and went on to make 97. There are lots of stories in sport like that.

I rate Mark's Edgbaston century as his greatest moment in cricket. Because of the pressure, the circumstances, everything that surrounded it, I place it above his 334. However, because of the emotion and the endurance factor and most of all the glorious coincidence, I accept that the innings in Pakistan will live longer in cricket's consciousness.

I honestly can't think of anything that compares with Mark's Edgbaston 100 when it comes to 'last throws of the dice' in Australian sport. Perhaps Kieren Perkins' back-from-the-dead win in the Atlanta 1500-metre freestyle gets closest. But even that is in the shadow of what Mark achieved, I believe. The weight on his shoulders was staggering. He carried the pressure and expectation of a nation in this one last chance. And he scored 100. It was Australian icon stuff.

I watched almost every ball on television, and it was a fine innings, notwithstanding the struggle at times on a wicket that wasn't easy. That aspect—the fact of a testing wicket—has probably faded into the background in the glow of the achievement itself.

The certainty was that England would have chosen to bowl if they had won the toss.

But Mark knew he had to bat first, to give Warnie the last crack at the Poms on a wicket that would take spin, late. As an opening bat under huge pressure it would have been so easy for him to take the easier road and send England in. On a juicy wicket, such a decision would have been easy to justify. I will just say this: there is no Australian captain who opened the batting who would have batted on that wicket. I think it was the bravest decision Mark Taylor ever made. To choose to bat under those circumstances was a tribute to his courage and to his quality as a 'team' captain. I watched every ball of the innings and when he reached his 100 early that Aussie morning both Kay and I were dabbing our eyes.

The 334 in Peshawar was at the other end of the spectrum, confirmation that batting in cricket is a pretty weird and wonderful thing. For those two memorable days Tayls could do no wrong. On such special (and rare) days, even if a chance is given you can bet London to a brick that it will be put down. When a batsman is in control as Mark was against the Pakistani attack in that innings, he could put some linseed on his old fella and still get runs. There was no way he was going to get out.

And the decision to call it off at 334? Undoubtedly correct. There were some rotten comments made—such as one that Mark's decision to declare was akin to Sid Barnes's famous sacrifice of his wicket on the same score as Bradman in the Second Test against England in 1946, linking his name forever to the Don's. The implication was that Mark decided not to bat on for the same reason, so that he would always be remembered with Bradman. Taylor declared because Australia had 599 runs and because you shouldn't bat into the third day for whatever reasons—although Bob Simpson did just that when he scored 311 at Old Trafford, Manchester back in the 1960s.

To declare was absolutely right—the team didn't need any more runs. Let's look at the Taylor view: what if he had batted on—and got out for 340, short of Lara and Hutton and Sobers? He would have looked a bit of a goose then. And what would he have done then? Closed the innings as soon as he got out? No, he pulled the right rein—absolutely.

The 334 undoubtedly added extraordinary late lustre to the Taylor cricket career. Already popular and widely acclaimed for his ability, his sportsmanship and his leadership, he became overnight a national celebrity of remarkable appeal. Just an example: in early 1999 I picked him up one day at his home in a cab, heading for the airport. We were off interstate for a Shield game. The cabbie was Chinese, a friendly fellow with not too much English. 'Where you go?' he asked me. 'I'm just heading off to watch a game of cricket,' I replied. 'Ooooh, you have a good life,' he said with a big smile. Anyhow, we rounded the captain up and said goodbye to Judi and the boys at Ryde. We were in the back seat yarning away and I could see the driver eyeing Mark off in the mirror. Finally, he couldn't hold back: 'Your face . . . I know your face . . . I know your face,' he said. 'Well, I do catch a lot of cabs,' said Mark. As I paid the tab at the airport, the penny dropped. 'Taylor!' the cabbie exclaimed. 'Is that Taylor?' I told him it was. 'He's a good-looking man,' said the cabbie. 'Good looking!' I replied. 'You're obviously talking about the wrong Taylor!'

The story is a small one, but illustrates a large truth. Since the 334 Mark has become amazingly recognisable. No way can he walk from the lobby to the bar of the hotel. Invariably someone will stop him. 'Excuse me, Mark, I'm over here from Essex, could you just sign this? That was a great innings you played . . .' A few paces further on he's stopped again. 'Mark—could you just sign this for my son?' Funny that. It is always for 'my son'.

In recent years as Australia's captain he has always been in considerable demand. Television guarantees that for our major sportsmen and women. But for Mark, the magic number of 334 has taken it to another level. I must say that with his easy-going nature he handles it all remarkably well, although it must become wearing at times.

Another thing that speaks for Mark is that he has stuck with his friends. When he had a barbeque at home after Australia had won the Frank Worrell Trophy in 1995, the guests comprised old school friends, a few old uni mates and team-mates from Northern District. Ordinary people. Apart from Mark it was a celebrity-free zone. In no way has he ever stepped away from his roots, or his old friends. Yet being Australian cricket captain and possessing one of the most identifiable faces in the land can be very useful at times, too. Steve Small was telling me of an occasion in Canberra a year or two back when he and Mark had a few beers with Ricky Stuart and Mal Meninga—Ricky being in the same management stable as Mark and a good pal of his. When going-home time finally arrived—pretty late in the evening, by all accounts—Steve and Mark were out the front of the pub, looking for a cab. There were none to be seen—only a police car. 'Excuse me, mate,' Steve said to the constable at the wheel. 'Can you tell me where we might get a cab? I've got to get the NSW captain back to his hotel because we've got a big match tomorrow.' 'You mean Mark Taylor?' asked the walloper. 'Yeah,' said Steve. 'Hop in,' said the cop—and off they went, siren blaring.

Mark and I are just mates. That's the way I like to look at it. Sometimes it gets a bit embarrassing when I am listed as being his 'mentor' or whatever. The fact is that the young bloke I first saw at Northern District's practice all those seasons ago is a much more important person than me, and now knows more about the game than I ever did. I'm not his great advisor or anything like that. We're mates. We talk. I'm proud of Tayls and Judi—and cricket should be too.

334 *and* ALL THAT

It was two o'clock in the morning before I knew finally what I had to do, and would do. Room 428, Pearl Continental Hotel, Peshawar—17 October 1998. I had woken from a brief and fitful sleep to the hum of the big city which sits just below the Khyber Pass, in Pakistan's north. What a day it had been . . . and what a time in my life.

For six sessions, two full days, on a beautifully tailored wicket at the Arbab Niaz Stadium, I had batted and battled on—in draining thirty-degree heat partnered by soaking humidity. Rarely before in my life in cricket had I been so much in what Greg Norman has called the 'zone'. For one of the few times in long seasons spent trying to master the art of batting, I was in total, absolute control, sure there was no way they could ever stop me. I had scored 100, 200, 300 against Pakistan's attack. Somehow—in no way contrived—at the end of the second day, I had arrived by unbelievable chance at a magical figure spoken of in tones of hushed reverence in Australian cricket, 334—the score achieved by Donald Bradman in his legendary innings against England at Headingley on 11 and 12 July 1930. The Australian Test record. There was just one difference between Sir Donald and me. I was not out. Back home, as

I later found out, openline callers to radio stations were urging me to 'bat on' . . . to the world record—Brian Lara's 375 for the West Indies against England in Antigua in 1994.

Between Lara and me were five players: Walter Hammond 336 not out (England v New Zealand, 1932–33), Hanif Mohammad 337 (Pakistan v West Indies, 1957–58), Sanath Jayasuriya 340 (Sri Lanka v India, 1997–98), Len Hutton 364 (England v Australia, 1938) and Gary Sobers 365 not out (West Indies v Pakistan, 1957–58).

I woke with a start, my mind crystal clear. Getting to sleep at all hadn't been easy, even though I was physically exhausted; my mind was buzzing. Now, at 2 a.m., one thought dominated—an old philosophy which had underpinned Australian cricket throughout the seasons of my experience. During my years in the Test team we had lived by the 600-run philosophy—simply, that if we could make 600 runs in a game, we were going to win a hell of a lot more cricket matches than we lost. The score on the board at Arbab Niaz Stadium stood at Australia 4–599. We were there, we had arrived at our team goal. I knew then there was only one choice: to declare and set about trying to win the match. On one hand, cricket is a game about individual achievement and goals. But much more than that it is a team game—and in my time as Australia's captain I had tried always to put the team first, eventually taking the individual out of any equation. I would declare. The decision made, I slept a dreamless sleep, waking in fair shape despite the long haul of the innings, and a shorter-than-usual sleep.

Since those two days in Peshawar—days which I will never forget—I have fielded literally hundreds of enquiries about my 334. Because of the magical link to Bradman there seems a greater fascination about the fine details of this innings than about any other individual event in my career. Contemplating the journey involved in telling the story of my life in the pages of this book, it seemed the ideal place to take block. Many people rate my century at Edgbaston in the second innings of the First Test in 1997 as the finest achievement of the Taylor career in cricket. Under the pressures that weighed me down at that time, perhaps it was. It enabled me to go on and achieve the other things that my career brought me—including the 334. But people love a fairy tale. And Peshawar's monumental coincidence was one of those, in the sporting context. So, to begin the journey of *Time to Declare*, I will take you back to Pakistan and try to reconstruct from the happy jumble of my mind over those days just how it was. And why it turned out the way it did.

THE INNINGS—DAY 1

The news greeting us in Peshawar was that Wasim Akram, Pakistan's main strike bowler, was out of the Test with injury. The home side would go in with two young guns, Shoaib Akhtar and Mohammad Zahid, as their opening bowlers. We won the toss and batted on a wicket that suggested some early life, but gave promise of settling into a beautiful batting strip. The two young Pakistani quicks were fired-up, and early on bowled as fast as anyone I faced in my career (my suspicions were confirmed with the release of figures in May 1999 which showed Akhtar at 155 kilometres per hour as the fastest bowler in the world and Zahid at 149 km/h equal third-fastest). My first runs came from a nick off the inside edge which shot past the off-stump, beat the keeper and raced down for four. It was the only boundary in the first hour. 'Slats' (Michael Slater) went early— and we were 1–16.

It was a hostile opening. Ahktar and Zahid were not as *good* as I have faced, obviously lacking the experience of the likes of Akram, Younis, Walsh or Ambrose. But, by gee, they were quick that morning . . . really steaming in.

I was dropped in the covers at 18, off Mushtaq Ahmed, a back-foot drive off a loose delivery which I hit in the air. It was a tough one-handed chance to Saeed Anwar which went to ground. Not long afterwards, Saeed dropped a sitter at bat-pad. Mushtaq Ahmed deceived me a little in flight and as I lunged forward the ball took pad, then bat and headed straight for Anwar's belly-button. He dropped it. I was 25 at the time. The next chance I gave was on 325 . . .

From that point on, I was in the 'zone'. It was a slow first day, the light gloomy and bad enough to cost us an hour of play. At stumps, I was 112 not out and we were 1–224 with Justin Langer on 97.

THE INNINGS—DAY 2

We started half an hour early the next day, and on Fridays in Pakistan the first session is traditionally two and a half hours anyway, for reasons to do with religion. This was the toughest period of my innings, the heat oppressive and wearing through the three hours. But I was okay; I have never been the world's fittest-looking bloke, but I have always been pretty strong and able to stay out there for a long time. I had worked hard on my fitness before Pakistan, with physical fitness guru Kevin Chevell, and in the last forty minutes or so of that session I picked up fifty runs, with the heat affecting the bowlers more than it was me. Through a long stay like that I drink plenty of water and Powerade. The elongated session provided an important opportunity. In the three hours before lunch I managed to score exactly 100 runs, taking me to 212 at the break. 'Well done, Tubs,' said the guys when I came back in. 'You know the best thing about it?' I said. 'That's 100 in a session!' 'Turn it up,' they said. 'Bullshit—that was three hours!' 'It doesn't matter,' I said. 'It was a session, between the start of play and lunch.' It's a joke (and a point of contention) that has carried on ever since. I reckon I've got 'em on a technicality.

At lunch, I sat next to Michael Slater. As old Wagga boys and opening partners, we're pretty good mates, and he was really pumped up for me. Before that day we had shared equal top scores in first-class cricket—219. 'You're going to get past me today, Tubs,' he said. 'Bloody oath I am,' I replied. 'I'm going to give you something to chase.' I was feeling great—a little weary, but still sharp.

Not long after lunch I nudged a ball away for a single, and was on 220. I looked up at Slats in the stand, and gave him a little wave. I then went on ... and on, feeling pretty much invincible. In the short session between lunch and tea I pushed on to about 260.

I had by now reached a point where I honestly didn't believe I could get out. It just wasn't a factor. It was bloody amazing. I had spent a whole six months of my career in 1997 trying to work out how I was going to get a run. Any run I got then was pretty much unintended. I'd try to play a straight drive—and it would finish up at backward square leg. But in Peshawar, I knew exactly where they were going. Even though they had five men on the boundary I could still picture myself hitting a four—and would do it.

It was only when I got to the 290s that I started to get a little nervous. All of a sudden I was a bit weary and overwhelmed. More mentally tired than anything else, I suppose. And the thought of a Test 300 is a somewhat sobering one for any batsman. Three hundred is the equivalent of a bowler getting 10-for in a game.

At 298, I got a short one from Mushtaq Ahmed. The moment was a perfect example of how well I was hitting them. They had fieldsmen at deep long-off, deep point and at cover. I knew if I could beat the bloke at cover, I would get two at least. I hit it exactly where I wanted to hit it, centimetres past the diving cover fieldsman and down to the fence for four.

From there to stumps it was a bit of a haze as batting milestones kept looming up ahead of me. I got past Bob Cowper's 307 scored at the MCG in 1965–66 and at 310 I got a thickish edge off Aamir Sohail to jump to 312, passing Bob Simpson's 311 scored against England at Manchester in 1964. The boys on the balcony cheered; Simmo, of course, had been the team coach in 1986–96. Ricky Ponting, who was batting with me at the time asked me between overs: 'What was that about?' I told him that I was now past

Simmo's score. 'Who's left?' he asked. 'Well, the only person I can think of from an Australian point of view is Sir Donald Bradman with his 334,' I told him. We were twenty minutes from the end of the day's play. 'I plan to be here at stumps,' I told Ricky. I almost wasn't. On 325, Aamir Sohail, bowling left-arm round the wicket, speared one down the leg side and I got a feather touch which went straight into Moin Khan's gloves—and straight out again.

So it was that nearing the end of the long, hot day, I was on 334, with two balls to play. Aamir Sohail was firing his left-armers in with three blokes on the leg side to cut off the singles—a mid-on, mid-wicket and a sort of short fine leg—with a couple out in the deep. He bowled me two identical balls pitched on leg stump and I played almost identical shots—to Ijaz Ahmed at mid-wicket. I tried to hit the last ball of the day a bit finer, to squeeze it past him, but he had moved a little squarer and there was no chance. So 334 it was and I was delighted as I walked off, bone-weary and three kilos lighter than I had been at the start of it. I honestly didn't have a clue what I was going to do at that stage.

THE MYTHS

That afternoon at Arbab Niaz Stadium, I didn't plan to finish the day on 334. I didn't do what Sid Barnes did—deliberately sacrificing his wicket when on the same score as Bradman, 234, in the same innings against England in Sydney in 1946–47. I didn't think about throwing my wicket away or set out deliberately not to take runs off the last over. All that sort of speculation is wrong.

People have said and written subsequently that it was a noble gesture for me to declare on the same score as Sir Donald. I appreciate those thoughts—and yes, of course I am proud of the wonderful historical co-incidence of that day, and that score. Yet, you know, all of it was fate. I ended up on the same score by chance, then finally decided to declare—as I'm sure Sir Donald Bradman would have done—for the good of the team.

THE AFTERMATH

The room at stumps was a blur of congratulations and talk of the 334 and the Bradman factor. It wasn't long at all though before the conversation moved on to: 'What are we going to do tomorrow?' I can reveal now that my initial thought was to bat on for twenty minutes or so. That had nothing to do with breaking records or getting past the Don or anything like that. It was to do with making it difficult for their openers—so that they wouldn't be padded up and comfortable and ready to start the day but would have to field for a while, then hustle on the pads. The more I thought about it, the more I came to the conclusion that the idea wasn't so brilliant. You know as an opener that if the other mob has batted for two days then you're going to be out there quick smart anyway— whether straightaway or half an hour into the day. It wouldn't make much difference. So I filed that one away.

Steve Waugh and I had a quiet talk in the room. 'What are you going to do?' he asked me. 'To be perfectly bloody honest, I don't know,' I told my vice-captain. We ran through the options. 'If you declare now, on Bradman's score, you know that's something that will be remembered for a long time,' said Steve. 'And if you bat on and get the record, on your own, that will be remembered too.' Someone else chipped in: 'What about the world record?'

I killed any talk of that straightaway. I knew that if I went after Lara's record, we could kiss the Test match goodbye. I needed 42 more runs—so I would have been looking at a minimum of an hour's batting, probably more. They would have taken the third new ball, and chances are the over rate would have been slow. Say they had bowled twelve overs in the hour and I had made 25 or 30 more runs to get to 360. What to do then? Declare? Or keep going? No, the world record was gone right away. It wasn't a rea- sonable option, for me or the team. Perhaps if it had been the last Test of the series and we had been up 1–0, the temptation would have been there to push on and grind the Pakistanis out of the match, and the series. In Test two at Peshawar, it wasn't. There were only two choices: to declare, or to go out for a twenty-minute bash the next morning to unsettle their start to the day.

BACK HOME

I was leg-weary and worn out and a session with our trainer-masseur Dave Misson was one of the first items on my agenda back at the hotel. I was on a bench with Dave really ripping in when our coach Geoff Marsh came in. 'Who have you spoken to?' he said. 'Have you talked to your Mum and Dad and Jude?' Swamp was really fired up about the sort of day we had had. 'No, I'll ring them back later,' I answered. 'No, c'mon . . . let's ring them now,' said Swamp, brandishing his ACB charge card. 'Put it on my room bill.'

So the coach made the calls for me while I was still on the massage table, handing me the phone in each case after he had had something of a chat himself . . .

TONY TAYLOR: *Judy and I saw Mark get his century on the first day—on a giant screen at Wentworthville Leagues Club in western Sydney. We were on our way back home from Canberra and I said to Jude, 'Let's call into Wenty Leagues and have some dinner and save having to cook when we get home.' We walked in and there was this huge screen—with Mark in the middle of it! It was about 2– 160, and he was on 80 or close to it. So we stayed at the club until he got his 100, then headed off home, absolutely delighted. For us, that was that. We haven't got Foxtel.*

It wasn't until the next night that we learned the full extent of Mark's extraordinary innings—when we switched on the TV to watch the evening news. I then sat up until 1.30 a.m. to watch the Channel 9 replay. As I was getting into bed about ten minutes later the phone rang. 'Hello, I'm looking for Mark Taylor,' said a strange voice. 'I haven't been able to find him all day.' I thought, who is this idiot?

I could hear the sound of laughter in the background. 'It's Geoff

Marsh, Tone,' the voice said finally. 'I've got a bloke here who wants to talk to you.' It was Mark, apparently stretched out on a physio table after his marathon innings. After all the congratulations and what have you, I said to him: 'Well . . . 334 . . . what are you going to do now?' And Mark said—and I agreed with him—that the main thing was the game had to be won. He said: '599 is plenty. If we are good enough, we'll win from here.' I believe he had pretty-well made his decision by then. But he told me: 'The boys want me to go on. They reckon I should forget about the game, go for the 375, beat Lara.'

I still think he made the right call. He considered the options, then made up his mind. It was the way Mark operated as captain.

I asked my wife Judi what she thought about the decision I faced. 'I've got no idea,' she said. 'What do you think?' I asked my mum and dad the same question. 'Gee, we don't know,' they said. 'Well, that's not much bloody help,' I said from my horizontal position. They were right of course: the decision rested entirely in my hands, based on the circumstances in faraway Peshawar. The funny thing is that the fact it was *me* on 334 made it a bit easier. If it had been, say, Steve Waugh or Michael Slater, it would have been an even harder call. That would have been tougher—to say to another player: 'Look, I'm sorry. But I'm going to have to cut you short of a world record.' Obviously no-one in cricket would ever get dirty about circumstances surrounding an innings of 334. But I suppose if a captain did declare on someone on that score there might be some lingering regrets in the years ahead. But that was not how I ever played the game—and it was not the way I wanted the Australian side to play the game either. The team was my only focus and in the end the decision was not so tough at all.

My sister Lisa was one who thought the other way. After she had spoken to Mum and Dad as I lay on the rubbing table she sent me a fax: 'I keep hearing about you declaring. You've got to be kidding.

You go out there tomorrow and bat you bloody idiot!' Lisa had no doubts what I should do.

I didn't get to talk to my sons, William and Jack, the hour being way past their bedtime. But Judi told me how William, then aged six, had stuck it out until I got to about 290, lying on the lounge in front of the TV. He saw the list of highest Australian scores come up, starting with Graham Yallop's 268 against Pakistan in Melbourne in 1983–84 and with Sir Donald Bradman on the top with 334.

She told me later how William had come in at first light the next morning to find out what had gone on. 'What do you reckon Dad got?' she asked him. '335,' said William. 'No, 334—but not out,' said Jude. 'Oh,' he said, 'he's got to get one more, he's got to make 335.'

TONY TAYLOR (fax to Mark): *You never scored 300 in the back-yard, even against my bowling!*

THE MORNING

Early the next day, I broke a personal rule which I applied during the years of my captaincy—not to conduct media interviews during a match, apart from the regulation post-stumps press conferences. Beside the pool at the Pearl Continental I did a 'live' cross back to Australia, talking to David Hookes on Foxtel. Heading inside for breakfast after the interview, I took a phone call in the hotel foyer. It was Prime Minister John Howard. 'What are you going to do?' he asked me. 'I'm going to pull up stumps,' I told him. 'Yes, I thought you might,' he said.

There were a few calls from some Pakistani journos and some from India, too. Was I going to bat on? they asked. I answered honestly—and then wondered later in the light of all the bribery and betting allegations whether that had been the right thing to do. Maybe there was some wagering going on whether I would chase the record or not? Some of them seemed quite shocked that

I was leaning towards a declaration—a reaction that reflected the different attitudes towards the game in different places. Then, and in calls and questions I answered from local journos at the end of the third day's play, there was quite apparent disbelief that with 334 on the board and the bowling at your mercy, you wouldn't go on and get the world record. There was a feeling that the record belonged to the West Indies through Lara and if there had been a chance to grab it back for Pakistan (or India), it would have been taken with both hands. In Australian cricket we look at things a bit differently. As I told the media at the time: 'It is the only chance I will ever get to be compared with Sir Donald Bradman and that will do me.'

During the 1999 series between Australia and the West Indies I noted a sign held up in the grandstand at Trinidad one day. It read: *Happy Fifth Birthday 375*. It was the fifth anniversary to the day of Brian Lara's record-breaking innings. Could you imagine that happening in Australia? I don't think so. But it's very much how people on the subcontinent and in the West Indies feel about world records in cricket, and the prestige of having them in your country.

That we went for the win in Peshawar and didn't achieve it leaves me with no element of regret today about the decision I made at 2 o'clock that morning. I owed it to the team and to Australian cricket for us to try to win the match, and not to place a personal laurel higher than that. So I declared—and they set about giving us long hours of hard work on a benevolent wicket, amassing 9–580, with Saeed Anwar making 126 and Ijaz Ahmed 155. When we batted for a second time, I found myself immediately back in the 'zone', hitting them better from the start than I had in the first innings.

I was back in record territory. Much was made of the fact that Graham Gooch's Test record aggregate of 456 (against India at Lord's in 1990, when he scored 333 and 123) was realistically within reach. To beat it, I needed an innings of 123. And when I got to 90 without a hitch, it was looking a genuine chance. I was hitting them so well that maybe I was a bit over-confident and at 92, with Aamir Sohail bowling his left-arm tweak, I tried to pull a ball of full length, caught an inside edge and dragged it back onto my stumps. So I ended up 31 short of the record—after the only record-chasing I did in the match, the chance of a result being by then long since out of the question. I had, perhaps, never hit the ball better in my career. Peter Roebuck wrote a piece in the *Sydney Morning Herald* at the end of the fourth day, when I was 13 not out, in which he suggested he had never seen my feet move so well in my entire career. I was seeing the ball like a watermelon. Middling every one, whether on front foot or back. Loose and confident, I went for them after lunch and got to my 92 pretty quickly, before Aamir Sohail sneaked that one past me. Sohail, the Pakistan skipper, did a fair bit of bowling that last day and managed to keep his sense of humour. Now and then he would make a passing comment— 'Mark, I think we've seen enough now' . . . 'Can't you save some for the next game?'—things like that. So it was a draw . . . in this match that I will surely never forget.

It wasn't until I got home at the end of the series that the impact my 334 had obviously made back there really hit home. Peter Roebuck had written at the time, 'As Taylor batted on and on, one could sense a whole nation at one with him', and it seemed as if it was true. The reaction of both the public and the media to me at this late stage of my cricketing career was extraordinary. I suddenly had to come to terms with the sort of attention that Shane Warne had to live with all the time. I was the same bloke, but it seemed that people now saw me in a new light.

Out of the avalanche of attention came a single, wonderful item—a letter from Sir Donald Bradman, with whom I now shared a new bond. We had both captained Australia at cricket, and now, amazingly, we had both made 334 runs in a Test innings. His had come from 430 balls in 378 minutes, mine from 564 balls in 720 minutes. He hit forty-six fours, I hit thirty-two. I hit one six, he hit none—but I probably lost the battle there too; Sir Donald always reckoned that you should keep the ball on the ground. Then came his letter, replying to an earlier one of mine concerning the Bradman Museum:

16 November 1998

Dear Mark,

I thank you very much for your kind letter of Nov. 11th.

It is very kind of you to be associated with that small photographic effort which will substantially benefit the Bradman Museum and I am of course happy to lend my signature to the project.

Might I take this opportunity of congratulating you on your wonderful batting performance overseas during which you equalled my 334. It was extremely generous of you to declare when our scores were level—a most sportsmanlike act—when you could have so easily gone on to take the record for yourself.

Your recognition of the interests of the team will never be forgotten.

May I wish you personally and the team the best of luck in the forthcoming Tests.

Yours sincerely,
Don Bradman

I will always treasure that letter, and, just as much, the memory of my visit to Sir Donald's home the following December, the story of which is told in Appendix 2 to this book on my life in cricket. For me all of it was culmination, of a cricket journey begun long ago. And far away . . .

Chapter 1

OPENING UP

I was born at the beginning of a cricket season, at a place of which I remember very little. Leeton, a town in the heartland of the rice country of south-western New South Wales designed by Walter Burley Griffin, was my first home—a whistle stop along the way for my mother Judith and father Tony as the family roamed the State in the 1960s, with Dad climbing the ladder as a valuer with the Rural Bank. I opened my innings there, in Leeton hospital, on 27 October 1964. My elder sister Tina was born in Goulburn, and my other sister Lisa arrived later, in Mildura, during the brief time we were living in the small town of Dareton, just across the border in New South Wales. A few years ago I went back on a speaking engagement to Leeton, surrounded by its irrigation crops of rice, peaches, citrus fruit and grapes. It was an eerie experience—to return to the place where you had been born and lived for almost two years . . . and to remember not one thing of it.

Dad was from the Hunter Valley, from Scone, and so was his father, who was the district's first health inspector. My grandmother on my father's side was a direct descendent of Captain John Piper, the richest man in the colony at one stage in Sydney's early days— and after whom Point Piper was named. Way back on the Taylor side too was a female ancestor who had sixteen children and lived to eighty-nine. There are Taylor links all the way to the First Fleet.

As Dad has said to me now and then, we come from pretty tough stock. My Mum, Judith Nield, was a Sydney girl, born in Crown Street Hospital, and from the suburb of Beverly Hills. They met when they worked in the old headquarters of the Rural Bank, at 51 Martin Place, Sydney. Mum was assistant librarian, Dad a cadet valuer who had first joined the bank in Maitland. When he was transferred in his job to Goulburn the pair of them decided they couldn't live apart—so he came back to Sydney and they got married. And the travelling began, back to Goulburn and then on from there.

TONY TAYLOR: *When we made the move after I had been transferred from Goulburn to our next stop, Leeton, it was a January long weekend. Stinking hot. We had no car—and we took the train with Tina, Mark's older sister, in her basket. We had to change trains at Junee. We were sitting there on Junee station in the late afternoon, facing the setting sun and looking out on the big wheat silos and one or two houses, and just open country. As Judy told me later, she was thinking: 'My God, this is Junee and it's supposed to be fairly big. Whatever will Leeton be like?' I looked across at her and the tears were trickling down her cheeks. So, I said to her: 'C'mon Jude, we'll go for a walk.' We headed out of the station on the eastern side, and straightaway we saw shops. Junee township happens to be on that side of the railway station. Our spirits lifted immediately. Soon afterwards we were on our way to Leeton.*

Leaving a succession of towns was never easy. We lived in friendly places in which it was easy to get deeply entrenched, very quickly. To leave Leeton, Dareton, West Wyalong, Wagga—each one of them—was a wrench. Country towns tend to grab you with both hands.

JUDY TAYLOR: *In small towns you get very close to people. You need people more. And I believe you meet them in deeper ways than is often the case in a big city.*

I was born at Leeton in October 1964, and christened Mark Anthony Taylor. I lived the first twenty months of my life in Leeton, in a cottage owned by the Rural Bank, in Church Street. Number 53.

JUDY TAYLOR: *He was a boisterous baby—very boisterous. It's hard for me to believe that the livewire baby he was then is the calm person of today. He just about wrecked a playpen—by shaking it. He just didn't want to be in there. I never took him to church. I'd take the girls occasionally . . . but Mark was a monster.*

TONY TAYLOR: *Mark was one hell of an eater—he used to eat like a horse. He probably hasn't changed too much in that regard.*

Unremembered by me, but very much a part of family lore, is the fact that at about twelve months I gave Mum and Dad one big scare. There was a night when I stopped breathing, and they thought they had lost me . . .

JUDY TAYLOR: *That was an awful time. As a baby, Mark used to get croup, and while we were living down in those irrigation areas he seemed especially susceptible to it. 'In those days they used to drive around the streets spraying indiscriminately for fruit fly,' Tony often reminds me.*

One day at home in Leeton Mark had what seemed like an asthma attack, and started coughing up blood. We panicked, naturally enough, and rushed him to the doctor. 'I don't think it's croup,' he said after examining him. 'I think he's got something stuck in his windpipe.' They x-rayed him, found nothing, and the doctor finally said, 'We'd better send him off to Wagga.'

At Wagga Hospital we gave them permission to use a bronchoscope on him, to suck out any foreign object that might be stuck in his throat. It turned out to be the worst thing possible—causing his vocal chords and windpipe to swell to the extent that he couldn't breathe. We honestly thought we were going to lose him. He was placed in an oxygen tent with tubes inserted to keep him breathing. Mark was in the oxygen tent for ten days or so, and they fed him through a tube in his leg. They had his hands strapped so that he couldn't touch his face.

It was a terribly difficult time. We were living in Leeton and didn't have enough money to stay over in Wagga. We'd ring at various times through every day and make the trip over every two or three days. Finally he recovered enough to come home. But they pumped him full of penicillin and for a good couple of years after that I was really terrified for him.

If there was some bug going around he'd pick it up and couldn't seem to shake it off. He'd pick up colds at the drop of a hat. There was another night when he had breathing problems and we had to put him in overnight at Dareton Hospital. Thankfully, like a lot of little kids, he grew out of it.

It's Dareton, not Leeton, which gives me my first life-memory. But it's no more than a fragment—of a thick grapevine reaching across the carport at our house. Somewhere way back, too, is a memory of Mum taking me to preschool one day, and me crying my eyes out. I don't think I ever went back, although I did subsequently begin kindergarten there. I was eighteen months old when we shifted to Dareton—four when we moved on again, to West Wyalong, 500 kilometres due west of Sydney.

JUDY TAYLOR: *Mark has always had an amazing memory. Yes, there was a grapevine at the house at Dareton, across a huge trellis in the backyard. Dareton has a desert climate and the grapevine provided beautiful shade. Lisa was born in Dareton and I used to put her under the grapevine where there'd be a little cooling breeze, and some shade. She's like Mark, with an amazing memory—and can actually remember little things about Dareton. We lived in some nice towns. We were lucky. Dareton was a really pleasant surprise. It only had about 900 people. In the bank they used to laugh at anyone who got sent to Dareton. You must have blotted your copybook, they would say. But it's a dear little place—right at the junction of the Murray and the Darling Rivers, and only about thirteen kilometres from Mildura.*

TONY TAYLOR: *I'll never forget the day I started work in Dareton. It was 6 June 1966—6-6-66. Easy to remember. It was there that Mark started to want to play cricket. I remember ordering him off the field during an Apexians' cricket day. He wanted to stand in the middle of the pitch. He was three or four.*

It is from my early days as a little fella at West Wyalong that the mist begins to lift on the beginning of my journey through life . . . and cricket. It was there that I started school, at West Wyalong Primary where Mrs Putton was the headmistress and Ms Scammel my first teacher. The school playground at West Wyalong Primary back then was just a bare stretch of ground covered with little red rocks. School Rule No. 1 was that the one thing you didn't do was throw the little red rocks. However, there came a certain day when I got pinged for doing exactly that. My punishment was to spend every lunchtime and recess break for a week standing outside Mrs Putton's office.

This was a pretty shocking thing for a five- or six-year-old, and I couldn't bring myself to tell Mum and Dad about it. It worried me so much that late in the week I threw a sickie. 'What's wrong?' Mum asked. 'I just don't want to go to school today,' I told her. Mum couldn't figure it out; she knew how much I liked going to school. Finally Tina spilled the beans: 'Mark's outside Mrs Putton's office every recess and lunchtime for throwing rocks and that's why he doesn't want to go.'

In the latter part of our stay in West Wyalong, we lived at 42 Kurrajong Street—right opposite the municipal pool, which was handy considering that West Wyalong summers can be bloody hot. I received a letter only this year from a youngster who now lives in our old house. 'Is it really true that you used to live at No. 42?' he asked. 'Yes, it's true,' I wrote in reply.

Our first house was near the railway line, and we used to cross the tracks and climb down to a creek where we caught tadpoles. On the back porch rested one of the first presents I can remember getting as a kid—a bug-catcher. It just happened that my little sister Lisa was terrified of butterflies. On one summer's afternoon I went out and caught a whole jarful of butterflies in my new bug-catcher. I waited until Lisa went to the toilet, then I opened the door, stuck the jar in with the lid off . . . and bolted. I can still picture her on the throne there, screaming. Lisa hasn't forgiven me for that.

Life was good and simple there, the way it is in country towns. With my mates Ben McCormack and Tony Pilon I'd ride my bike, and just knock around . . . unworried by anything, happy to be alive. We always found things to do.

Sport started for me in West Wyalong . . . but in my own memory, not cricket, not competition cricket, anyway. I played some rugby league with a tiny tots side—and fairly hopelessly. I think I was too small. There were a lot of bigger blokes and they pretty much hogged the ball. I was forever being pushed in to play dummy-half, or left hanging out on the wing. I didn't play league again until I went to university, and only then because I got bloody-well conned into it.

TONY TAYLOR: *We bought a plastic cricket bat and ball for Mark in West Wyalong. His first bat. Out in the backyard at Kurrajong Street we had a pitch, with an ever-deepening hole where the batsman stood. He was always a left-hander with the bat—a left-hander in fact in anything that required two hands, like an axe or a shovel . . . except golf.*

There are things from West Wyalong days that stick in my mind. I remember the floodwaters backing up in Kurrajong Street, which was sort of dish-shaped, and I have a clear impression that there seemed

19

to be as many hotels in the town as there were houses, West Wyalong being a sort of half-way stop along the road from Sydney to Adelaide. And I remember, too, a day when we packed up our things at 42 Kurrajong Street, said goodbye to our friends, and moved on.

It was in Wagga Wagga, a city of nearly 60 000 people nestled beneath rolling hills on the banks of the Murrumbidgee River, that cricket really came into my life. We shifted there in 1971, Dad taking on a senior valuer's role with the bank, covering a huge area of territory. Mum and Dad settled the girls and me in to South Wagga Primary School, and all of us started down the track of our new lives.

Not counting the backyard games down a worn strip in West Wyalong, I 'officially' began playing cricket in Wagga, at the age of eight. Dad kick-started that for me. Being new in the town and a bit unsure, I wasn't going to enrol in the school team, even though I was beginning to really like the game. Mum and Dad never pushed any of us kids hard with sport—they preferred to let things take their course. But I think my old man knew that I really wanted to play and just didn't have the ticker to put my name down. So he took me back up to the school, and enrolled me. And that's how it began.

TONY TAYLOR: *We were a bit worried about Mark when we first moved to Wagga from West Wyalong. It took him quite a while to settle in. He seemed to want to stay home a lot, didn't really want to mix. We tried a few things—Police Boys' Club and so on—to help him settle. But in the end Mark pretty much found his own way, and that's always been his way. He started playing soccer—then he was right from there. We were proud of the way the kids handled the moves. It wasn't too easy at times.*

JUDY TAYLOR: *We've been pretty lucky. Mark always got on well with his two sisters—and they're real close now. I think the fact of the moves we had to make drew them all closer together. Mark was a bit of a peacemaker with the girls. Tony thinks that's where his diplomatic skills come from.*

People have asked me over the years where my love of cricket came from, and from which Taylor ancestor I got my ability to play the game. Well, I can't really answer those questions. My mother and father both liked sport, and I'm sure that Dad would tell you he had a *great* sporting background, if you cared to ask. Mum was a darned good tennis player and Dad played some cricket at school—batting number ten and first-change bowler, he says—and was a good tennis player and golfer. But cricket of a serious nature? Dad tells me of a cousin of his, Ray Taylor, who was a more than useful opening bowler in the Hunter Valley a few years back. That seems to be about it. But then, with cricket I don't think it's necessarily the way it is with racehorses—that it's handed on in the genes.

I'm sure that in the story of Mark Taylor and cricket, the way things were, and are, in the town of Wagga played their part. People have pondered the long list of outstanding sportspeople to come from this town in the heart of the Riverina—Michael Slater, Geoff Lawson, Tony Roche, Greg Hubbard, Scobie Breasley, Kim Horne (Robinson), Diane Jenkyn, Paul Hawke, Wayne Carey, Paul Kelly, Peter Sterling, the Mortimer brothers, Steve Martin, Eric Weissel, Greg Brentnall, Beresford Ellwood, Jim Lenehan, Ken McMullen, Steve Elkington (he was there for a few years) and all the rest—and concluded there must be something special in the Murrumbidgee water! My own theory is that Wagga is just the right size—the perfect mix of town and country. It's big enough to have all the facilities for a rich sporting life and small enough to have that country way about it in which people almost by necessity get involved in sport—because if they don't they're left behind in the life of the town. The range of sports and the choice they offer are amazing. Michael Slater, for example, loved his hockey before cricket became his sporting life. It had, and has, all the amenities of a city, without being so big that you get lost. Its position helps too—the fact that it's roughly halfway between Sydney and Melbourne. Over the years there have been any number of blokes who played Aussie Rules on a Saturday and rugby league on Sundays.

In Wagga, the sporting mix is just about dead right, and there are other keen sporting towns within comfortable reach—Griffiths, Leeton, Junee, Cootamundra and so on. Any weekend of the year the playing fields of Wagga are full of people doing their thing. So it's not for nothing that it's increasingly known as 'the city of good sports'.

TONY TAYLOR: *He made South Wagga Primary Under-9s Australian Rules side and I bought him a new pair of boots. He was picked in the back pocket and an early training run coincided with a sex education lecture at school. I had to operate to get the boots off him.*

I was thinking after the lecture: Now, I'm going to get all the questions. As we walked up to the car, he said: 'Dad?' 'Yes son,' I replied, taking a deep breath. 'Does a back pocket punch or mark?' We talked football all the way home.

We lived in a rented house in Bolton Street, in our early days in Wagga, then shifted up to Mt Austin—16 Fraser Street, the first house we owned. It used to be the last house in the street. Not any more.

My earliest cricket—with the school and with the Lake Albert Club which I joined—was played on a variety of wickets. I played school cricket on grass mown just a little bit shorter than the surrounds, real rough turf wickets. I played on concrete with matting over the top, and on bouncy malthoid and in the yard at home. And I played, and played, and played . . .

TONY TAYLOR: *I can remember quite a number of times when I was umpire at both ends, and scorer. Now and then I had to give a decision on a run-out at the other end, which was always interesting.*

Mark argued with me more than once on a decision. As we say, he has never been out in his life. I remember, too, occasions when we turned up late at matches. We might have been shopping or something after dropping him off at the game. We always knew whether he had scored some runs or not. Just the look on his face . . . We didn't have to ask.

As captain of Australia he became renowned as a gracious loser. And he was. But he'd be burning inside—plotting the opposition's downfall next time.

JUDY TAYLOR: *In those days he was not a good loser. Tony reckons 'he's not a good loser now, but nobody knows it!' Even if that's so, he hides it. He dresses it very well. I liked what someone said recently in the paper—that he'd smile at you while turning off the support system for English cricket. I thought that described him very, very well. He's always had an amazing competitive spirit. I remember that as a three-year-old we took him on holidays to Adelaide. And we kept this elderly man amused for ages because the kids, he and Tina, wanted to race. From Mark it was: 'C'mon mum, I'll beat Tina.' He was sixteen months younger, so we'd give him a bit of a start and she would clear off and beat him every time. And he would do his block. Absolutely do his block. He'd throw himself down on the ground . . . just* hated *losing. And we'd say: Okay, you can start from* here *this time. And Tina would win again—and he'd throw himself down again. And this old chap was watching, and laughing his head off. There was a repeat performance over several afternoons, and the man started to come back to watch the show. Mark was a very determined little boy—he'd never give up.*

Every kid in my class at school had one of those Polyarmour bats. They weren't too cheap, costing around fifty bucks or so, but the thing about them was that if your bat got chipped, you could get a repair kit to fix it up. Later I had an old Gray Nicholls, although I'm not sure now where that came from. But as the seasons went past, what I really wanted was one of the ST. PETER Master bats that Rodney Marsh and Tony Greig used in the World Series. One day I went along with my old man to a sports store in Wagga. The bat I wanted was $104. 'Okay, you can have that for your birthday, provided you save half the money,' Dad said to me.

In the weeks that followed I worked flat out doing odd jobs and gradually scraping together the dollars I needed. On my thirteenth birthday I got my ST. PETER bat, although there were still another two agonising weeks to wait. We left it at the shop for the bloke to roll it and prepare it. When I finally got it—and with a new pair of gloves—it was fantastic. It was my first senior bat—and I wish I still had it.

TONY TAYLOR: *The bat was all he ever wanted. But I remember he took it to school to try it out—and it got damaged. It hadn't been rolled properly. That nearly killed him. He came home and he was quite distraught. The bat had been badly marked by being hit with a six-stitcher, caught right on the corner of the bottom edge.*

The great thing about the house in Fraser Street was that it had a carport with a concrete floor. When we shifted the car out into the street, it was like an indoor cricket centre. And that's what it became. Bowling was down the driveway, and Dad did his fair share of that. Batting there, I learned an important lesson—to keep the ball down.

TONY TAYLOR: *I think the marks are still on the garage wall at our first place in Bolton Street, behind where we'd set the stumps up. There'd be endless cricket, with me bowling much of the time. Occasionally he'd get the huffs and walk off . . . head into the house and watch TV for a while. But he never took the pads off. After a while he'd come back to me. 'Have you got a bit of time, Dad? Can you come out and throw a few at me?' And we'd start all over again. It was never-ending cricket—until the football season came around.*

I'm sure every young cricketer in Australia then—and probably now—had heard the story of Don Bradman and the water tank. Every cricketer I knew in Wagga performed variations of that—got out a stump or bat and bounced a golf ball against something. I sure did. I also practised my catching with a garbage-tin lid or a little wooden stool we had in the house. The trick was to get the ball to clip the edge of the lid or the stool as it bounced back from the wall. A lot of times it would miss—but every now and then one would nick it, and that was the one you had to catch. I have no doubt that early drill in Wagga helped my reflexes, and my catching later on. It taught me patience, too—the knowledge that only one in ten or so would come off.

TONY TAYLOR: *Rod Pilon, our butcher in West Wyalong and a great friend, was probably the first to predict that Mark would play for Australia. He was over in Wagga one day, watching Mark and the other kids at Lake Albert. Most of the kids were swiping and swishing, but Mark was there, playing dead straight, which he always did—almost from as soon as he picked up a bat. 'That boy will play for Australia,' said Rod.*

JUDY TAYLOR: *I have a clear memory of one of the first games he played in Wagga. It might have been the first. I know they were trying to get the boys into the right positions on the field. I haven't got a clue who the opposition was. Anyhow, a batsman on the other side hit the first bowled ball—and the whole of the team took off after the ball. It was one of the funniest things I've ever seen.*

From early backyard games in West Wyalong, I was always a 'leftie' when it came to batting. In the overall picture though, I'm pretty much two-handed. I bowl right-handed, throw right-handed and play golf right-handed. In that regard I'm pretty much the same as Tony, my father. The only reason we both finished up as right-handed golfers, however, was that there were only right-handed clubs around and, well, no-one seemed to play left-handed back then—apart from Bob Charles, who won a British Open. Swinging a golf club left-handed in fact feels pretty comfortable to me, and I reckon I could play that way. But if I try to bat right-handed, it feels terrible.

ALLAN BORDER, 'This is Your Life', 1998: *Mark has been a tremendous ambassador for cricket. But Mark Taylor the golfer is an absolute shocker. He swears and carries on and does all the worst possible things a golfer can do. He is a club thrower. I remember playing with him one time in India and he was carrying on like a good sort—how he always gets the worst lie, how lucky I am, etc, etc. Next hole he teed up. Now, he's got this bit of a nancy-boy swing and it was the usual result. He donged it on the top of the clubhead and it went about twenty yards. Here we go . . . Mt Vesuvius. He went to throw his club after the ball—but hung on a bit too long and it went whooshing into the air, and over a big high fence. It was an interesting sight—to see the Australian captain clambering over a five-metre fence to try and get his hired club back.*

My favourite cricketer in my early days was Rod Marsh. I felt a bond with 'Bacchus'—the fact that he was a left-hander. And I also liked the fact that he was what we kids used to call a 'bash artist', which I wasn't. In fact, I turned out the exact opposite of that. But I really liked the way that Marsh swung from the hip as a batsman. Kepler Wessels and Allan Border—'AB'—were other favourites. All the lefties.

One day Dougie Walters brought a coaching clinic to Wagga. At the end of it they were to pick half a dozen kids to come to Sydney for two weeks of coaching at a clinic at Cranbrook School. The outcome was one of the early disappointments of my life as a cricketer. I reckoned I was one of the best cricketers in the district—but I didn't get picked. I was bloody disappointed . . . it really hurt. It was only later that I realised just how tough a job that is—to roll into some town, watch a bunch of kids you've never seen before for a couple of hours and then try and pick the best of them.

JUDY TAYLOR: *He was terribly disappointed. But life went on and we thought, 'Oh well, maybe he's not meant to be a cricketer.'*

In the late 1970s a World Series Cricket (WSC) country touring team—'The Cavaliers'—came to town, featuring the likes of Ian Chappell and Clive Rice. It was the only time I recall ever collecting autographs. The members of the team signed a bat to help raise money for junior cricket in Wagga, and it was my job to go around the ground selling raffle tickets.

It's fair to say that in Wagga sport dominated my life. I can't remember too much else outside the pattern of going to school, coming home and watching a few cartoons on the TV—then heading out to play whatever game happened to be in season. At school the conversation was endlessly about sport—your last game of cricket or footy, or the next. In an early winter season down there I took on soccer with the Tolland Wolves, and was pretty fair at that, and made the Wagga rep side. I played until I was ten or eleven. But around the time I befriended Paul Hawke I was getting a bit tired of soccer, and he said to me: 'Come and play Aussie Rules.' Paul made that game his sporting life, with Collingwood and the Swans. He was a terrific player, and I loved the game too. Really loved it. I played a couple of seasons with Wagga Tigers when I was twelve and thirteen and kept going with the game as a centre or ruck rover when we shifted to Sydney. My old man will tell you that for quite a time in my life he thought I was going to make it as an Aussie Rules player, rather than as a cricketer. In Sydney I even had a couple of trial goes for a place with the Swans. I was playing with Pennant Hills, but each time the talent scout came to see me in action they were pretty shocking games and I failed to shine. In fact they were two of the worst games I ever played. It just wasn't meant to be—I wasn't going to be an Aussie

Rules player. But when by necessity cricket finally took over in Sydney, I was sad. I loved my footy, and the likes of Hudson, Matthews and Jesaulenko were my heroes.

In Wagga there was never any problem playing the two seasons, and I did it with relish, switching over to footy—soccer, then Rules—the instant the cricket whites were put away. In between there was half-court and full-court tennis . . . and marbles. Marbles was big at South Wagga Primary. Every day you'd head into uncertainty—never knowing if you were going to lose the favourite in your bag. That was like losing an arm, except there was always the chance you'd win it back next day. I played a lot of marbles.

As a kid, cricket came easily to me—and from pretty early on I found I was able to bat for a long time. I wonder now about the kids who didn't do that, who might have been late developers, but were ultimately lost to the game. We didn't have Kanga Cricket back then, which I think has been just great in providing opportunity for more young fellas to enjoy the game. However, the balance must always be there—to avoid holding back the good player and give him opportunities to fulfil his potential higher up the ladder. Anyway, before long I made my first big breakthrough.

DAILY ADVERTISER, Wagga, 13 November 1978:

WEATHER DID NOT DAMPEN MARK TAYLOR'S BIG DAY

A young star emerged out of the rain-sodden third series of Wagga Cricket Association on Saturday. He is Lake Albert's Mark Taylor, who scored a century in Juniors on Saturday morning and 68 in third grade in the afternoon.

Taylor made 116 against Leagues in Juniors as his team's score of one for 182. Taylor's 68 against Leagues Club third grade helped the team to four for 142.

I guess I'll never forget that—my first 100. It was down at Bolton Park, one of the big open grounds of Wagga, containing three or four near full-sized cricket fields. Before the game the kids would go around and put out the flags to mark the boundary. With 180 runs in a single day, my dreams were happy ones that November night. And I sure slept well.

Third grade was as high as I went as a youngster in Wagga, although I was in the town's Under-14 rep side in the Bell Shield.

There are a couple of things that stick in my mind about that 100 at Bolton Park. One of them is that Geoff 'Henry' Lawson was there, being back in town for a few days to see his folks. The second thing is that I was out when I was on 80, or thought I was. I was run out by a metre or two and was walking off when Bernie O'Connor, one of the umpires, called me back. 'You're not out,' he said. 'Why not?' I asked, knowing that I had been. 'The keeper knocked the bails off before he had the ball,' said Bernie. 'You're not out.' Recalling that game some years later, Geoff Lawson wrote about me in the *Sydney Morning Herald*: 'He was a tubby little fellow, even back then.' Well, at least I made some impression on him.

That day, and always, I was an opening batsman. I'm not exactly sure why. It was just the way I started out—and twenty years after Saturday mornings at Bolton Park I was still walking out first through the gate.

In the classroom, I was no genius, but I guess you'd say a pretty solid student. I had good teachers at South Wagga Primary, and they live on in my mind: Mrs Walker (second grade), I really liked her; Lex Bittar, the principal, a man who was strong on discipline but a really nice bloke with it; Mary Millard, who became Mary Murphy (fourth grade), who coached my two sisters in softball. I helped out with the coaching one year just for something else to do. I enjoyed my school years. From South Wagga Primary, I went for Years 7 and 8 to Mt Austin High, Geoff Lawson's alma mater. I became captain of South Wagga Primary, as I did at Chatswood High some years later.

When I think back to Wagga, I think back to a couple of blokes in particular. Both of them, sadly, are dead. Derek Rogers was a good cricketer and bloody good Aussie Rules player, a good sportsman who was a fine coach of kids. He certainly helped me. Derek was killed one evening in a head-on collision as he came home to Wagga from a football game. It was a great tragedy for the town. Bernie O'Connor was the coach who helped and influenced me most, and was a good mate. He looked after the junior side at Lake Albert. Bernie loved his cricket—he was an umpire and a coach, and a fan. He became headmaster at Yerong Creek Primary School. But cancer cut Bernie down in 1994, when he was only 40. It was so cruel. There is no doubt it was these sorts of blokes who lit the flame in me, Bernie particularly. It really knocked me around when he died.

JUDY TAYLOR: *It was Bernie O'Connor who told us that he was quite convinced Mark would go somewhere with his cricket. When we came to Sydney he gave us a letter. 'Mark will want to play cricket—give this to one of the guys where you put him in,' he said. The letter outlined Bernie's belief that Mark had great potential.*

I struggled with all sorts of emotions when we left Wagga, in 1978. Dad had gone as far as he could go as a valuer there and when a chance to step up to a spot on the bank's Rural Assistance Board came up, he accepted. We had been in Wagga seven years then. And when you're fourteen and loving the life you lead, the prospect of such change is not easy to accept. When I look back on it, I don't think any of us really wanted to go.

We had, however, been neatly conditioned to Sydney life by the regular Christmas holidays we took at Bondi. Each year of our stay in Wagga we'd book one of the flats owned by the State Bank, in a solid old building above the bank premises in Campbell Parade, Bondi. Right across from the beach. Every day would be spent on the beach, or maybe on an occasional trek into the city for a movie, or some sightseeing. Every Boxing Day, the portable radio accompanying us to the beach when the Test got underway in Melbourne. The summer holidays of 1974–75 Dad took me to my first Test match at the SCG. It was Rick McCosker's first Test for Australia, and he scored 80 on debut, against England. I remember him being caught behind.

> TONY TAYLOR: *I remember standing on an Esky in front of the old Brewongle Stand. Mark was squirrelling his way through the crowd and down to the fence, then coming back to me. It was a terrible day, crowded and uncomfortable and the toilets were awash. Finally, late in the day, Mark said to me: 'Dad, it's on TV now. Do you want to go?' And off we went.*

Bondi in the hot, holiday summers when the city is at its most relaxed was our only taste of Sydney life. We knew, of course, of the other side—of the crime and the crowds, the bustle and the traffic. And from my point of view, at fourteen, I wished down deep we could stay where we were. In Wagga, 'the place where many crows congregate'.

Chapter 2

....

MAKING *the* GRADE

Things are rarely as bad as it sometimes seems they might be: not even the shock of confronting the 'big smoke', after years of living an idyllic life in the gentle pace of a country town. Even my father-in-law Arnold, Judi's dad, might agree with that. He's about as countrified a country bloke as I've ever seen. Just won't leave his banana plantation, south of Grafton. When Judi and I got married he said to us, 'If you have any kids I'll come down to Sydney and visit.' He's never done that. We've always gone up there to Halfway Creek, where he lives. But a couple of years back Arnold had no choice but to come to Sydney to have some medical tests done. He was absolutely pooping himself at the prospect. He hadn't been to Sydney for thirty-something years, and he didn't want to come. Well, on arrival we rounded him up and took him home to our house in Ryde, a middle-class suburb, certainly not the most luxurious in town. 'Gee, this is not too bad,' he said, looking around at the trees. Later we took him up to North Ryde RSL for a few beers, and I think it really shocked him that there was this nice, friendly club, with trees around. In his mind I'm sure Arnold had pictured Sydney as a big prison, a terrible concrete jungle of a place.

So it seemed to us back in 1978. Leaving Wagga was a sad occasion for sure, slamming the car door for the last time. The knowledge that this was really it. But the move was not as painful as those lonely 3 a.m. thoughts of the nights before suggested—and the pleasures of the big city became apparent soon enough. I had my doubts and fears though, that's for sure. I'd read all about the violence and the gangs on the street and the drugs. I'd lie awake thinking: 'What's going to happen to me? I'm bound to get beaten up three or four times before anyone gets to know me. Will I be able to avoid the drugs?'

It was such a step for all of us. Dad came up to Sydney in the August of that year, to find a house and begin work in the new job. That left the four of us—Mum and us kids. Mum wanted us to finish off the school year, to bring something of a completion to our life down there. So we stayed until December before saying our goodbyes, and setting out on the trek up the Hume Highway.

Dad had done well. The house at 17 Grosvenor Road, Lindfield, owned by the bank, had a long, level backyard—close on twenty metres or so. You could just about play full-length cricket out there. It used to take me an hour to mow the bastard, though. Competition cricket disappeared from my life, for a time—although Dad would trundle away against me in the backyard in Grosvenor Road. New in town, I didn't have a club, didn't know anyone, and after my last game in Wagga, I didn't play another match in the season of 1978–79.

Chatswood High became the new school for Tina, Lisa and me. I was in Year 9 by then. I remember my first day there in 1979 well. The morning before I had gone to the barber's and—wouldn't you know it—the bloke had given me the shortest haircut I'd ever had. This is the last thing I need, I thought. I'm going to go to school and they'll be saying: 'Look at this kid from the country with his short hair—a real hick!' Of course it didn't turn out like that at all. On the very first day I met some really good people who showed me around the school. 'This doesn't seem to be too bad,' I was soon thinking. Within six months I was right in the thick of Sydney life—with sport playing a big part in the process of easing me in.

As I've said, I was a solid rather than a brilliant student. I was always good at Maths—ultimately tackling three-unit Maths and Physics at high school—but English, with its Shakespeare and poetry, was never a speciality and the 50 per cent I scored in the HSC was a fair reflection of that. I'll never forget a day in Year 9 at high school when I was chosen to take a part in the reading of one of Shakespeare's plays. I haven't a clue now which character was given to me but the way it worked was that you had to stand up in class and read out your part. When it came to my turn, I was hopeless. I was never a good reader at school—and I certainly wasn't that day. I fumbled and stuttered and finally the teacher, Mrs Dunn, said to me: 'Mark Taylor—sit down. You can't read.' With that, she stripped me of my part in the play.

I'm sure now that Mrs Dunn would shudder at the thought that this is my *third* book. 'Mark Taylor writing books!' she would say, somewhat aghast. I'm still not a great reader now; I'd rather tackle a mathematical puzzle than a book. I think it's probably because I have always been too energetic through my life to sit down long enough to read. One of my other high school English teachers, Mrs Foster, remembered years later some of the problems I caused her.

MRS FOSTER, 'This is Your Life', 1998: *We locked horns over Shakespeare—and I didn't succeed. I note he has wonderful punctuation and grammar and spelling in his books. This is the whole irony. I could hardly get him to write a few paragraphs in an essay and now here he is writing books—and I'm buying them and asking for his autograph. However, I could have predicted the kind of man he would become, because even at school he was a fine character.*

Tina and I both went on to complete our schooling at Chatswood, even after we moved to the house in Epping where Mum and Dad still live. From there, it was a nightmare getting to and from school, an hour or so each way by public transport involving bus and train changes—although things got better in my last year when one of the Geography teachers at the school, Mr Grudinoff, who lived out at Seven Hills, used to give me a lift each day. Lisa did her last four years of schooling at Carlingford High.

JUDY TAYLOR: *Mark's competitive spirit shone through, even at school. I can remember days when he'd come home and I'd ask him: 'Did you have a good day?' 'Yeah Mum,' he'd say, 'except that so-and-so beat me at Maths. I got 92 but he got 94. Can you believe that?' For me, a good pass or being second-best was pretty good. But Mark was so competitive. He had to win, had to be best. And that was in everything he did. But don't get me wrong—he always enjoyed himself. In the 1998–99 season when I missed seeing him bat for NSW for the last time at the SCG I was really disappointed. 'Never mind, Mum,' he said. 'But d'yknow I really feel sorry for these young guys (his NSW teammates). They haven't experienced what it's like to win.' He was really upset at the likelihood that he was no longer going to be there to gee these new teammates up, to help give them the chance of knowing what winning is like. His competitive spirit has always been very much a part of him. A gift, I think.*

Cricket was soon enough back in my life. I joined Lindfield Club, where I played two years of Under-16s, including a couple of Green Shield games one year, and during the week I played at school. I scored some runs with the club—three or four centuries, I think. By fifth form at school I was going well enough to make the CHS (Combined High Schools) Second XI for a carnival in the country town of Young in which I did pretty well. Subsequently I got to play for the CHS Two's against GPS and CAS (Combined Associated Schools) and I also got to play one game in CHS Firsts, together with two young blokes named Waugh, from Bankstown. The trials for that CHS carnival were conducted at Queen's Park, Waverley, on a grey Sydney day with misty rain falling. I tell the story now and then about the Waugh boys that day. I reckon they were already in the side, and the way I like to tell it now is that while the rest of us had to go out and show our wares in the rain, Steve and Mark just sat there and watched us. Very cosy. Even back then everybody knew about the Waugh boys. I told the story with some relish at Steve's wedding.

With that experience under my belt I figured I was a shoo-in for the CHS teams the next year. But along with a pal of mine, Dave McLean, the star cricketer at Chatswood High, who had also played CHS Seconds, I somehow didn't get the message that following year that the trials were on at North Sydney. We didn't go—and so we didn't get picked. I was a bit dirty about that. Dave was one of those enormously talented young blokes who didn't quite carry on with a sports career, once life got in the way. He played for the Australian Under-16s and second grade with Manly and Gordon as a young bloke, and had all the necessary potential. But he gradually fell away from the game as his working life with Australian Airlines became more demanding. There's nothing wrong with that—there are lots of similar stories.

In late 1981, I joined Northern District Club—choosing them ahead of Gordon for a couple of reasons. Firstly we were building the new house at Epping, so they were within closer reach, and secondly because they were a very strong and high-achieving club. And it was at Northern District, that I first met Neil 'Harpo' Marks, one of the great blokes of cricket.

Years later, when they made me a life member of the club, Harpo stood up and gave me a glowing tribute for ten minutes or more, presenting the case for me becoming a life member, etc. I thought to myself: is this the same bloke who bags me all over the place? When I responded, I told the now-famous story of my first real encounter with Harpo.

When I arrived at Northern District as a seventeen-year-old, he was one of the guns. He'd played State cricket with some distinction, was one of the senior blokes, was a club selector, club patron, etc,

etc, etc. There came a day when I was playing third grade, and we lost a player from the team, fairly late. Instead of pulling someone up from fourth grade, it was decided that Harpo would come out of retirement and play. He ended up captaining the side. Harpo loved nothing better than pulling the boots on for one last game.

And, of course, it had to be that day I turned up late to Asquith Oval! My sister Tina was just about to go for her driving test, and it was decided that she could run me up there, and Mum would give her a lesson along the way. Well, it took us forever. By the time we pulled into the ground it was just five minutes to the start of play.

Harpo was waiting for me—and just nailed me. He gave me the best dressing-down you've ever heard. 'If you think you're going to turn up at this time of the day and play for this club you've got another thing coming, my boy!' he spluttered. 'You either get here half an hour before the game or you don't come at all.' It was a real good work-over. Things didn't get much better, either. I was out for seven, and I remember standing out there during the afternoon and thinking: What a bloody awful day this is! Thankfully, things got better between Neil Marks and me. He's been a terrific ally and friend over the seasons. Although when we're together we continually bag each other. At District I made steady progress: 1981–82, third grade; 1982–83, second grade (with one first-grade game); 1983–84, first grade.

SUNDAY TELEGRAPH, 11 March 1984: *He [Mark Taylor] has impressed officials so much that club stalwart and former Sheffield Shield star Neil Marks says he's the club's best batting prospect in 25 years. 'I know I'm sticking my neck out, but I believe he is a near certainty to play Sheffield Shield cricket,' said Marks. 'His technique is sound and his application is first rate.'*

TONY TAYLOR: *Neil Marks is a wonderful fellow. He has always treated Mark like a second son. Strangely enough, it was a distant relative of mine, Cyril Burke, the former Wallaby rugby union halfback, who gave him his nickname 'Harpo'. Cyril's mum was 'Auntie Hazel' to me and my mother and Auntie Hazel and I used to go to the pictures together. I remember the first time Cyril met Neil he summed up his fuzzy hair and the Marx Brothers link and said: 'We should call him Harpo.' It stuck.*

The two paths of my teenage life—heading towards my HSC at Chatswood High before tackling University life, and making steady progress as a cricketer through the grades with Northern District—ran a fairly smooth parallel course. After playing a full season in thirds, I went up to seconds in 1982–83 and was called up for firsts for one game—against a University of NSW side, minus 'Henry' Lawson. We played at Waitara Oval, before a crowd of about thirty. I made 20-something. But in fact I was out when I was five, caught behind. I stood my ground and was given not out—and the Uni blokes were getting into me. After the game I went back to seconds, to complete the year with a highly successful team. We went on to win the competition.

My second first-grade game in 1983–84—my first was against North Sydney—was against Bankstown at Somerville Oval, Epping, a ground without sightscreens that day. I was just nineteen. Firebrand fast bowler Len Pascoe had just been dropped from the Australian team and was on deck for Bankstown that weekend. He was fuming from the moment he arrived at the ground. In my first game I had gone in at No. 7, because we had a pretty-well set top order. One of the openers, Neil Howlett, couldn't play in the Bankstown game and our skipper Ross Turner had a yarn to me about where I would bat. 'You've only just come into first grade—you don't have to open straight away,' he said. But my thought was that if I was going to be an opening batsmen, well, I had to be an opening batsman. 'No, I'd like to open,' I told him. The realisation that Lenny Pascoe was in the other side then hit me. I gulped.

The wicket at Somerville Oval was as green a track as I've ever seen—perhaps matched only by a greentop I was to face in Trinidad much later, in 1995. Bankstown won the toss and batted—and we ripped through a side which included the likes of Steve and Mark Waugh and Rod Bower and bundled them out for 66.

Then it was our turn. Jack Moran faced up to Pascoe and was out first ball, a fate that awaited him in the second dig too. Lenny was steaming in, his face like thunder. On five a flier clipped my glove and I was caught behind. Not out, said the ump. The next ball was short, and I pulled it for four. Lenny's comments were unrepeatable. The next was even quicker, rearing up and catching my glove, on to the keeper. This time I was out, Lenny's ringing words accompanying me as I walked. 'You're like the whole bloody team—you're a so-and-so cheat!' he said . . . among other things.

We passed the Bankstown score nine-down, went on to make 120 and then knocked them over for 91. Jack Moran's king pair for the game brought Ross Turner to the wicket and Pascoe promptly felled him with one under the rib cage. 'Oooooffff!' I could feel it at the other end. We battled on, not needing many, working our way through the minefield. When I was on about seven or eight, Pascoe dropped one short and I nailed it right in the middle, and sent it looping over the square-leg fence. I was thinking 'No! No!— Don't go over!' I was sure that Lenny would kill me now that I had hit him for six. Next thing, someone shouted from the fence: 'That's it. We've gone past them!' Then someone else yelled, 'Just finish the over out.' 'No way!' I thought, and walked off, my gloves soaked through with sweat and terror. Lenny was fierce that match, and quick—on a nightmare of a wicket with no sightscreens.

Len Pascoe was always an angry fast bowler, a fairly common characteristic of the breed. But he was *really* angry in that match—and the manner of his dismissal in the second innings didn't help things one bit. He got one from Kerry Mackay that seamed about a foot, clipped his back leg—and he was given out caught behind. I can still picture Lenny standing there as umpire Rocky Harris raised his finger. 'No way!' he shouted. 'Rocky, that can't be out . . . can't be!' It was—and I had to face the same bloke ten minutes later. It was quite an initiation, my first game as a first-grade opening bat.

Later, I got to know Lenny Pascoe well—a real nice bloke. And the blokes I know who played with him all say the same thing: 'Yeah, Lenny was *mad*—but if there was one bloke you wanted in the side, it was him.' The bloke had a huge heart. I was with him one day at a coaching clinic associated with a Country Cup match and he asked a bunch of kids: 'Why do you think I bowl short so much?' The true answer of course was that Lenny was out to kill the bloke at the other end. The kids were too scared to answer, so Lenny told 'em. 'I tell you why I do it,' he said. 'Because all the fieldsmen are behind the wicket and they have to deflect the short ones. They can't hit me down the ground, that's why'. He was straight-faced at the time. It sounded quite convincing.

By the time of my early days at The Districts, cricket had placed a pretty firm headlock on my life. I played for the school during the week, and for the club on Saturdays. On Sundays there would be Poidevin-Gray (under 21s) or something else. It was cricket, cricket and cricket. Yet all of it was by choice . . . my choice. Over the years many people have asked me: 'What sacrifices have you made to play cricket?' I have always answered: 'None.' And that's the truth—I never saw any of what I did as 'sacrifice'. I just loved playing. In those early years in Sydney one of my mates had a place up the Central Coast, at Terrigal, and during summer a bunch of people would go up there at weekends. There'd be a big night out on the Saturday, and a day at the beach on Sunday. I didn't make that trek too often—almost always there was cricket to attend to. And it has occurred to me more than once over the years if I hadn't been like that, I wouldn't have got to play for Australia for ten years.

I have long been aware that one of the best things I ever did in my career was to decide to go to Northern District. They were a very strong club, based around a core of talented senior players. Today it is a much younger club in terms of personnel, lacking the sort of experience that I was fortunate enough to run into back then. The way it was at that time, with the likes of Mark Clews, Ross Turner, Kerry Mackay, Neil Howlett, Jack Moran, Dennis

Lynch, Peter Taylor and Steve Whitfield in the club, I really was the 'kid' when I was called up to first grade. All the rest of the team were experienced grade cricket hands, in their mid-20s or above. We had a terrific run of success. For most of the 1980s we were in the semis, and in with a chance of winning. We were premiers two years in a row.

NORTH SHORE ADVOCATE, 24 December 1983: *'You've got to hunt pretty hard to find a better timer of the ball in Sydney grade. Mark seems to have so much time to get into position. He has the gift of being able to see the ball so early. We're extremely enthusiastic about his future. One gets the feeling we won't have him our grade ranks for much longer. Senior cricket might be his bag before long.'— Northern District captain Ross Turner after an unbeaten century by Mark Taylor against University of NSW at Waitara, his first for the club.*

Nonetheless, for quite a while cricket and football continued to wrestle for my full attention. I played a season of rugby union at school, while on weekends I played Aussie Rules with second-division side Parramatta. Then I had a season of first division with Pennant Hills, at $50 a win and $25 a loss, in which I found the enjoyment factor a lot less than when I was kicking around with my mates at Parramatta. By then I'd left school and was enrolled at the University of NSW, and it was a real struggle trying to juggle my studies at Kensington with two or three training sessions out at Pennant Hills. After one season I decided I'd take a step back, and just enjoy my football. But Pennant Hills wouldn't grant me a clearance, and I had to wait six weeks or so into the season for an official ruling. Finally they said okay. But time was starting to beat me then when it came to football, and I gradually realised that much as I loved it, Aussie Rules was not going to be my game.

My working future had been settled as early as Grade 10 at Chatswood High—or so I thought. I always took my school studies seriously, although I never saw myself as a doctor or a lawyer because with cricket's place in my life I was never going to be able to give that sort of thing enough of my time. I guess you could rate me a 'slightly above average' student. That was about the level at which I studied too, and it suited me nicely. As part of the Year 10 curriculum all of us had to go out and find jobs for two weeks to get work experience, without pay. We were still living at Lindfield then and one afternoon I walked around to a place called Proust & Gardner Surveyors, with offices on the Pacific Highway. Any chance of a couple of weeks' work experience? I asked them. Sure, come around, they said. So I had two enjoyable weeks' work with them, going around to various sites as a sort of second fieldhand, including a terrific day up in the Blue Mountains. This is for me, I thought. I had never pictured myself as a bloke who was going to sit in an office five days a week. After the fortnight ended I went to a Careers' Officer and asked what subjects I had to take on to become a surveyor. They steered me into Maths, which I was good at, and Physics, which I didn't much like but took on board all the same. To get into surveying at the University of New South Wales I needed a Higher School Certificate mark of 291. In the HSC of 1982 I got 305, and so I was away, *en route* to the job I had decided two years before was for me.

Five years later I completed that journey, having made an absolute mess of my first year at Uni. Funnily enough, that was the year that my cricket commitments were at their lightest. By second year and after I was playing Sheffield Shield. That first year, though, I just didn't knuckle down. I was bloody terrible—didn't go to lectures and tutorials, just couldn't get into it. I was more likely to be found on the beach than at the Uni. The travelling was a real struggle—getting from Epping to Kensington was an hour or more's trip, and I didn't like the Maths they were doing. When it came to the crunch—exam time—I failed Maths and a couple of other subjects, and so failed first year. I lost a complete year. I had effectively turned a four-year course into a five-year one.

I persevered, balancing the different aspects of my life better after that first year. I remember saying to myself: 'I'm going to bloody-well get into it and pass this course. It's time to get serious.' As it turned out, I didn't fail another subject, despite the increasing demands of cricket on my time. In 1988 I graduated as a surveyor— after some late complications, caused by cricket. The final part of the course was a big survey camp, two weeks away during which you were put through a series of surveying exercises. By then, I was in the State team—and to go away would have meant missing two Shield games. My lecturers very kindly agreed that I could under-take a separate test, in January 1988. It turned out to be a huge job, which I had to do solo—virtually re-surveying the various survey marks at the university. It was a nightmare, involving far more work than I would have had to do in the survey camp. But I got a credit for the project and so passed my final year. I was a surveyor. The only thing was that instead of heading out to get a job, I went to England and played league cricket as a professional.

One of the odd stories of my years at University was how I won a State jumper ... at rugby league! In June 1985 I had a call from a mate, Jack Hughes, who was later to be best man at my wedding. Jack was a keen league man. 'Mark, we're really struggling,' he said. 'We're short on numbers for the inter-varsities competition. How about having a game?' I said to him, 'Mate, I haven't played league since I was five years old!' But, I agreed anyway.

Having spent a season playing rugby union at Chatswood, I knew I could handle the rugby codes okay. I could catch and kick and I knew how to come into the backline, and that was a good start. So I played fullback for University of NSW and if I say so myself, I had a pretty fair game. The next weekend they played again, but I had other things on and couldn't make it. The next thing I knew I got a phone call at home. 'I've got some good news for you, Mark,' a voice said. 'You've been picked at fullback in the NSW Combined Unis side to play Queensland Tertiary Institutions, up at Lang Park in Brisbane.' 'Not me,' I said. 'I'm a Rules player.' 'Naa, come on,' said the caller, 'it'll be a great trip—you'll love it up there.' I ended up talking to Jack Hughes and a couple of others and they were very persuasive. 'What the hell,' I finally decided. 'I'll give it a go'.

And so I played fullback for NSW in what is known as 'The Cauldron', as a curtain-raiser before 12 000 or so people, in the lead-up to a Test match between Australia and New Zealand. We got beaten by the Queensland Unis, 18–10 I think, but I enjoyed the game. Afterwards we had prime seats right down on the fence near the players' race. And it was right smack-bang in front of us that Kevin Tamati of New Zealand and Greg Dowling of Australia traded punches in one of rugby league's most notorious moments after being sent from the field. In the photo of the fight, which has been published many times, you can see me in the front row, almost within touching distance. One of our team had bought a special T-shirt as a memento of the Test night and we were so close to the stoush it finished up splashed with blood—from either Dowling or Tamati, or maybe both. That night was both the beginning and the end of my career in rugby league.

During the five years I spent at the University of NSW, my cricket career gained momentum. Late in the 1983–84 season I was chosen to play for Australia in a Youth Series against Sri Lanka. Also in the side were the Waugh boys and Craig McDermott. I had had an excellent Under-19s carnival for NSW that year in Melbourne, and was then picked in the Australian side. Our skipper was Jamie McPhee from South Australia; he and one of his teammates, Daryl Wallis, had been stars of the State carnival which the South Australians had won, and were tipped to be the two who would go all the way to the top. Funnily enough, as cricket can turn out, neither of them went on to higher things.

It was a special experience, my first taste of flying around the country to play high-level representative cricket. We played three Tests against a Sri Lankan side which included Aravinda De Silva, Asanka Gurusinha and Roshan Mahanama. For the Sri Lankans it was the beginning of their coming of age in cricket. Mine too. We played at Manuka Oval in Canberra, the Adelaide Oval and the MCG. It was quite a thrill. We won the first game in Canberra and in the Melbourne Test I scored 86 before holing out to mid-wicket off their spinner—just at the moment I was starting to think, 'Wow! I'm going to score a century on the MCG.' It was a good series. I think the expectation was that we would wipe the floor with them, but they played very well in the drawn games in Adelaide and Melbourne.

Being a member of the Australian Under-19s sort of made it official. I was on my way.

Chapter 3

....

PLAYING *with the*
BIG BOYS

By 1984–85 I was playing with the big boys ... or practising with them anyway. As an Australian Under-19s player I was automatically part of the NSW Sheffield Shield squad. At weekends I was accumulating some runs for Northern District— three centuries in four digs at one stage, and 717 runs for the year— and on two days during the week I was out at the SCG No. 2, training with Henry Lawson, Mike Whitney, Dave Gilbert and the rest. I remember thinking that when Dave Gilbert hit me on the foot with the first ball I faced against him in the nets: Hang on, I'm out of my depth here.

There was one more stepping stone before I received the thrill of a call-up to Shield ranks. Early in the 1985–86 season I was picked for a NSW Second XI against Victoria at Manly Oval—to open the batting with Mark Waugh. Mark went third ball for a duck, I got 102 in 289 minutes. The match was played at a time when NSW cricket had been hit hard by the decision of John Dyson and Steve Smith—the regular openers—to join the rebel South African tour of that season. We knew spots were up for grabs. The word was out that Mark was a sure bet to join brother Steve in the State side, and my century in front of State chairman of selectors Dick Guy was obviously a great boost to my chances.

On 21 October 1985, six days before my twenty-first birthday, rumour became fact. I was named in the team to play Tasmania at the old TCA ground in Hobart. Celebrations were muted; I had an astronomy class at the Uni to attend. The selectors had by-passed more experienced players in Steve Small and Trevor Chappell to squeeze M. Waugh and me into the side. I could barely believe it . . .

DAILY MIRROR, 22 October 1985: *NSW selectors made their bravest decision for many years by pitching 20-year-old rookie opening batsmen Mark Taylor and Mark Waugh into this weekend's first Sheffield Shield clash, against Tasmania.*

It *was* a brave decision. To pick two new openers who had only opened together once was certainly a gamble. After all the much more experienced Steve Small was on hand—and incidentally soon back in the team—and they could have gone with him. But I think the selectors just contemplated the hole caused by the absence of Dyson and Smith and decided to bite the bullet. 'Here's your chance . . . away you go': that was the message to 'Junior' Waugh and me.

Hobart did its worst for us. It was absolutely freezing for the four days of the game. The top temperature was around fifteen degrees and most of the time it was well below that. I started what was to be a fourteen-year life in Sheffield Shield cricket with 12 and 56 not out. (It's also interesting to note that my first-class career ended in Hobart as well, but at a different ground.) The fifty was atrocious . . . well, not flash anyway; I was dropped twice and had more than my fair share of luck. I'll take it, though.

I remember this: I hit my first ball in first-class cricket for four, off West Indian paceman Winston Davis. I was so nervous out there, trembling from a combination of cold and nerves—and just hanging onto the bat wondering what was going to happen. Big Winston generously started with a slowish half-volley on the leg stump, and I clipped it sweetly away for four. Right in the middle. 'You beauty! I'm away,' I thought. I wasn't there for too long— soon on my way, caught at fine leg, trying to hook. We played a draw in a high-scoring match, with David Boon putting together 196 to keep us at bay. Steve Waugh got his first 100, and Greg Matthews a big 100. I'll always remember Boonie for what he did during that match . . .

The third day of the game coincided with my twenty-first birth-day and the night before the big day, the NSW boys put on a dinner celebration for me at a place called Maloney's. David Boon, estab-lished Test player and captain of his State in the three matches he played for Tassie in 1985–86, including this game, came along and joined in the night. He wouldn't have known me from a bar of soap, but there he was singing 'Happy Birthday' and joining in the celebrations. I thought it was fantastic, and I've always had some-thing of an affinity with the bloke ever since.

The story continues—and it is one that I tell now and then in my guest speaking sorties. That night Steve Waugh and I headed on to the Hobart Casino and did what I assume plenty of newly-arrived twenty-one-year-olds have done over a lot of years: I had a few beers too many. Tugger and I finally got back to the hotel in fragile condition at about 4.30 a.m. It seemed I had barely put my head on the pillow when the phone rang. It was our coach, Bob Simpson. 'Mark, the bus left for the ground ten minutes ago,' he said. I was sure it was a 'gee-up' organised by one of the other guys who knew about the big night out. 'I suggest you check your watch,' I said to the coach. I then politely suggested that he 'piss off' . . . before checking my watch. It was ten past nine. I flew down to the ground—where the coach had waiting for me one of the most strenuous catching workouts of my life. Thankfully, I survived the birthday and its aftermath.

Our next game was against Victoria in Newcastle, and introduced me for the first time to the formidable presence of Swervyn Mervyn Hughes. I bought myself one of those big plastic visors, specially for the occasion, figuring that Merv would give me a warm reception—which he duly did. He was bowling quick back then. I got 77 and 7, and I was pretty happy with that first innings. Included was a hook shot off Simon O'Donnell for six, my first in first-class cricket. Whenever I get the chance I remind 'Scooba' of that day.

I was on my way as a first-class cricketer. I don't know that Mark Waugh ever forgave me, however, for what happened in the next game against New Zealand in Sydney. I'd been going all right—50 in Tassie and 77 against the Vics—but Mark hadn't yet got among the runs. Against the Kiwis I hit one to mid-wicket and called 'Yes'. He was run out—and for the next game he was dropped. He always believed the run-out cost him his spot. He did make it back, though (and how!). In later years I've told him once or twice that the fact was he just wasn't equipped to be an opening batsman . . . never quite had the technique to handle it. We've been joshing about that for quite a while now.

That first toe in the water of international competition was a moderate game for me. The scoresheet tells me I scored 29 and 5, but it was not a game that sticks in my mind. Something that does though, is the story of Greg 'Moey' Matthews and the patent leather black shoes. Mo was going great guns at that time. He was also a metre or two ahead of me in the fashion stakes, news that will come as no surprise. I was a pretty ordinary dresser back then and people will tell you that I'm a pretty ordinary dresser full stop. But in my uni days there wasn't much money around, and I dressed plain. Moey's shoes caught my eye one day, and I commented on them. 'Hey man,' he said. 'If you can get 100 before Christmas, these shoes are yours.'

Soon afterwards, we played South Australia in Sydney, and bowled them out for 175. We then got stuck right into them and were 6–438 before our skipper Dirk Wellham declared. It was Saturday

14 December 1985—and a special day in my life. After 356 minutes at the crease, on the second day of the match I ground out 118 runs, my maiden first-class century. I had nudged past Steve Waugh's maiden century score of 107 against Tasmania, and Tugger declared that he was going to beat my score. Wellham batted on until Steve got to 119. The competitive edge that has gone hand-in-hand with the friendship between Steve Waugh and me started right there.

Sometime later I was sitting in the dressing room after a practice session when Greg Matthews walked in, black leather shoes in hand. 'There you are, man, they're yours,' he said, plonking them down. They fitted like a glove—my first decent pair of black shoes. Knowing Moey, they would almost certainly have been imported Italian leather.

We had our moments, Mo and me. He was a cricketer with a difference—very much his own man, and a bloke not inclined to toe the line just for the sake of it. When it came to cricket and the men who play it, Mo's knowledge was very good. The problem with him sometimes was that he could work out the game very well, but then didn't necessarily follow his own theories. A rebel? Well, yes, to an extent. Mainly just very different from the mainstream. We played a lot of cricket together and in the last four or five years we understood each other very well. I knew where he was coming from . . . and he knew where I was coming from. I didn't always agree with Mo Matthews and the things he did. But I would defend forever his right to be different within cricket's framework.

There's a further story I can now reveal about my century against the South Australians. We cleaned them up on the first day with Murray Bennett and Bob Holland getting four wickets each. Overnight, I was 23 not out. That night happened to coincide with the twenty-first birthday party of my best mate Jack Hughes at Randwick. It went late, as twenty-firsts tend to, and after a few beers, I decided to bunk down at Jack's place, rather than make the trek back to Epping. I slept—if you could call it that—on a skinny lounge with my feet hanging over the end. When I awoke in the morning, I felt bloody awful—not so much from the grog, but from a crick in my neck from the way I had slept—and with my feet numb. I thought to myself: 'Geez, I'm glad I've got 23 already . . . I'm going to be struggling to get too many more.'

Jack rang me that night after my century. 'How the hell did you manage that?' he asked.

SUNDAY TELEGRAPH, 15 December 1985: *Mark Anthony Taylor sipped quietly on a 2.2 Tooheys Lite last night and said: 'I'm glad that's over. It is a great relief to break the three-figure barrier.'*

Lite beer? Certainly—Tooheys were NSW sponsors that year. My long stay (356 minutes) and the style of the innings that day were a prelude to the way it was, and would be—for me as a batsman. During that long stay, I used the devices that became part of my make-up in the seasons ahead. For starters, I relaxed between balls, something I always tried to do. When you look at 356 minutes 'cold', it's a bloody long time, almost six hours. But in any long innings, I would always break it down into personal slices. I would set myself short-term targets. For example, in that knock I batted for an hour and a bit the night before. The next morning as I carried on, I increasingly targeted the lunch break, encouraging myself by thinking, 'C'mon, it's only half an hour to lunch. You can get to there, and then you'll get forty minutes off, have a shower, get something to eat and drink.' Always, through my cricketing life, I worked that way . . . half an hour to drinks . . . forty-five minutes to tea. Never would I think: 'Geez, if I'm going to get 100 I'm going to have to be still out there at 5 o'clock.' Breaking it down into 'manageable' bits worked for me. It was one of my secrets as a batsman.

Hot days, I reckon, can be as tough on batsmen as they are on bowlers and fieldsmen. For starters you're wearing more gear—pads, a helmet maybe, protective stuff. And you're in the game the whole time—whereas a skipper can shuffle his bowlers around, give them three overs at a time and so on, keep them relatively fresh.

The South Australians proved to be fruitful foes that first year for me in Shield cricket. In the return game at Adelaide Oval I made 92 and then 100. I was bowled around my legs in the first innings— and I was really spewing. To this day I swear that the umpire must have given me the wrong guard. Andrew Zesers was bowling medium pacers and I went to clip one over the top. I couldn't believe it when the ball hit leg-stump. Throughout my career my guard never changed. Two legs.

That Adelaide match turned out to be a fiery encounter with one of our batsman, Rod Bower, fined for dissent and another, Mark O'Neill, who scored a terrific 170-odd, involved in a dust-up with South Australia's English import Gladstone Small. It was just one of those things. 'Gladdy' is a great bloke, real easy-going, but in the second innings when we were giving them some hammer he went right off at Mark O'Neill, the talented son of a famous father (Norman O'Neill). He ended up running through the bowling crease and letting go a real quick bumper from about eighteen metres. O'Neill and Small exchanged heated words and were mentioned in the post-game reports. It was nothing too dramatic, but as is the way of those things, it captured some headlines. Sledging and drama on the field always do—and I'll have some more to say about that.

It turned out to be a grand Sheffield Shield season for NSW, with a brilliant finale. We fought it out with Queensland, in two fiercely waged and exciting struggles. We needed to get at least first-innings points against them in the last match of the competition itself to ensure that the final was played at the SCG, and I was delighted to play a long—if rather stodgy—part in achieving that. I was out there for something like six hours, for 89. When Jeff Thomson finally got my wicket he uttered the immortal words: 'Now, piss off!'

The final, at the SCG, was a terrific game, with Bob Holland and

Murray Bennett hanging on for the last ten overs to secure a draw—just when it looked like the Queenslanders might beat us. I scored 41 and 30. For a young bloke from the bush it was a dream start to a career in first-class cricket.

The next night, the NSW team left on a seven-match tour of Zimbabwe. We won the one-day series 3–2 and also won the first-class series with one win and one draw against a Zimbabwe side which was much on the up-and-up. It was the first of my three trips to the country—the others being in 1987 and 1991—and the thrill of the game parks or a day at Victoria Falls never dims for me.

The chance to see 'other places' really is a wonderful bonus to being a first-class cricketer. I have experienced places that a more normal working life would surely never have taken me anywhere near. Zimbabwe and South Africa in particular are brilliant places to visit, high on any holiday list, I would imagine. Others like Pakistan and India are more difficult, but fascinating all the same. For a keen young surveyor my first glimpse of the majestic symmetry of the Taj Mahal was mind-blowing.

The Zimbabwe tour was a further confidence-building exercise for me when I headed into my second Shield season with NSW, 1986–87. The year produced its usual cricketing mix of the good, the bad and the frustrating. Against the West Australians in Perth I batted for seven hours for 98—and then was second-last man out, caught off my pad! The ball from Bruce Reid went nowhere near my bat. In the same session of play I was out for a duck when we followed on, adjudged lbw to Ken MacLeay. Again, I didn't agree.

The seven hours at the crease in Perth and a long second-innings haul in Sydney for 186 against South Australia confirmed something that now and then would surprise people about my career as a batsman. I have never been an overly fit-looking bloke, although the truth of it is that I often worked hard on my fitness. But there always seemed to be some people who expressed surprise when I dragged out a long innings. The fact of it was that my concentration was always pretty good, and my fitness far better than it apparently looked. Batting through a day was always a possibility for me.

That and my physical appearance might have something to do with the nicknames I've been 'blessed' with during my career, none of which has been what you would call 'flash'. Early on some of my team-mates used to call me 'Helium Bat'. This was much to do with my inclination to soldier arms, raise the bat skywards and let anything outside the off-stump go. They reckoned my bat was forever up in the air over my shoulder. Back then I played the pull and the square cut and an occasional glance—and that was about it.

'Helium Bat' sort of faded away—and I became 'Stodge' or 'Stodgy'. Blokes reckoned that was the way I played—that I was out there not playing shots and pretty much giving the opposition the squirts. At the twenty-first birthday party the boys in the NSW Sheffield Shield team gave me in Hobart, I seem to remember that the message on the cake was 'Happy birthday, Stodge'. 'Stodgy' disappeared around the time I started playing for Australia.

Greg Matthews was behind my becoming 'Tubs' or 'Tubby'. We were mucking around at training one day, using people's initials to make up nicknames. When 'MT' came up someone suggested 'Mighty Tub'. My memory tells me it was Matthews. 'Mighty Tub' soon became just 'Tubby'—and it stuck. I've got a feeling that it's going to be with me forever, too. People have said to me: 'That's not a very complimentary nickname, Mark.' But it's never worried me. Provided a nickname is not an absolute shocker, a four-letter word or whatever, I reckon you've got to live with it, and I've had a few variations: Helium Bat, Stodge, Stodgy, Tubs, Tubby, The Tubster, Tayls ... even Beefy. Occasionally, I am even known as Mark.

The 1986–87 season produced something unique for me—one of those things on which you can easily win money in a pub bet. I opened the bowling for NSW! During the match against WA in Sydney fast bowler Dave Gilbert suffered a recurrence of a bug he had picked up while on tour with the Australian side in India. We had three spinners in the team—Bennett, Holland and O'Neill—and just two quicks, Gilbert and Mike Whitney. When the second innings came around Dave was crook and I said to our skipper Dirk Wellham: 'I'll bowl a few overs for you if you want.' So I went out and bowled these cosy little right-arm outswingers and finished 0–1 off three overs . . . two maidens! I'm sure the reason was that the WA openers, Michael Veletta and Mark McPhee, both of whom I knew very well, were absolutely pooping themselves that they might get out to me. It was that, rather than my bowling, that kept the runs down.

For me, in 1986–87 there was no 'second-season syndrome'. Although it was not a great year for NSW after the premiership-winning achievement of 1985–86, I was pleased with my own contribution. I held my place in the NSW team, made 765 runs at 40.26 and took ten catches in slips.

For me, the first 'slump' in the rollercoaster years of my career was still a season away. It was a beauty when it came, though.

....

Chapter 4

The Case
of the
Two Taylors

On an unforgettable morning in January 1987 I was in the Australian Test team. Well, sort of . . .

I was in the middle of a pretty fair Shield season, averaging around 50 at the time, and had been mentioned in dispatches as knocking on the door for Test selection. The Poms were here for a Test series, and were giving us something of a working-over, winning in Brisbane and Melbourne to have it all parcelled up before the final Test was played.

Just before the team for the fifth Test was selected, NSW played a game in Newcastle, against Tasmania. Neither I nor the off-spinner Peter Taylor did particularly well. Peter, a member of the winning Shield side the previous year, was back in the team for his first match. On the night the game finished in Newcastle a few of the press guys grabbed me and asked me about the Test and what I reckoned my chances were, etc, etc. I played a diplomatic straight bat.

The next morning—very early—I took a call from a young woman at Channel 9's *Today* program. 'Mark, you have been selected to play for Australia,' she said. 'Could you come into the studio for an interview?' 'No problem,' I said coolly. 'Wow, fantastic . . . how about *this*!' I thought. I hopped into the shower and was getting dressed twenty minutes or so later when the phone rang again. It was the *Today* lady again. 'Mark,' she said. 'Is there a P. Taylor who plays cricket for NSW?' I told her yes, there was a Peter Taylor. There was a pause. 'Well . . . could it be *him* who's been picked and not you?' she asked. 'Yeah, it could be,' I said.

Then we got into some cricket talk. She told me that David Boon had been dropped, and Dirk Wellham selected. That was an opener out, and a middle-order batsman in. 'And is Greg Matthews still in the side?' I asked. Yes, he was. Hmmm, an opener out, and two 'offies' in the team. 'Could it be you?' she asked again. 'Well, I don't know . . . it could be,' I said. Anyhow, she asked me whether I'd still come into the show, and I said no. 'Look, I'd better not; I don't want to be telling people how great it is that I'm in the team, and then finding out that I'm not,' I said. So I didn't go.

At 9 o'clock NSW captain Dirk Wellham rang me and told me what I suspected, that I wasn't in the team—and Peter Taylor was. It had been a strange three hours, sitting there wondering whether I was an Australian player or not.

During that morning I had a yarn to 'PT' (Peter Taylor) on the phone. We were then, and are now, great mates. We talked about the mix-up and I congratulated him and wished him well. 'What are you doing?' I asked him. 'Oh, the bloody phone hasn't stopped ringing and everyone wants to see me,' he said. 'I was thinking of having a hit of golf . . .' I said.

So the Taylor boys, one a Test player, one not, headed quietly out to Moore Park and played nine holes of golf before State training on that rather strange day.

In the years since no-one has ever really answered the sixty-four-dollar question: did the selectors, as some newspapers suggested, get the wrong Taylor? To this day, I don't know. No-one has ever walked up to me and said it was a mistake; and no-one has ever walked up to me and said no, they definitely got the right side. My assumption is that the right side got picked. Greg Chappell was a selector at the time and the story was that he was very impressed with PT. Peter had had an excellent Shield final the year before with four wickets in an innings and 42 when the pressure was right on in the second innings.

> SUN PICTORIAL, 7 January 1987:
> ### THE GREAT AUSSIE COCK-UP!
> *The shattered Aussies have dropped the biggest clanger in cricket history. They've named the wrong man to face England in the fifth Test! Almost unknown spinner Peter Taylor is in the squad for Friday's clash in Sydney instead of opening batsman Mark Taylor.*

To be honest, I wasn't too disappointed. Even though I would have loved to have played and certainly wouldn't have knocked it back, I knew deep down that I wasn't yet ready to play for Australia. I was a second-year Shield player and I was doing all right. But I had a long way to go. I wasn't a dominating batsman by any means then and when I look back on it, I still reckon it was best that I didn't get picked then.

In season 1987–88, the wheels fell off my career for a time. Unaccountably, just when people were expecting me to continue to score good runs for NSW (and so was I!), I struggled. Not until a 70 against Queensland in January and then a century against Tasmania right near the end of the season, in March, did I get going.

> SYDNEY MORNING HERALD, 4 March 1988: *Then came the heebie-geebies that seem to afflict all batsmen at some time in their careers. A succession of low scores saw Taylor's face droop until his jaw nearly reached his navel. The NSW selectors were also starting to appear perplexed and heated, wondering whether Taylor, whose average had dropped below 20, deserved one more chance.*

I was in my final year at the Uni, but it was no excuse. I had been studying hard each year. I just couldn't get myself going. It was a shocker of a season. I remember a game against Western Australia in Sydney where I was on the brink of being dropped. I went cheaply, and as I walked off the field I was thinking: That could be it for me. I was dropped from the one-day team during the season, replaced by Scott Hookey who promptly went and got 70 in Brisbane to rub it in.

I sure tested the patience of the selectors—and it was fantastic that they stuck with me. I didn't really deserve it; I just wasn't playing well enough. Much was made of the century I finally scored against Tassie—and the fact that I wore a 'lucky' white floppy hat that day. In fact, superstition never played much of a part of my life in cricket. On any hot day I was naturally concerned about the burn factor and would wear a floppy hat if the spinners or medium-pacers were on. But that 140 against Tasmania dug me out of the mire, gave me fresh hope.

Judi and I were together then and I said to her when my struggling season at home finished that I wouldn't mind having one crack at earning some money in England, before my life as a surveyor began. My year with NSW had been so poor that I was really starting to think I wasn't cut out for it. I signed for Greenmount in the Bolton League in Lancashire, a £3000 contract for five months plus airfares and we flew out to try our luck in the UK. I was twenty-three and the 'pro' at a club which had a lot of senior blokes. Quite a bit is expected of the pro; you are not captain, but you are pretty much expected to run the team.

Early on, I was just one of the boys—sitting back at practice sessions, having a bat and a bit of a bowl. But one afternoon I realised that it all had to change. A big lump of a bloke named John Ashworth walked past me and made some muttered comments. I had started to think by then that I was going to have some trouble with Ashworth, a big-hitting left-hander. He was about my age, and I had the feeling that he harboured some resentment towards me: I was being paid, and he wasn't. At a rather lacklustre session Ashworth brushed past me with words to the effect: 'This is @#$#&!!! roobish.'

He was pretty right, and I realised it was up to me to do something about it. I clapped my hands. 'Everyone come in,' I shouted. They all wondered what was going on, and as soon as they gathered I got on the front foot with them. 'The nets are crap at the moment,' I said. 'We're not training properly. It's gotta change.' And it did—from that moment. I took over the sessions on NSW Shield lines, with fielding exercises, short catching, high catching, allocated time in the nets, etc. I decided almost in an instant that day: if I'm here to do the pro's job, well, I've got to do it. Almost immediately things got better. Practice sessions became keen and enthusiastic and the team spirit got stronger and stronger. John Ashworth ('Ashie') and I became good mates—and Greenmount went on to win the League.

BURY TIMES, 3 June 1988:
SPELL-BINDING BATTING BY THE WIZARD OF OZ!
The Greenmount record breakers were at it again on Saturday for the third successive weekend . . . Mark Taylor was once again in sparkling form, hitting his second century in three games and taking his personal tally over the 500 mark which makes him the first batsman in the history of the league to achieve this target before the end of May.

It was a dreadful English summer weather-wise, raining most of the time, but Judi and I had a ball. We lived in a semi-detached house in the town of Bury. Before our last game Greenmount already had the trophy parcelled up, so the team headed out on a whopping pub crawl and turned up hungover to the final match. Somehow I got 100—and I haven't a clue how. It was my sixth hundred for the season, a record for the club, and the League.

The experience of what the English apologetically called a summer that year was no doubt a help and an education in what lay ahead for me on Ashes tours. But the League wickets really didn't have much in common with the first-class wickets of the big tours that followed for me later. In League cricket you play on wickets that you would normally not even *dream* of playing on—totally uncovered and at the mercy of the elements. The challenge they presented was certainly a help to my approach to batting, via the need to develop a technique to play balls you knew were going to burst the surface and go all over the place. On the other hand, anything short on those wickets was fruit for the sideboard. It was as if we were playing the way cricket had been played for a hundred years or more. More than anything else I think that the months with Greenmount gave me a deep down feel for English cricket, and cricket culture. It also left Judi and me with some wonderful friends. The people we met were just terrific, and the friendships endure to today.

EVENING NEWS, 29 August 1988:
TAYLOR-MADE! AUSSIE'S CENTURY EARNS PLACE IN RECORD BOOKS
Mark Taylor's fifth century of the season kept Greenmount at the head of the Bolton League's championship chase. Australian opener Taylor's unbeaten 108 put him into the League record books alongside Rod Bower, Parvez Mir and Mark Waugh, but more importantly for his side it earned them an eight-wicket win over Eagley.

The experience done and the trophy won, I was at the crossroads in my life in cricket when Jude and I headed home from England. I came home a more confident person and, I think, a more rounded cricketer. Being the pro at Greenmount had made me more positive in my batting; over there I found that I was expected to set the pace. There was a spring in my step and a new sense of adventure in my approach to batting. For a time blokes like Mark Waugh renamed me 'Slogger'.

But heading into the Shield season I knew that I was at the crossroads. I had graduated as a surveyor and now needed two years of practical experience, plus Board exams, before I could be registered. One morning before the season started I said to Judi: 'I've made a decision. I'm going to give State cricket my best shot this year. If I don't do well I'll give it away and concentrate on my surveying.' I decided deep down that if I had a Shield season like the previous one, that would be it for me as far as serious cricket was concerned. For Mark Taylor, cricketer, it was down to this. The rest, I'm happy to say, is history.

The 1988–89 campaign ran positively for me. I started with a century for Northern District on day one, followed with another for NSW against Combined Country . . . and ended the season as a Test player. When NSW played the touring West Indians in November, I scored 82 and 49, out sweeping in the first innings and run out by John Dyson, the so-and-so, in the second just when I was hitting them sweetly in the centre. I had two early cracks at the Pakistanis too, who were also out here—scoring 62 against them for NSW and then 99 for a NSW Invitation XI in Newcastle. I remember that 99 well. Against an attack that included Imran Khan, Wasim Akram and Abdul Qadir, I hit the ball as well as I have ever hit it in my life. I was out, caught at mid-wicket off a full toss from Wasim which I tried to despatch into Hunter Street. The score-board at the time showed me on 95. I was, in fact, 99, so could just have pushed a single anywhere and got my 100.

Two paths were gradually converging in my life as mid-summer arrived. Australia's Test team was in deep water, really struggling against the West Indies' pace barrage—and I was getting among the runs.

One night in January, 1989, the two strands came together . . .

Chapter 5

THE REAL THING

On the evening of 21 January 1989, I was in a restaurant in downtown Melbourne, about to tuck into a nice bowl of pasta, if memory serves me correctly. Around me were members of the NSW team, in town for the Shield match against the Vics. Steve Waugh was there, although very likely I wasn't speaking to Tugger. That afternoon he had run me out cold—at just the point in the match at which I had seen Merv Hughes off. And my memory is that Mervyn had bowled very quick and fiery that day. But when I was on 40, Steve blocked one back to Simon O'Donnell and called 'Yes'. Foolishly, I responded. Simon snared the ball and threw down the stumps at the keeper's end, with me two metres out of my ground.

I can't pinpoint where we had our team dinner that night. But it would be hard to forget the arrival of a couple of cricket journos with their news: 'Mark, you've been picked to play in the Test in Sydney.' My first reaction was: 'Are you *sure* it's me?' I wasn't taking any chances after what had happened two years before. 'Yes, it's you,' they said. Taylor, M. Champagne was called for, and glasses distributed. In the middle of a tough series (the Windies led 3–0), after all the games and all the hopes and all the dreams, I was a Test player.

I played the Fourth Test in Sydney and the Fifth in Adelaide, failing to place any great imprint on proceedings, but relishing the taste of the 'big time' all the same. In Sydney, I breathed a private sigh of relief when Allan Border lost the toss, and we fielded. To be out there soaking up the Test match atmosphere gave me a chance to settle in. The Windies started out as if they were going to get a squillion. But this was a typical Sydney wicket, i.e. a turner, and when AB chipped in with a seven-for, grabbing all the headlines, we had them all out for 224 at the end of the first day.

I didn't sleep well that night, spending much of my time checking the clock. Finally daylight, breakfast and 11 a.m. came. The hour had arrived. My first run in Test cricket came off Curtly Ambrose—a ball I gloved onto my hip, then down to fine leg. On 5, Ambrose bowled me a perfect yorker which got underneath my bat and smashed down my stumps. I was ready to go when I heard the call, and saw umpire Len King's arm extended. No ball! Big Curtly wasn't pleased. In disgust he kicked the wicket, leaving a scar that ran for forty centimetres or so. I battled on, slow but focused. At lunch I was 21 not out, having survived my first two-hour session as a Test opener. Straight after lunch I hit a nice cover drive for three off Courtney Walsh. 'Wow! This is more like it,' I thought. But I was soon gone, for 25. Ambrose produced exactly the same ball that had knocked me over in the morning. This time the umpire did not signal and Curtly did not kick the wicket. But it was nice to read in the *Australian*, 28 January 1989: 'Taylor played admirably and more heroically than 25 runs suggested.'

Curtly Ambrose bowled the best yorker of all the quicks I ever faced, although there were other good ones—Darren Gough's later on, for example. But the Ambrose yorker was a lethal delivery because it came from such a height. Your first reaction was that it was a full toss. Next thing . . . bang! . . . It was through.

It was quite an experience, facing the Windies' fast men in the Test arena. I remember thinking that they were definitely quicker than they had been when NSW played against them. They didn't give you a breather: Ambrose, Walsh, Malcolm Marshall, Patrick Patterson. The trick for an opener, and especially a new one, is to get over the initial shock and the fear factor against such a barrage. I remember the New Zealand opener John Wright saying to me once that the worst time to face the West Indies was in bed, the night before. How true that is. The fear (of just about anything) is so very often worse than the reality. They were quick, for sure. But it's amazing how you can get used to even that and how your reactions and reflexes can get you out of trouble. In Adelaide I hooked Patrick Patterson sweetly for four and remember thinking that I must be a reasonable player if I could manage that.

We won in Sydney, and went on to Adelaide in some hope. There, in my third and fourth Test innings, I was run out, both times by a whisker. In the first innings it was my call—a deflection off my legs in front of square. The outfield was a little slow after overnight rain and I assumed it was a certain two, but Courtney Walsh—not renowned as having a great arm—flicked it in, right over the top of the bails. I thought I was safe, but there was no third umpire in those days—and I was given out. And the TV replay showed I probably was, although by only an inch or so.

DAILY MIRROR, 3 February 1989: *Australian opener Mark Taylor, the fortunate rookie of the SCG last week, literally ran out of luck in the fifth Test at Adelaide Oval today. Taylor was far too slow completing a second run on his own call to give Australia a bad start in the final shoot-out of the summer against the West Indies.*

In the second innings, when I was on 36 and we were effectively 0–244 after building a nice first innings lead, Geoff Marsh— 'Swampy' to his mates—dabbed one down and called 'Yes'. I responded, and slid the bat as Gus Logie hit the stumps with his throw. Again it was a desperately close photo finish. Again I was padjudged out. Swamp and I had put on 98.

During that match, and at other times too, I wondered whether the perception of me reflected in those nicknames ('Tubby', 'Stodge', 'The Tubster' ... even 'Beefy' occasionally) contributed to some of the run-out decisions given against me. I was generally thought of as a big lad, not too quick between wickets. It was something I had to live with. In the same Test Dean Jones, who scored a terrific 216, was run out by a good third of a metre—and given not out. I reckon Deano's was more out than both of mine—but he was a quick bloke and was given the benefit of the doubt.

Frankly, I am not a great fan of the TV replay 'third umpire' in some respects, but I do think it's a winner when it comes to run-outs, in that it takes away any pre-conceived ideas the human umpires may have about a particular batsman.

I put down a couple of catches at first slip in the Adelaide Test. My confidence level wasn't great. I was twenty-four, young, fit, keen—but still thinking deep down that I'd rather the ball didn't come my way. Ten years later when my physical skills as a slipper shouldn't have been as good, I loved being in slips, relished the chances I got and caught more of them than I had at twenty-four. Put that down to confidence and experience.

Late in my career I wouldn't get that little flutter of the heart when a ball caught the edge. Most often I'd just let my instincts go to work, not panic—and catch it. Increasingly over the years I became a calmer slips field, and a better one. When your heart races your technique can fall away a bit, and you can tend to snatch at the ball. As the years went by, I became more relaxed, my hands 'softer', ready to snare whatever happened along.

Not long after the Adelaide Test I took what I believe was one of the very best catches of my entire career. It came late that season when I was back in the Shield, feeling—and playing—like a batsman who had all of a sudden gone to another level. I came out of the Tests thinking, 'Now I really am an Australian player.' My mental attitude seemed to have changed completely. People I had been playing against six weeks before suddenly weren't so daunting.

I had taken a giant leap in my career. Two centuries against the Western Australians at the WACA and another three weeks later against Queensland at the SCG provided a spectacular end to my domestic season.

It was in Perth that I took *the* catch. We set WA 395 to get, and by stumps on day three, we had them 4–40, with their best men back in the pavilion—Marsh, Veletta, Wood and Moody. The game was as good as over. Well, it looked that way. Buoyed by my two centuries and the state of play I stayed out far longer and later than I should have that night. Lack of sleep and associated problems had me in pretty ordinary shape by the time we got going on the last day. By lunch they had lost only one more wicket, and put on 120 runs. Then Wayne Andrews and Tim Zoehrer got together—and Zoehrer, in particular, really trashed us. He scored 163, Andrews made 78 and suddenly late in the day they were 7–312, only 80 or so short. A game that had looked a real gimme had turned into a battle.

As we took the second new ball I was wondering how the heck we were going to get these last three out after the sort of day it had been. Then Steve Waugh bowled a ball which Chris Matthews tried to flick down the leg side. Phil Emery, our keeper, followed it across, but the ball nicked the *outside* edge of the bat and flew fast and high, way to my right. I dived full-length, and somehow it stuck. Matthews was out for 14, the last two followed him quickly and we had won the match, by 60-odd runs.

The events of that day and the previous evening taught me two important lessons: (1) That in cricket, it's not over until the last batsman walks. (2) Late nights in the middle of a game are not such a terrific idea.

Near the end of the season, two or three days before the team was picked for the Ashes tour, we had a 'sweep' in the NSW dressing-room. Each of us threw in ten bucks and set about picking the seventeen for England. I remember writing my own name down and thinking: I hope I'm right. A glance through the other sheets indicated that everyone had me on the list. My hope had to be that the selectors were thinking the same way. I had made 1241 runs during the first-class domestic season, had played the last two Tests against the Windies and picked up three centuries since. But in the business of cricket selection you can never be 100 per cent sure.

I was in my car, parked under a tree somewhere in the eastern suburbs when the news came through. I had been heading into town, and pulled to the side when it got to about 10.55 a.m. I knew the team would be announced on the 11 o'clock ABC news. It was—and my heart literally jumped when my name was read out. To make an Ashes tour is the dream of every Australian crick-eter, and has been for over 100 years. And it had become my dream. I just sat there alone for a few minutes and let it sink in . . .

LAURIE SAWLE, team manager, letter to Mark Taylor, 16 March 1989:

Dear Mark,

Congratulations on your selection for the 1989 Ashes Tour of England. We leave from Melbourne on the 29th April. We have a huge task ahead of us—to regain the Ashes. Australia has not won a full Test series in England since 1964, so there is quite a challenge ahead for the 1989 team. We need to start preparing for it now.

Chapter 6

THE UNSINKABLES

The omission of NSW left-armer, and considerable character, Mike Whitney, was the big talking point of Ashes selection day, 1989. 'Whit' had had a terrific year, taking fifty-eight wickets in thirteen first-class games, thirty-seven of them in the Sheffield Shield, and sustaining his form throughout the season. His credentials were exemplary, but there were several elements working against him. The selectors seemed to think that as he didn't swing the ball back in to the right-handers but generally pushed it across them, he would not get a lot of wickets in England.

In addition, four quicks (Geoff Lawson, Terry Alderman, Merv Hughes and Carl Rackemann) pretty much picked themselves for the tour, leaving just one spot open. There was an old theory that in such circumstances a young guy should be picked as fifth pace man, for blooding purposes, and so Greg Campbell from Tasmania came into the picture. At thirty, Whit was seen as approaching veteran class.

The fact—or perception—that Whitney was not getting on too well with a few of the establishment also was not in his favour. I remember Greg Chappell had a bit of a dip at him in a newspaper article before the Adelaide Test against the West Indies. Whit took it on the chin, went right out there and got 7–89—and had a few words to say after the game.

My own view is that Mike Whitney was desperately unlucky. On what he had achieved he certainly deserved a trip to England more than Greg Campbell did. The outcome did not vindicate the selectors' choice. If Campbell had gone on to become a leading Test bowler in the seasons ahead, the controversy would have quietly faded away. But Greg's career never really took off, even though he played the First Test at Headingley on the tour, and another three later against Sri Lanka, Pakistan and New Zealand, finishing with thirteen Test wickets. He never really kicked on. It was a selection punt that attracted big headlines but unfortunately didn't work.

My own tour started slow and scratchy. I batted poorly in the warm-up games, and just as poorly in my first couple of county games. Six or seven innings into the tour I had a top score of 23—against a League side—and was, to put it mildly, struggling. At about that time I remember saying to one of the other players: 'Well, at least I can say I've made *one* Ashes tour.' For a time it was how I felt, so low was my form—that I could sit back and enjoy the experience of travelling around with the guys, because there wouldn't be another chance. And it was quite an experience at that.

MARK TAYLOR, letter to parents, May 1989:
We've been practising twice a day at Lord's. It was fantastic to go there for the first time, and I was amazed at the slope on the ground. You won't believe it when you see it. After practice yesterday we had the official MCC welcome dinner . . . I was very fortunate in that I was seated next to Denis Compton CBE and had a great chat about horse-racing and golf. He is a lovely bloke and signed my menu, which was a real bonus.

There was a bit more to it, actually, and a story I tell now and then. I didn't know too much about Denis Compton back then, except of course that he had been a special cricketer and a very good sportsman generally. When I saw his card on the table I thought to myself, 'This is a good seat first-up.' He was very laid back and friendly. The dinner got underway and the guest speaker got up, Lord so-and-so from somewhere or other, very pukka. The dinners at Lord's are all-male affairs, and very traditional, with cigars and port and everyone wearing the bacon-and-egg tie—the whole lot. At the end of his speech the special guest concluded: 'Gentlemen, let us hope that at the end of this forthcoming series that it's not Australia or England who are the winners . . . but that *cricket* is the winner.' At this there was loud applause, many 'Hear-hears' and the rapping of cigars and glasses on tables. As it subsided I felt a tap on my shoulder. It was Denis. 'What a load of #$&$#@!!! crap!' he said. I *like* this bloke, I thought. I was happy to share his company a few more times after that, on this tour, and the next.

At Somerset, the whole tour changed for me. And it changed on a single ball. We lost the toss, and were sent in and I was out there, plugging away, on 8. A guy named Rose bowled one that was short and wide—and I cut it high and not too hard, straight to gully. 'That's out!' I thought, the moment I played the shot. But the gully fieldsman lost the ball in the background of the crowd, ducked for cover and it flew safely through for a couple of runs. It didn't get anywhere near the boundary, that's how poorly I hit it.

After that let-off, I suddenly started to middle them and play some shots until sometime in the early afternoon I tickled one and was out caught behind for 97. In the second dig, when we were chasing quick runs, I picked up a fast-moving 58, including a couple of sixes. This was better.

Derby, the game before the First Test, came and went as a real trial for all of us. I scored 5 and 28 on a wicket that was a real horror, against a Derby pace attack that included Ian Bishop and Devon Malcolm. The top score by either side in the match was 228, by Derbyshire in the first innings. We won outright by 11 runs. My credentials for first Test selection were brief: one good game.

There was much conjecture about the Test team. Would Allan Border and the other tour selectors stick with me? Would they reunite Boon and Marsh to open and bring Tom Moody into the middle order? And the pressure was on a lot more than just me. We had been lambasted by sections of the English press which suggested that we couldn't bat, couldn't bowl and couldn't field, all of these inadequacies being something of a drawback for a cricket team. What's more, we had a popgun attack, led by Terry Alderman who was 'past it'. So were Henry Lawson and Carl Rackemann. Merv Hughes was just huff and puff. And Greg Campbell? Greg who? they said. And with Tim May and Trevor Hohns as our spinners how the hell were we ever going to bowl *anyone* out?

In the days before the game, with the debate still raging, I went along to the tent of Ladbroke's, the bookies, and checked out the odds for different players: who'd get most wickets, score most runs, make the first 100, etc. I ran a finger down the 'most runs' list, down to 33/1—Moody and Hughes! I didn't even make the list. But at least, a day or two later, I made the team, a real show of faith which I was determined to do my best to reward.

Cricket's history now records the fact that despite what Ladbroke's reckoned, I *did* make most runs in the First Test of 1989, played at Headingley, Leeds. After a rain-delayed start, I was 96 not out at stumps, sharing good partnerships with AB and Dean Jones. Just before stumps David Gower dropped me in the gully, an easy chance when I was on 89.

DAILY MIRROR, Sydney, 9 June 1989:
HOWZAT FOR OPENERS
Australia's batting hero Mark Taylor said he would sleep well despite being a shot off his first Test century. 'I'm happy with my effort. If someone had told me yesterday I'd be 96 not out at stumps, I wouldn't have believed them.'

Very early days. Tina, Lisa and I (left to right) pose for the camera. How about the bow tie and check shorts!

Tina (left), Lisa and me with our 'Nan', Mabel Taylor, in her home at East Maitland, 1976.

In Canberra with the Wagga junior representative side in the 1970s. That's me second from the right. On the far left is Paul Hawke who went on to achieve great things in Aussie Rules. At the back is our manager Bernie O'Connor, who was such an influence on my early cricket career.

A snapshot to mark my naming as school captain of South Wagga Primary.

Tina, me and Lisa (left to right) with Mum on holidays in Sydney, 1977.

Ready for school, 1977—my first year at Mt Austin High, Wagga.

The Taylor family at home, Grosvenor Road, Lindfield, August 1978. I take no responsibility for the pyjamas … a present, I'm sure.

Toasting the move to a new house in Epping in 1981—with Mum, Dad and Lisa.

The NSW Universities rugby league team, which played Queensland Tertiary Institutions at Lang Park in 1985. The fullback, Taylor, is fifth from the left in the front row. Nursing a bloodied nose and various other aches and pains after the game, I decided cricket was a far better career path! (Photo courtesy of Paul Samanay)

Padding up, NSW practice, 1985.
(Photo courtesy of News Limited)

The late spring of 1985—and a posed shot for the Sydney Sun after I had made the NSW Sheffield Shield team. (Photo courtesy of Fairfax Photo Library)

Going for it against South Australia at the Sydney Cricket Ground, 14 December 1985, during my maiden Shield century (118). (Photo courtesy of News Limited)

A happy memory. The winning of the Sheffield Shield in 1986, after the hard-fought drawn final against Queensland. No prizes for guessing the sponsor. Our skipper, Dirk Wellham, is up front on the left, his arm draped around Mark O'Neill. That's me on the far right.

With skipper Greg Dyer (background) doing the honours, I meet Robert Mugabe, Prime Minister of Zimbabwe during the tour by the NSW team which followed the 1985–86 season. Graham Smith is the player next to me on the right.

With Peter Taylor (left) and Steve Waugh—celebrating my selection for Australia in 1989. (Photo courtesy of News Limited)

Checking my flexibility. A fitness testing session at the University of New South Wales in 1986. (Photo courtesy of News Limited)

The Greenmount Cricket Club, 1988—with the Aussie professional Taylor third from right in the front row. Over my left shoulder is Neville Neville ('Neville squared'), who became a great family friend.

Getting one away to leg (above) during my debut Test innings against the West Indians at the SCG in the fourth Test of the 1988–89 series. (Photo courtesy of News Limited)

Just married and I'm off to England! A traditional 'packing the bag' shot with Judi after my selection for the Ashes tour of 1989. (Photo courtesy of the Sydney Morning Herald)

A great day at Trent Bridge (above), 1989 Ashes tour—clipping one away en route to the 301 that Geoff Marsh and I put on in a day's play in the fifth Test. The 'keeper is Jack Russell; Ian Botham is behind me and Robin Smith on the right.

With my dad Tony and the Sheffield Shield—won comprehensively by NSW in the final of 1990.

Cricket in the backyard at Mum's. Having a hit at home in Epping, season 1989–90.

Hoiking one away during the first innings of the Sheffield Shield final of 1990 (against Queensland)— my first game as NSW captain. With a century in each innings and the winning of the Shield it was a game to remember for me. (Photo courtesy of the Sydney Morning Herald*)*

Tired but proud—acknowledging a generous reception from the SCG crowd after my Test century, v Pakistan, 8 February 1990. (Photo courtesy of the Sydney Morning Herald*)*

A happy snap at home with Jude after my naming as NSW Sports Star of the Year in March 1990. (Photo courtesy of News Limited)

*Weary, unshaven, happy—
on reaching my century v
West Indies in the Fifth
Test at St John's, Antigua
in April 1991. I scored
144. (Photo courtesy of
Allsport)*

Some fun with a couple of stars from another game—rugby union's Glen (left) and Gary Ella, before a testimonial match for Mike Whitney in 1992. (Photo courtesy of News Limited)

A champagne toast and a happy day. Celebrating my appointment as Australian captain in 1994. (Photo courtesy of News Limited)

A very small field invader at Stellenbosch, South Africa in 1994 (Australia v Boland). Batsmen Taylor and S. Waugh enjoy the moment. (Photo courtesy of Allsport)

Street scene, Pakistan, 1994. Cricket there is a passion and a way of life. (Photo courtesy of Allsport)

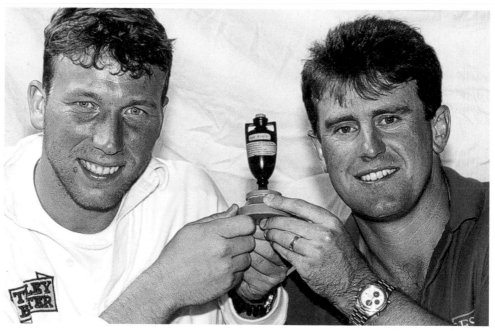

Mike Atherton and me and the glittering prize, November 1994—with my first Ashes series as Australian captain coming up. (Photo courtesy of Allsport)

William Taylor gets on with the game while I chat with some fans at the SCG, December 1994. (Photo courtesy of News Limited)

A cheesy grin and an armful of fruit. Shopping in St Vincent, West Indies before the fourth one-day international, March 1995. (Photo courtesy of Allsport)

A day out in Jamaica in 1995, with Michael Slater (left) and Tugger Waugh. (Photo courtesy of Allsport)

A quiet moment, but a glorious one. Alone with the Frank Worrell Trophy after the fourth Test in Jamaica, April–May 1995. (Photo courtesy of Allsport)

Chatting with a legend. Sir Garfield Sobers on the West Indies tour of 1995. (Photo courtesy of Allsport)

The great day of the ticker-tape parade in Sydney in 1995 when we brought home the Frank Worrell Trophy from the West Indies. (Photo courtesy of Allsport)

Mark Taylors as far as the eye can see! With NSW team-mates and some funny masks, part of a promotion for an MMI one-dayer at North Sydney Oval, late 1995. (Photo courtesy of the Sydney Morning Herald)

Forcing on the off. Second Test against Pakistan, Hobart, November 1995. (Photo courtesy of Allsport)

An uneasy ending to an edgy series. My handshake offer to Sri Lankan players at the SCG is ignored at the end of the 1995–96 World Series. (Photo courtesy of News Limited)

Not everybody was impressed, however. Geoff Boycott, cornered in the carpark after the first day's play, was reported as saying about me: 'From what I've seen, he's a limited player with limited shots . . . I don't think he's going to be a great player. But so what, there are very few who are.'

The night that followed was a long one for me. Mum and Dad had flown over for the Test and they took me out to dinner. And the more time I spent with them the more nervous I got. The conversation kept drifting back to just how I was going to make my first Test 100. I slept fitfully. At two o'clock I was wide awake thinking about just how I might get the four runs.

TONY TAYLOR: *We had Mark's club secretary from his Greenmount days, Neville Neville, with us for dinner. Judy asked Mark the key question: 'Why didn't you get the other four?'*

JUDY TAYLOR: *I was just disappointed for Neville . . . pacing up and down, wanting to see Mark get his first century. 'Why didn't you get your hundred?' I asked Mark. 'Mum,' he said, 'it's hard work out there!' And I said to him: 'You* think *it's hard work. We've slaved all day!'*

After all that, I was relieved to walk through the gate next morning, and get on with it. Twenty minutes or so into the second day Derek Pringle bowled me one just outside leg—and I glanced it down to the fence for four, and my century. The reception from the crowd was amazing—a standing ovation. They really are generous fans, the English. I know that in the stand Mum and Dad were moved pretty close to tears by the reception the Headingley crowd gave me.

I got 60 more in the second innings, and we blasted them out for 190 on the last day to win the match—and cause some hasty reassessment of our qualities as a Test team.

Streaking was a popular pastime in those days and with just a dash of poetic licence I have often told the story of one (a female) who flashed into the picture at Headingley one afternoon during the Test. Judi and I were married only three weeks before I left for England with the team. After the Headingley Test she flew to England to stay at Bury. I was given the next match off and drove across the Pennines from Leeds to Bury, in the north-west. My new wife met me brandishing a copy of the *Bury Times* and demanded: 'Have a look at page three.' Which I did. On page three was a pic of the Headingley streaker with Geoff Marsh and me in the background, arms folded and with what looked suspiciously like smug expressions on our faces. We were not looking at the seagulls. I survived.

At Lord's, we won again. And what a thrill that was for a boy from Leeton, NSW—to walk out onto that famous turf in a Test match. By then I was thoroughly tapped into the ancient and wonderful thrill of the Ashes 'journey' and was loving every minute of the campaign. I scored 62 and 27 at Lord's. Our victory, by six wickets, was decisive after a last-innings chase for 118. Back home, under a headline reading 'Taylor's finishing school: Extraordinary mixture of flair and fallibility', the *Australian* said about my first dig: 'A less organised personality would never have survived the foothills of screaming uncertainty which Taylor negotiated on his way to a major innings.'

Just before the Third Test, at Edgbaston, Birmingham, I was in the wars. During fielding practice on a rough piece of ground outside the oval, a ball bumped nastily on a tuft of grass and hit me flush in the mouth. I had a couple of stitches inserted in my top lip, just before the Test started. I scored 43 and 51 there, in a Test in which the weather had the final say. Two days of rain cost us a victory in a match highlighted by Dean Jones's great century (157).

In the Fourth Test at Old Trafford, Manchester, I scored 85 before off-spinner John Embury had me stumped as I went after him. Embury got me out a few times on that tour. Richie Benaud interviewed me on television at one stage and posed the question: 'People are saying that you have a problem with off-spinners?' I agreed that indeed I had been out now and then to the spinners, but added: 'I hope I keep getting out to the spinners for the rest of my life, because it means I am making runs.' For an opening batsman, it seemed a reasonable ambition.

In the second innings at Old Trafford I scored 37 not out and was there when David Boon swept the left-arm spinner Nick Cook for four to win us the series, and the Ashes. We were three-up, with two to play. What a moment that was—and what a celebration in the dressing room when we made it back there. XXXX was there in some quantity, both in the cans and out of it as the spray flew. There was a problem, though, when it came to partying. After the Test we were booked to travel to Nottingham for the county match which began there the next day. In 1989 the Tests still included a rest day, which meant that there was no break before the next fixture.

I'm sorry that the games' brass dropped the traditional rest day from Test match programs. Those days were not only a welcome respite for the teams but helped to develop a spirit of sportsmanship and camaraderie between them. The rest day gave you a chance to mix more with the opposition. The tradition was that on the third day of the game the teams would get together and have a few beers at the close of play. Very often the players from the two sides would arrange to meet again at some bar or nightspot later in the evening. Some warm friendships and a feeling of mutual respect came out of those get-togethers—although the 'edge' of an Ashes series was never any the less sharp for it.

En route to Nottingham in the bus there were a few sherbets consumed, as you can imagine. And when we reached the hotel, the word was: 'Righto—up to the rooms, then straight back down. We're going out!' I can tell you not much more than that it was a *big* night and one befitting an Ashes victory.

The hard part came next day—a clear sky . . . no bloody rain when you needed it . . . and a crook wicket at Trent Bridge for the game against Notts. AB, of course, didn't play. You can make those sort of choices when you're captain. Geoff Marsh won the toss, and I had pleaded with him earlier to bowl if he called right. But he answered quite reasonably: 'We can't bowl—we haven't got enough players fit enough to bowl.' So we had to bat. Swampy and I headed out there, David Boon had the pads on and was possibly awake—and everyone else was asleep, bodies strewn around the dressing room. Somehow we constructed a win out of the wreckage. Boonie made 76 and 102 not out, Swampy got 16 and 66, I scored 33 and 30 against a pretty fair attack that included Franklyn Stephenson. Despite the headache we managed a decent first innings, then knocked them over, made some more runs, knocked them over for a second time and took the match. It was an interesting experience: cricket played on memory.

The wicket for the Fifth Test at Trent Bridge was a far superior strip. Flat, and potentially full of runs. Thankfully, we won the toss. On three, I nicked one between first and second slip. A reaching English hand flicked the ball, but I survived. I went on to make 219—and the scoreboard at the end of day one became headline news all over Australia (and England). With Marsh on 125 and Taylor on 141 it stood at 0–301, a new record for an Australian opening partnership in an Ashes series, surpassing the 201 Bob Simpson and Bill Lawry had put on at Old Trafford in 1964.

We ended up putting on 329, and I was finally out for 219 about forty-five minutes after lunch, trying to slog Nick Cook into downtown Nottingham. It was a wild and woolly shot; I was doing it easy at the time. What I remember most of all about the whole day was David Gower at lunch. The two teams lunched together on that second day and David, always a bloke with a bit of style about him, ordered a glass of champagne! 'I am celebrating our wicket,' he explained. We were about 1–370 at the time.

David Gower was one of my heroes, but he played very strangely in that series. He scored 100 at Lord's, but generally was decidedly cavalier in attitude. He kept playing these 'nothing' shots down leg side and getting caught. Geoff Lawson focused on a line about fifteen centimetres outside leg-stump and Gower just couldn't seem to resist the lure. It wasn't the real Gower, that's for sure. He was such a graceful, sweet-timing player at his best. He had destroyed Australia in 1985.

When I was finally out that day, charging down the wicket to Cook and missing, I felt physically fine. I wasn't too tired at all. That night when I had a beer with AB, he complimented me on my innings. 'Fantastic . . . well played,' he said. 'How were you feeling when you got out?' I told him I was just a little bit weary—but really, pretty good. 'Tub, d'you know something?' he said. 'You had a unique opportunity today to get a 300 in a Test match.' In Pakistan on a day ten years later, I thought back to that conversation.

The London *Daily Mirror* went over the top. Their headline after my 219 read THE NEW BRADMAN and journalist Chris Lander wrote: 'Mark Taylor's marathon 219 in the Fifth Test at Trent Bridge yesterday put him on a par statistically with the one and only Sir Don Bradman. No higher compliment could be paid to Australia's batting discovery of 1989.'

We smashed them in that Test match. I think Gower's gesture showed they were pretty demoralised. We batted on into the third day, made 6–602, then got them out for 255 and 167. Terry Alderman had 2–1 in his first over in the first innings, and that sort of set the standard. He had a great tour—forty-one wickets in six Tests, on strips that I thought were beautiful to bat on. They were wickets that didn't seam a lot, but the Englishmen just played them very badly. Alderman bowled much as Adam Dale does today, from very close to the stumps. He was always being warned for running on the wicket. He bowled very straight, with just a little movement off the seam now and then. The Poms were continually trying to whip him away through mid-wicket . . . and missing. Half Terry's wickets were via lbw.

By The Oval Test I was seeing them like a watermelon. I should have made more runs than I did, and that's not being big-headed in any way. I made 71 and 48—and got out to two wides, on a wicket that was simply a beautiful batting track, with a bone-white, hard outfield that was full of runs. In the first innings I slashed at Alan Igglesden and in the second at Gladstone Small when we were chasing fast runs. Caught behind both times.

That first Ashes series is obviously a great memory for me, and undoubtedly the turning point in my career. In four and a half months I went from Mark Taylor, Sheffield Shield player, to Mark Taylor, Test player. I made 839 runs at 83.9, and if I had been more methodical it could have been some more. But who's to gripe about 83.9? Amazingly, it placed me second on the Ashes list to Don Bradman's 974, scored in seven innings in 1930. The funny thing was I didn't play that well in the county games. I made 100 against Gloucester, and no other centuries. So 1669 first-class runs, and happy memories galore, including some golf when time allowed.

In many ways the summer of '89 in England was a golden one— for me and the team. To have flown out of Australia described as the worst side to have ever left our shores and then to have equalled the 4–0 series record of Sir Donald Bradman's 1948 side was just a fabulous result. And it could have been 6–0. It's fair to say that rain saved England at both Edgbaston and The Oval. If both Tests had been played out to the limit there would have been only one winner. Us.

The people of Sydney gave us the final nod—with a wonderful ticker-tape parade that was a thrill for every one of us, and made us realise just how much people back home cared about what we had managed to achieve. One of the papers tagged us 'The Unsinkables'.

I consider myself enormously fortunate to have been on that Ashes tour of 1989. The world of cricket was changing. That tour was a link with the past, with the way it had been. It was four-and-a-half months in duration, and full of the special 'extras' that then went towards making up an unforgettable package: the golf games into the English twilight after play had finished for the day in this county game or that, the special dinners, the special places, the people who made us so welcome. I had an absolute ball, and thoroughly enjoyed the social side of the campaign. It was a unique tour in a balmy English summer.

My subsequent tours increasingly came into the category of 'harder business', although much enjoyed and valued all the same. In 1989 I was just one of the team, a new chum on tour and with only one responsibility: to make runs and to put my stamp on the side. To be there for eighteen weeks or so gave you a sense of the 'endless' English cricketing summer.

In 1993 things were changing. The rest day during Tests had gone, and the program was trimmer. By 1997, the tour had changed a lot. It had changed in one way for me because I was captain, with all the extra pressure and responsibility that the job brings. But the tour by then was streamlined to three-and-a-half months—yet still with six Tests and three one-dayers. The county program had been reduced and, as a result, so had the 'relaxation factor' of the tour. The county games were serious, of course, but played in a different spirit to the Tests, and at different places. I think the media regret the change, too. I'm sure it was of great interest—and news value— to see a team take shape over the period of the longer tour. For them in the future it'll be more and more a question of 'Bang— there's the team, stick 'em out there and we'll just comment on what they do.' I honestly feel a little sad for today's players, that they won't get to experience what I did back in '89.

More and more, cricketing life in the 21st century will be about professional cricketers flying out to do a job, with the high-level matches they play on increasingly tightly scheduled programs beamed across the world. No longer will young cricketers be going to England to meet people or to tour around and visit places. They will be there to play cricket, and a fair bit of one-day cricket at that. Possibly it will get down to a two-and-a-half-month tour, with back-to-back Tests. Perhaps the traditional five or six Test Ashes format will be down to three Tests. The days of the long, drawn-out tour, unfolding through the summer, will be only a memory. More and more it will be tight and bright, in and out—then on to the next commitment in some other country. I won't judge that trend as either good or bad. It is just the way cricket is going.

The danger of excessive tampering with cricket's tradition is one reason why countries are wary of handing over too much power to the ICC. Pass on total power to one body and they may well say something like: 'Hang on a minute. Because of the overall programming in world cricket there's no way we can afford to have England play Australia over four months.' That fear is precisely the reason the ACB and the English Cricket Board are hanging back.

I don't want to sound like an old fogey, hankering for the 'good old days', but I value greatly the chance I had in '89 to be part of cricket's disappearing world. I won't forget it.

····················

Chapter 7

A Tale *of* Two Summers

The true value of the mental side of cricket really hit home to me in the crowded domestic summer that followed the Ashes series of 1989. I came back to face Kiwis and Sri Lankans and Pakistanis as an established Australian opening bat. No longer was I a part-timer trying to forge a place in the scheme of things. On the Deloittes World batting ratings I had jumped from ninety-seventh to seventh, and I received a cheque for $5000 and a silver platter when named their 'Rising Star'. Now I was the bloke that the likes of Wasim Akram and Waqar Younis had to get out.

I had taken sport's quantum leap. And recently, at the occasional times when I have looked back on the very tough series that year against the Pakistanis in which I did well, the thought inevitably occurred to me that I seemed then almost a different human being from the struggling batsman of season 1996–97. Physically, I looked the same, but mentally the Taylor of 1990 and the Taylor of 1996–97 were worlds apart.

The mental side of cricket (and sport, generally) is enormous. When you're struggling, out of form, and make a mistake you agonise: 'Oh no, here we go again. I'm gone.' But when you're in the groove and you make a mistake you merely think, 'Oh well, it's just one of those things—I was due for a low score,' and you immediately think about what you're going to do to them next time you get out there.

In the home summer of 1989–90 I was mentally ready. The challenges we faced came in all shapes and sizes. In Perth Mark Greatbatch batted for 655 minutes for 146 as we played a draw against New Zealand. Then the First Test against the Sri Lankans in Brisbane on something of a green wicket turned into a pretty boring old draw, although it was a good game for me via a 164 in the second innings. I was heartened to receive a fax from my parents after the match congratulating me on a particular milestone it marked.

TONY AND JUDY TAYLOR, December 1989: *It seems that the footwork and aggression have returned. Even more impressive is the unprecedented record of over 1000 runs in your first Test season. While the press don't seem to share our feelings at this feat, rest assured that your family along with friends with a knowledge and appreciation of cricket are just 'over the moon' and feel it is a just reward for your hard work, dedication and, above all, ability.*

The Second Test against the Sri Lankans, in Hobart, was a cracking game, though. I can still picture in my mind the screamer of a catch that Ian Healy took down the leg side to get rid of Ratnayeke as the match hung in the balance. He had scored 75 and looked as though he was going to save the game for them. But he got a lot of bat on one down the leg side and Healy took one of those catches that can be the winning, and losing of Test matches. It was a good game—with our victory coming only in the last twenty minutes of the final day. Another 100 down there (108 in the second innings) added to the growing quality of my summer. In scoring it I joined a very select band—the '3000 Club'—batsmen who had scored more than 3000 first-class runs in a calendar year. In fifty-five innings in that truly remarkable year in my career I accumulated 3092 runs at 58.34 and became the first batsman to top the milestone since Bill Lawry with 3122 in 1964. To join the likes of Bradman, Harvey, Macartney, Trumper, Lawry, Simpson and Morris was a tremendous thrill for me.

The legendary Bill 'Tiger' O'Reilly offered a tribute in print— and it meant a lot to me. In the *Sydney Morning Herald*, Bill wrote, generously: 'Mark Taylor, the country boy from Wagga Wagga, turned out to be this country's best contribution to international batsmanship since the Second World War.'

With Wasim Akram, Waqar Younis, Javed Miandad, Mushtaq Ahmed and the like in the ranks there was never any doubt that the Pakistanis who awaited us subsequently were going to be very tough. I believe that the Test in Melbourne on a difficult wicket was one of the greatest of my career. Wasim bowled absolutely beautifully in the match on a pitch providing encouragement and finished with ten wickets for the Test. But we got home late on the last day via a great catch at point by Geoff Marsh to remove Ijaz Ahmed.

I had a game to remember—52 in the first innings after I had taken a knock from Wasim which I thought had broken my arm, followed by 101 in the second on a really tough wicket. In addition, I finished with five catches.

SYDNEY MORNING HERALD, 15 January 1990:

MARVELLOUS MARK MASTERS THE 'WOLF'
The wolf was at Australia's throat again in the first cricket Test yes-
terday, but Mark Taylor stood as immovable as the great tram jam
clogging the streets of Melbourne. In three days Wasim Akram (6–62,
4–77) proved himself the most explosive young fast bowler in the game.

Wasim and Waqar were quick and dangerous throughout that series, Wasim was probably the best bowler I had faced up to that time. For Waqar it was his first campaign out here and he was a real steamhead, sharp and awkward to play. I got 77 and 59 against them in Adelaide and Dean Jones scored two 100s in a Test in which, after looking like we were going to bolt it in, we had to hang in for a draw on the last day.

The rains came in Sydney and washed away any chance of a result. But there was enough cricket for me to pick up 101 not out. I was delighted with what I had achieved: 52, 101, 77, 59, 101 not out against a really high-class bowling attack. Only in my beginning as a Test player, against the West Indies, had I faced bowling of such sustained quality. At the end of the series I was named No. 1 batsman in the world under the Deloitte's Rating system.

The domestic first-class season proved a successful one for me, too. I got 199 in Adelaide one day—and we went on to win the Shield final, with myself unexpectedly as NSW captain for the first time. Sharing a long partnership of 263 with Mark Waugh (172), I had a ball in the game against South Australia. But I still rue the way I got out, just as I was ticking off the double century on an easy wicket I gave one chance—dropped by the 'keeper off big Phil Alley on the leg side at 70. That apart, I never had a moment's worry. Then on 199, I was facing leg-spinner Peter Sleep. They had one slip and everyone else in the ring, and Peter wasn't bowling that well. I was just coasting along, thinking that I would hang on until he bowled me a bad one and deal with it accordingly for the 200. I blocked a couple, then he bowled me a regulation leggie—and I nicked it straight to David Hookes at slip, and was gone.

In the Shield final of 1989–90, we played Queensland. There was a lot of speculation about our skipper Geoff Lawson, who was struggling with a crook shoulder. The papers were wondering who would be captain if he didn't play. I honestly didn't think much about it all. I didn't realise Henry was struggling that much.

On the morning of the match NSW selector Neil Marks pulled me aside. 'I want you to do two things today,' he said. 'Yeah? What's that?' I asked. Said Neil: 'Well, I'd like you to make 100.' 'I'll do my best,' I replied. 'And you've got to win the toss,' he continued. Win the toss? What's he talking about? I thought. 'What do you mean?' I asked. 'Henry's out,' said Harpo. 'You're the captain.'

I went straight out there and lost the toss. But they put us in to bat and I got the 100 Neil Marks had requested, and another one in the second innings. We won by a squillion—345 runs to be precise.

Pitchforked without warning into the captaincy, I had only one tough decision to make. After we had made 360, Moey Matthews took 5–31 and spun them out for 103. Everyone was saying, 'Make them follow on. Let's get them in again, and nail them.' I gave it some thought. There were three days to go and I figured that the only way we could lose the game after leading by 257 was if they went in and made 400 or so, and left us 150 to get, batting last. 'Stuff that,' I thought. So we batted again, and I made my second 100 of the game—and we ended up setting them 654 to win. They didn't even get close. This was when Queensland were the perennial bridesmaids of the Sheffield Shield. Then in the '90s they spoiled it all by finally winning a couple of comps. The first time was as if North Sydney won the rugby league premiership (they last won in 1922). Domestic cricket had lost one of its great talking points.

In early 1990 the *Daily Telegraph* honoured me by naming me NSW Sport Star of the Year. An old pal, Laurie Pilon was so moved to see a country boy doing well that he burst into verse:

Amiable, affectionate and altogether affable
Cool, calm, collected—and certainly unflappable
Pulling, driving, sweeping
Playing cut shots to a T
Taking great slips catches,
Overhead, or on one knee,
Scoring century after century
The reasons are quite clear
Why the Telegraph *named Mark Taylor*
Sportsperson of the Year.

In New Zealand in early 1990, the Kiwis caught us on the hop. For the two days before the scheduled Test at Wellington it poured non-stop. It was still raining on the morning of the Test, and I recall that my roomie Peter Taylor made me a nice cup of tea as I stayed in bed with the rain tumbling down outside. The feeling was pretty relaxed. No way we'll play today, we thought. The word from the ground was continuing rain, with more forecast. There was speculation that if it kept up, we'd miss the first two or three days and instead of a Test the organisers would schedule a couple of one-dayers on the last couple of days.

Anyhow, we wandered down to the ground and just after lunch it stopped raining and blue sky appeared. They rolled off the covers and, surprise, surprise, there was no water underneath. We would play today.

At stumps on the first day we were all out for 110 and they were 0–18 in reply. We were in trouble. Eventually we knocked them over for 202. But we were still struggling, and got knocked over again for only 269, leaving them 178 to get, which we figured would be tough on a wicket giving some help. In fact they coasted home one-down, with opener John Wright getting 117 not out. So in the Test match that was never going to happen, we got badly beaten. Richard Hadlee bowled really well and was the main destroyer, with seven wickets in his last Test against Australia. Peter Taylor, better known as a bowler, had the distinction of top-scoring in both our innings with 29 and 87. At least, however, we had the satisfaction of winning a three-cornered one-day series against India and the Kiwis.

For me, the roller-coaster of my career so far seemed to have reached a peak. The Ashes summer that followed in 1990–91 was nowhere near as productive as the home summer had been. Physically, I hit a hurdle early and, mentally, I had somehow slipped out of the 'zone' in which I had dwelt for most of the 1989–90 season. In a Country Cup game before the first Test against England, I busted a finger, which was not the ideal start to the year. It happened in my old home town of Wagga, of all places. I went for a caught-and-bowled and took it right on the point of the little finger on my right hand. Probably there was a message there about me having a bowl.

I played the First Test in Brisbane with the finger strapped and wearing a special guard and got 10 and 67 not out. I came out of the slips and fielded at mid-on. I even took a catch there to dismiss Robin Smith—a different experience for sure with the longer wait for the ball to arrive than in slips. Geoff Marsh and I began the second innings chase for 150 to win the match—and got them, none-down.

At the end of the game, however, coach Bob Simpson walked up to me and tapped me on the shoulder. 'Mark, well done today,' he said. 'But I need to let you know the news that you're not in the one-day team.' One of the reasons offered was that my broken finger would inevitably hamper my fielding and the time off would give me time to recover. The message was roughly: give it a couple of weeks, and then you'll come back into the side.

I was very disappointed—and that was really the start of the ongoing controversy about me and one-day cricket. I had played in the one-day World Series Cup against Pakistan and Sri Lanka, the previous year, which we duly won and made a pretty reasonable showing. Now, I was sidelined—and the fact was that despite what was said I didn't step straight back into the side at all, only getting the call very late in the series when Allan Border pulled a leg muscle. I played both finals, against New Zealand, scored some runs—41 and 71—and won Man of the Finals. That, I can reveal, gave me a deeper sense of satisfaction than I showed publicly at the time.

I realised then, and now, that it wasn't an easy call for selectors. Geoff Marsh and David Boon at that stage were probably the form one-day openers. But from my point of view—with a reputation as one of the best batsmen in the world and the best opening batsman—it wasn't easy to take.

GREG CHAPPELL, *Sun-Herald*, 23 December 1990: *I don't care how they do it, as long as Taylor is in. He has the potential to be anything. Outside Bradman, who is in a category of his own, Taylor could become the best batsman Australia has produced. I'm convinced he would develop into an excellent one-day cricketer and I believe one-dayers will improve his batting at Test level.*

The one-day snub planted a seed of self-doubt in my mind. I scored 60 in the first innings of the Melbourne Test, in a game we again won easily, but my summer was pretty much downhill from there, apart from the brief interlude of the one-day finals.

We won the Test series 3–0, but it was a closer battle than that—more hard-fought and evenly fought than the 1989 Ashes on their home soil. They missed significant opportunities in both Brisbane and Melbourne. In both matches we were level-pegging after the first innings (46 behind in Melbourne, in fact)—but each time they crumbled in their second innings just when they were poised to set up winning advantages. We chased fourth-innings targets on both occasions, of 157 and 197 respectively, and won comfortably.

Those matches were pretty much representative of the Test series I played against the Poms over the seasons. Never was it a case of us just rocking out there on day one and nailing them. In many games there was a sense of things being delicately in the balance at certain times—the chance that the pendulum could swing either way. There's no doubt that England have had their opportunities in recent years. But the difference between the two sides was always this: that when Australia had its opportunity, the chance was almost always taken. With England, more often than not, the chance was *not* taken.

Many theories about this have been aired. My own is this: that English cricket lacks a certain toughness within its current structure. In County cricket there are so many matches that I am sure that if a game gets away, well, it doesn't matter so much. Another one will be along in a moment. They play up to six days a week—and as a result the necessary hard edge which breeds hard players and tough teams is missing to an extent. Sometimes there must inevitably be a feeling that a game ahead is just another game. I have no doubt that the Sheffield Shield is a much more cut-throat operation—and consequently one of the secrets of our success. In the Shield there are six teams and ten games. There is not a lot of margin for error—every match counts.

I can assure you that Shield cricket is very hard cricket indeed. The extent of sledging that exists in cricket—even if it's not too dramatic—has a sharper edge in Shield games than anywhere else. State against State is tough cricket, taken very seriously by the men who play it.

At the moment, for varying reasons, we breed tougher cricketers and technically better cricketers than the Poms. And it's when closely balanced games are there for the taking that these factors come to the fore. It all adds up to England's problem ... and Australia's winning advantage. I do believe, however, that things are improving in England. More four-day games and a two-tiered system with promotion and relegation for the counties will lead to greater competition—and possibly a better English team.

Chapter 8

CALYPSO CRUNCH

My lasting impression of my first tour to the West Indies, in 1991, is of a non-stop barrage of fast bowlers—big, lean, mean blokes steaming in, wherever we went. The series was undoubtedly the toughest and hardest of my years in the game. By a mile. It goes without saying that the people of the Caribbean islands are wonderfully passionate about cricket in general. But at that particular time they were *especially* passionate about cricket played in the fast lane, their battery of quicks having ridden roughshod over most of the world through the 1980s.

Built on pace and aggression, the West Indians were the best team in the world—awesome. Every team we played over there had four quicks. In the Tests the quartet of Patrick Patterson, Curtly Ambrose, Malcolm Marshall and Courtney Walsh came at us relentlessly. Elsewhere blokes like Tony Gray, Ian Bishop and Kenneth Benjamin took over the running. The cricket played was about as physical as it can possibly get. Someone called the whole thing a 'dockyard brawl'—a colourful phrase, but probably not too far off the mark.

When I reflect on the series, which we lost 2–1, I think we were still scared to an extent—no, not scared . . . *intimidated* is a better word. There is no doubt that all of us gave 100 per cent in that series, but when it came to the mental game, they still had our measure. We didn't beat them then, or in 1992–93 because deep down we didn't *believe* that we could beat them. In 1991 they were the better side, with a better attitude. We competed, but they won fair and square. No doubt about that.

That tour, it was on from the word go. The first game against the West Indies Board of Control President's XI at St Kitts had blokes like Patterson, Gray and Benjamin lined up against us. It was a game I remember sharply, for a few reasons. For starters I scored a second-innings 100, which was a great way to begin the tour.

But it was not without incident. I remember at one stage cracking Patrick Patterson through the covers for four—a sweet shot that gave me considerable pleasure. But there was close enough to a deathly silence as the ball cannoned into the fence. Immediately, Patrick was after me. He bumped me next ball, and it was right on the money and sat me on my bum. This time the crowd went berserk, producing a tremendous roar that cascaded around the ground. Next ball was a bouncer, too, that had me ducking for cover. Again, a mighty roar went up.

It was at this point that I turned to the crowd and gave them an energetic two-finger salute. I was steamed up. 'So that's what you think of cricket,' I was saying to them under my breath. 'A bouncer gets a bigger cheer than a good shot through the covers.' I was fired up and, wisely or not, I let the crowd know what I thought. The next morning, back home one of the papers had a headline along the lines of 'Crowd brings Taylor to tears', which was rubbish. I certainly wasn't in tears. I was just bloody angry.

PATRICK SMITHERS, *Australian*, 21 February 1991: *Mark Taylor made a century yesterday in the same way a sick man pulls up the covers in bed and sweats off a fever. It was not a pleasant experience, but something he had to do.*

The tour was a tough and testing experience, as they always are over there, with incident and drama aplenty and intermittent rain to play its part in the Tests themselves. We got rolled 2–1 in the end, but in a series in which opportunities slipped through our fingers. In the First Test in Jamaica we had them 6–75 and later 8–166, with Gus Logie down at the hospital getting patched up after Craig McDermott hit him under the eye with a bumper. Curtly Ambrose hung around just long enough with Jeff Dujon for Logie to get back to the ground and, just when we had them on the ropes, he and Dujon restored the innings and they finished with 264. We had a great chance to grind them under when we were about 2–227. Boonie got 100, Geoff Marsh made 69 and I got 58, but we eventually lost our last five for almost nothing and the lead of 107 was not what it could have been. After the rains came the groundsmen put petrol on the wicket and set fire to it to try to get the match quickly back on track. But the weather won in the end, and it was a draw.

The sort of challenge I faced as an opener was at least on show very early. In Jamaica, the first three balls I received from Curtly Ambrose were bouncers. Here we go, I thought. This is the way it's going to be.

And it was. Most of the guys in our team believed that Patrick Patterson on his day was the quickest of the Test quartet, for pure pace. I didn't necessarily agree. The only one of them to actually hit me on the head was Malcolm Marshall, in Jamaica. Of the four, Marshall was the one pitching the ball up most and he just took me by surprise with a bouncer which clouted me on the jaw.

It was Curtly Ambrose, with his steepling bounce from a great height, who bowled me some of the quickest balls I had ever faced. I remember a moment late one afternoon in Antigua, in the Fifth Test. I was batting with Ian Healy, who had come in as night-watchman after Swampy lost his wicket. The light was fading, and Ambrose bowled me a bouncer that I just managed to dodge, by a centimetre or two, at eye level. It was travelling. I looked up the other end, and 'Heals' was smiling. 'Gee, that was quick!' he said with a grin at the end of the over. At that moment the umpires conferred, and called off play, owing to the light. The ball that Ambrose bowled me that late afternoon has always stuck in my mind. I think it was the most lethal bouncer I ever faced.

They smashed us in Guyana, particularly Richie Richardson who got 180. Our 348 faded into insignificance against their 569 and they knocked us over for 248 in the second, for a comprehensive ten-wickets win. Rain was the only winner in Trinidad for the Third Test—and the Fourth, in Barbados, again represented opportunities lost for us. We restricted them to 150 in the first innings and we were thinking that this was going to be the chance. They promptly knocked us over for 134—at which point Gordon Greenidge launched a one-man assault on our bowlers, supported by Richie Richardson's 99, and scored 226. Gordon had a weird series; I think he made 366 runs in total, but 226 of them came in this one knock. He was in full cry that day, a great player right on his game. Richie Richardson, too, was pretty devastating that game. They ended up beating us. I dug in on the final day, hanging around for a long time for 76. I was finally bowled by a shooter from Marshall which just ran along the ground. I got an encouraging fax from my parents that night, in which Dad said characteristically: 'Congratulations (at last)! You have apparently returned to reading my coaching manual. Give 'em hell from now on!'

In Antigua we got one back for a more respectable series result, after a game which my mum and dad will probably never forget. It was a darned good Test for Australia and for Mark Taylor—but not nearly so good for Tony and Judy Taylor who had flown to the Windies for the match. It was the Test in which we at last grabbed our opportunities after a strong first-innings batting display in which Mark Waugh got 100, Dean Jones 80 and AB and I 50s each. I copped a bad decision, which didn't please me. Trying to sweep Carl Hooper, I missed by a fair space and the ball flicked my thigh pad. I was given out caught behind. I was dirty.

The second-innings provided a terrific finale to my tour. In a struggling Aussie innings I managed to provide the meat, scoring 144 out of a total of 265. I went close to carrying my bat. I recall Courtney Walsh bowling beautifully that day. We were eight down when I was caught and bowled by Curtly Ambrose, trying to whip him over mid-wicket. The ball took the leading edge and fired straight back to the big bloke.

The West Indians started the fourth day chasing the formidable target of 455 to win the game. Mum and Dad summed things up and decided the fourth day would be something of a battle of attrition, with the Windies taking it slow and steady. They figured that shopping and relaxing at the beach were a preferable option. So it was that they failed to see us knock the Windies off their perch with the bowlers, headed by Merv Hughes's 2–49, sharing the load as we bundled them out for 297. They also missed seeing me get my Man of the Match award. 'How did it go?' they asked when I met them back at the hotel. I told them. There was silence and then . . . 'Oh, no!' I don't think Mum was all that bothered, but Dad was really spewing, mainly because he didn't want to go shopping in the first place. Swervyn Mervyn also had a few terse things to say to my folks re their absence.

The fierce nature of that series, on and off the field, came despite a pre-tour meeting at which Allan Border and coach Bob Simpson met West Indies skipper Viv Richards and Clive Lloyd, their manager, to defuse some ill-feeling that had emerged in the last series in Australia. They all agreed that it needed fixing, and that the two sides should get together for a beer after every day's play.

Well, that lasted one Test—in Jamaica. About half the blokes on each side would meet after the day's play. The two sides just managed to sustain the effort for the duration of that game, but that was it. By Guyana, they weren't coming into our room, and we weren't going into theirs. If there was any blame in that, it was shared 50–50. Out on the field, in the seething atmosphere of the grounds over there, it was more akin to a prize fight. The feeling between the two sides was really bad. It was tough and bruising cricket, played with great aggression. The spinners hardly took a wicket through the series. It was just quick, quick, quick. As my wife Judi can confirm, I was bordering on punchy when I got back home, and it took me two or three weeks to get back on an even keel. I had spent twelve weeks in a sporting war zone, and it showed. I had played every game except three one-dayers, opening the batting against the relentless assault that was the reality of West Indian cricket at that time. I came home ready to belt someone!

The series probably reflected pretty accurately the nature of the captains, Allan Border and Viv Richards—two tough, hard crick-eters who had played against each other many times. Neither was going to give anything away. Neither was going to be the first to take a backward step ... or even a *sideward* step.

I didn't see the best of Viv Richards, undoubtedly a very great player. He was right near the end of his career when I struck him in the two dead-rubber Tests back in Australia when I first played against the Windies, and then again in this 1991 series. I don't remember him playing the great and powerful shots for which he was renowned. I saw him when he was a cricketer near the end of the road. I have no doubt, though, of his qualities as a batsman— and even in 1991 he still had an air of arrogance about him. He walked the walk. In his own country he was a god.

At the end of the series Richards ripped into Bob Simpson at an extraordinary press conference. 'You treat people as you are treated and he ain't our cup of tea, man,' he said, labelling Simpson 'sour'. 'You can quote me as saying he is a moaner and a bad loser,' said Richards. Our coach declared himself 'amazed, disappointed and a bit shocked'. Richards's comments summed up the way that series had been—bitter, hard-fought, far more shade than light. There was little fraternising between the teams. It wasn't until later series when the cold war thawed that I felt I got to know (and like) some of the West Indian players.

Playing in the West Indies is a unique experience in world

cricket. People who have never been there, I'm sure, have the perception that when it comes to cricket it's a calypso carnival all the way—balmy weather, glamorous places . . . a tropical paradise. Well, that's not *quite* the way it is, although there are some beautiful islands and some fun spots to go to. The West Indian experience is a mixed bag, for sure, with some pretty edgy and uneasy spots on the itinerary. Kingston, the capital of Jamaica, for example, is a very tough town. When we first went there they told us it was known as 'K-town'—the 'K' being for killing. We spent a lot of time there in '91. Guyana is a struggling third-world country on the South American subcontinent. Not too much glamour there. At the other end of the scale Barbados is a lovely island; we spent more time there in '95 than we had in '91, and this helped the campaign. The weather throughout is certainly tropical, often unpredictable. I recall days in Trinidad in 1991 in which we sat on the balconies of our hotel rooms playing cards while the rain poured down outside. A drain outside the hotel had become a river. And despite the apparent closeness of everything when you look at the dots on a map, the travel can be a real problem as you hop from place to place; on my tours there were painfully slow days as we waited for this connection or that to take us . . . not far.

One certainty of a West Indies campaign is that you will find great passion for the game of cricket wherever you go. The people are just cricket mad—and their exuberance and desire to see their team do well create a truly gladiatorial atmosphere at matches.

I rate the 1991 Caribbean campaign as my toughest tour. Others might argue that the difficulties presented by the Indian-Pakistani subcontinent make a series there cricket's biggest test. But for all the enjoyment I have taken from the West Indies, it is in my view the tour, both physically and mentally, that brings you to ask the most questions of yourself. That's especially the case for an opening batsmen in this place in cricket's world where speed, undoubtedly, is king.

Chapter 9

ZIMBABWE *and* AFTER

Back from the West Indies for the home season of 1991–92 Steve Waugh and I did our darndest to get a young leg-spinner named Shane Warne to leave Victoria and come and play for NSW. We nearly brought it off, too. The three of us went with the Australian B side to Zimbabwe. I was captain—my first experience of leading an Australian side—and Tugger was vice-captain. This was the next generation, a side containing the likes of Warne, Paul Reiffel and Tom Moody. We took two leggies—Warne and Peter McIntyre, another Victorian.

Both bowled very well, but even back then there was no doubt Warne was going to be something extra special. In those days the most famous blond in cricket had more of a 'bluey' look about him: his hair had more of a reddish tinge than it does today. For a young leg-spinner, he just about had it all—even then. He was a big turner of the ball and his flipper was as good then as it ever got. He'd start it wide of off-stump and drift it back in. On the Zimbabwe tour I remember him bowling both Andy Pycroft and Dave Houghton, two players bound for Test status when Zimbabwe gained full international recognition in 1992, as they tried to cut him. Warne 1991 was not too different from Warne now—a bit of a larrikin, and an outstanding talent.

Amazingly, he was really struggling to get a game for Victoria. At the time they were strong in medium-fast and seam bowlers—the likes of Merv Hughes, Paul Reiffel, Damien Fleming and Tony Dodemaide—and the spinners were battling to get a look in. Steve Waugh and I told him he'd be sure to get at least eight games a season with NSW, with Perth and Brisbane the only two he might miss. Warnie was good mates with Steve's younger brother Dean and there was some strong lobbying from Bankstown club for him to come up too. Most importantly of all, Warnie was keen.

In the end Victoria got wind of the plan and headed it off at the pass. They started picking him for the State, and kept picking him. He progressed so quickly that by the middle of the season he was a Test player, and it was obvious he would never be playing for NSW. A shame really—Shane Warne would have had some fun on the SCG wicket. Notwithstanding, he went on to become the Grand Master of the ancient art of leg-spin.

The rebirth of the leggies helped change the balance of world cricket. Via the Australians in the '70s and the West Indies in the '80s, the established lore of cricket was that if you picked a battery of mean 'quicks' and set out to intimidate the opposition, you had the formula for winning cricket.

The change back to a richer, more varied approach took time. For years Bill 'Tiger' O'Reilly lamented the lack of leggies on the scene. It's sad that he wasn't around to see the full restoration of the art in recent times, headed by Shane Warne. On the world stage, Abdul Qadir emerged as something of a magician. Trevor Hohns played five of the six Tests for Australia in the 1989 Ashes series. And NSW had a fine exponent of the leg-spinning art in Bob 'Dutchie' Holland.

I didn't see the best of Qadir, although I did play a couple of games against him in the '80s. From all that I have seen and heard about him, I don't believe he was as good a bowler as Warne. One point: he didn't like bowling against lefties too much, whereas Warne has defied old beliefs about leg-spinners by building a high success rate against left-handed batsmen.

For a time, the theory given most support was that if you were going to beat the West Indies then you had to beat them with fast bowling. In fact, that's *not* the way to beat them. The way to beat them is to take them on at *your* game, not theirs. Many sides have failed by trying to beat the Windies at their game. I don't believe there's any doubt that the West Indies batsmen play better against fast bowling than they do against other kinds of bowling. It was in no small way because of the emergence of a leg-spinner of Shane Warne's quality that the balance gradually shifted on the international stage.

Through the colour, excitement and unpredictability they bring to the game, I hope the leggies thrive forever. England don't produce them, with their wickets and their system being against the breed. When you are playing as much cricket as they do over there, it tends to produce a lot of guys who bowl medium-pace, plonking the ball on a good line and length and virtually trying to entice a batsman into getting himself out with a rash shot. In Australia there is a very different philosophy, of using our spinners as a genuine attacking option. They're not just there to nag away—they're there to get blokes out.

The Zimbabwe tour of 1991 was a relaxing and enjoyable experience after the white-heat atmosphere of the West Indies campaign. On one memorable day a pilot named Captain Hook, with Mrs Hook as our flight hostess, flew us in an ancient DC3 over the Victoria Falls. On request Captain Hook got special clearance and took us on what they call the 'Flight of the Angels', down low through the mist, over the falls, then up the Zambesi River. Mrs Hook had thoughtfully packed several cases of beer which we drank on the way home. It was a fabulous day, the sort of experience that represents the icing on the cake when it comes to life as a cricket tourist.

Back home, a typically crowded year awaited: the Shield, a tour by India, World Series Cup, and then the World Cup. Cricket was becoming that way—moving ever-closer to an all-season global game in which the whites were never long in the wardrobe.

We had the Indians in trouble from the word go. In an early game in Lismore, on a bouncing wicket, we (NSW) whipped them in three days. That was the only lead-up game before the Tests began—and it was to be the story of the tour. The Indian team that year was laced with good players—Vengsarkar, Shastri, Tendulkar, Azharuddin, Kapil Dev—but for whatever reason they rarely clicked into gear.

We won the series very easily, 4–0. The only Test we didn't win was Sydney's, in which Tendulkar gave a glimpse of things to come with a really good 100. The nature of that century and one he scored at the end of the tour on a Perth wicket that was decidedly 'un-Indian' in character confirmed him as a special player, even then. In Brisbane, during a Test we won in quick time, I scored probably the worst 90 of my entire career. Talk about scratchy! But I pottered around and hung in there for a long time—and all of a sudden, on 94, I was a chance for a Test 100. At that point, justice was done. Trying to sweep one, I got no more than a top edge; the ball flew up and hit me in the chest and popped up for bat-pad. At the end of the day people were saying to me: 'Gee, you must be disappointed you missed out on the hundred.' 'No way,' I answered. 'I can't believe I'd got to 94!'

The Sydney Test was Shane Warne's first. When Ravi Shastri was on six, Warnie dropped him off a fairly straightforward caught-and-bowled chance. Exactly 200 (Shastri) runs later Warne had him caught at deep extra-cover to take his first Test wicket. Shane finished with 1–150 off 45 overs after that early lost opportunity.

That was a funny Test match. They won the toss and sent us in—which is something you *never* do in Sydney. We couldn't believe it. There's no way that you choose to bat last in Sydney. But as it turned out after we had scored 313 they just smashed us, with Shastri getting 206 and Tendulkar 148 not out. They passed our score only four-down and went on to make 483. In fact, *we* had to bat last—and hung on under increasing pressure on the last day to finish eight down for 173, but safe for the draw. This Test confirmed my theory that the toss of the coin—whether you choose to bat or field—rarely decides the outcome of the game. The side that plays the better cricket over five days does that. Apart from that, we had the wood on them pretty comprehensively, although Adelaide was a match that ebbed and flowed to an extent. In the end Boonie and I got hundreds in the second innings and we set them 372 to win, which proved beyond them.

In Perth, we won easily, despite some distractions. Australia's vice-captain Geoff Marsh was dropped and Victorian Wayne Phillips picked for what was to be a one-off Test match. Swampy was obviously very upset to be dropped for a Test to be played in front of his home crowd, but he was very supportive of Phillips, and said all the right things. The WACA crowd, however, gave Phillips a terrible razzing. It was pretty horrible stuff—and unfair. It wasn't Phillips's fault that he was there, and Marsh was not. On reflection, it was a mistake by the selectors. The match was a 'dead rubber' game and the dropping of Marsh was certain to be inflammatory. They would have been better off leaving Geoff there, maybe with a final warning: 'Get some runs here, or we're going to have to leave you out.' Instead, they created a nightmare for Wayne Phillips on Marsh's home 'patch'. The decision on Marsh ended his international career and led to me being named as vice-captain for my first series—against the Sri Lankans mid-year. For the first time there was public speculation that I was on track to be the next Australian captain. I was aware of the talk, and the thought was inevitably there somewhere at the back of my mind. But I never sat down and discussed it with anyone. Whatever was to happen was out of my hands.

The Indians never seemed happy or settled on that tour. They suffered from a complaint which once used to afflict Australian teams on the subcontinent, but which we became increasingly better at dealing with in more recent years. Australian teams used to tour there expecting everything to be so different that they could never approach it the way they would a home series. They automatically thought in terms of turning wickets, bad umpiring, crook food, bad spectators. These preconceptions are something we worked very hard to change on recent tours to the subcontinent, and I believe we achieved reasonable success.

I'm quite proud of the headway we made on that, and to have been part of it. The senior members—including the Waughs, Heals, myself and the two coaches, Bob Simpson and Geoff Marsh—concentrated on developing a more positive outlook. Sure you can get crook over there and the crowds can get to you if you let them. But there is much else offered by way of compensation. Our philosophy became: 'Okay, it's going to be very different from what I know back home. But it's the way things are there . . . and there is much to enjoy and learn. Going on this tour will make me a better, more rounded person.'

The Indians of 1991–92 suffered from the same sort of siege mentality that used to plague our teams on some tours. At the end of the series Sunil Gavaskar came out strongly in print, questioning the balance of the umpiring during the series. The statistics were that we got fourteen lbws to their seven during the Tests. Looking back, I can understand they would feel pretty ordinary about such a stat. The challenge of the tour generally, with the hostile crowds and the full-frontal approach of our team seemed to get under their skin more than it should have. I reckon the way to tackle tours is to accept the realities. For the Indians in Australia this meant they would get different wickets, some of them—such as Perth—with real pace, highly competitive opposition in any match they played, and crowds who loved nothing better than a hometown Aussie victory. Those things have to be taken on board and accepted as inevitable elements of the tour, and then a game plan mapped out within that framework.

I was interested to read some comments of Sri Lanka's captain Arjuna Ranatunga on some of these points during his team's last visit here. A tough nut in his own way, Ranatunga has generally been something of a critic of Australian crowds and aspects of an Australian tour. But this time he declared the challenge was no more or less than going to the subcontinent—accepting what the situation was, and making the most of it.

My in-and-out life as a one-day cricketer continued its uncertain path that season. I played little part in the World Series Cup, against India and Sri Lanka—and Merv Hughes and I were virtually 13th and 14th men for the World Cup that followed. My two call-ups in the World Cup produced scores of 13 against India and 0 against England—after which I faded out of the picture. Pakistan pipped us for fourth spot in the finals after a not-too-impressive build-up and went on to win the Cup over England in the final.

PETER ROEBUCK, *Sydney Morning Herald*, 11 March 1992: *Here he is, beside Desmond Haynes and maybe Graham Gooch as one of the world's leading opening batsmen, and here he is too—cast off as trenchcoats are by explorers entering the jungle.*

It was at the close of our summer, as eyes turned to Sri Lanka, and beyond that I made a decision to toughen up the way I prepared for cricket.

Chapter 10

....

THE FITNESS
FACTOR

After my first training session with a bloke named Kevin Chevell in 1992 my thighs burned as if they had red-hot pokers running through them. They hurt with even the lightest touch. Walking up or down stairs was agony. Yes, my introduction to the Chevell Method was memorable in its own, painful way. With time away from cricket after the World Cup I decided that with Aussie Rules gone from my sporting life, I had to substitute something else in the way of hard physical yakka. For much of my life, winter football had kept me fit for summer cricket. Now, there was just cricket.

So I joined my NSW team-mate Steve Small to link up with Chevell, a former fast bowler and a health and fitness expert who owned a gym at Penrith, on Sydney's western fringe. On and off (and with maybe not enough 'on') I trained under Kevin Chevell's guidance up to 1998, when he helped get me ready for what was to be my last first-class season.

I'm thinking that I should be with him again right now. Since I made my decision to retire from Test cricket the subsequent let-down has seen a few kilos piled on the Taylor frame. Kevin could get rid of those. I just don't know if I want the pain . . .

He's a hard taskmaster but, for me, proved a bloody good one. Once I had survived the first couple of weeks with him and my body got used to the fierce work-outs, the results were amazing. I was stronger, faster, fitter. There was bike-riding, rowing and weights. Upper- and lower-body work. You name it. In six weeks Kevin could transform me into the athlete I wanted to be. Well, pretty close. To a degree physical fitness transfers into mental confidence. But I have always been a believer that no matter how much work you do off the field there are no guarantees. Cricket is such a mental game that you still have to get the package right on the field.

Throughout my career, I probably didn't work physically hard enough often enough. At various times I worked harder than most other cricketers. But I tended to be spasmodic; on reflection, if I had worked twelve months a year, I would have been better off. I got into a rough pattern—hitting the gym, dieting, getting really fit leading up to a season, then tapering off during the season itself and feeling the strength and the fitness gradually ebbing away again. The next off-season, the cycle would begin again.

The dinner table was one of the trouble spots of my career. The problem was always pretty simple: that I love a good feed, and I love a beer just about as much if there happens to be one going. I would say that I'm easy to feed; I eat just about everything. And beer? I suppose I've tried most of 'em. Crown Lager rates highly with me, and I like the real beer taste of the good English 'bitters', having tried one or three on the various Ashes campaigns.

In my periods of training with Kevin Chevell, I watched my diet studiously. I'd be strictly on the fruit and vegies, and keeping a close check on my alcohol intake. The trouble for me always was an inclination to drift back to the things I like.

I happen to have these days a manager, John Fordham, who is a wine connoisseur and expert and who has something of a reputation as a luncher. And I have always found that a lunch or dinner with good food, a nice glass of wine and harmonious company is one of the most enjoyable things in life. I have had one or two of those with J. Fordham over the years, requiring me to redouble my efforts in the gym. Through John's enthusiasm and interest I am now also something of a wine enthusiast myself, with a keen interest in the subject, and a few in the cellar.

The timing of my first training program with Chevell in the autumn of 1992 couldn't have been better. In the first one-day match of our campaign in Sri Lanka, I struck the hottest cricketing day of my life. In Colombo that day it was an absolute stinker—temperature in the high 30s and humidity in the 90s. I batted for more than three hours, and scored 94. At that point, I was out—caught on the fence off their spinner. Reflecting occasionally on a one-day career that produced only one century, I have thought back to that match and to the fact that if I had just knocked it around for a few more singles and made 100 I might have got the one-day monkey off my back. I had done all the hard work—but I was so knackered I felt I just had to go for boundaries. I was at the peak of my physical fitness as a cricketer then, but it was such a brutish day that, even so, I had reached the point at which I could barely run.

Saturated in sweat and utterly exhausted, I went back to the dressing room and just slumped in a chair, barely able to move. There were twenty minutes to go in our innings, plus forty minutes more until we had to field. I had worked harder physically in preparation than ever before in my life, yet I was 'gone'. The last thing I wanted to do was field, but that, of course, was precisely the requirement.

There was some luck in the fact that the captain (AB) and vice-captain (me) of that tour were able to play at all. Both of us could so easily have finished up road-accident statistics in Colombo before we played our first lead-up game, in Kandy. One night a few of us decided we'd have a race back to the Hilton Hotel where we were staying, travelling in the little three-wheel taxis that abound over there. These are pretty basic little conveyances—one wheel in front, two at the back and steered by handlebars like a motorbike. A canvas canopy covers the passengers in the back.

Motoring along at about sixty km/h we were cut off by a big official-looking car with a flag fluttering in front. Within an instant we were over, flipped onto one side and sliding down a main street of Colombo—me underneath with my head down near the road and AB's weight on top. Finally, we slid to a stop—petrol pouring out of the tank which had been ruptured as we skated along the street. Shaken, AB and I clambered out. It was pretty amazing that the thing hadn't burst into flames considering the amount of petrol spraying around. Allan was okay and I had done nothing more than some damage to one ankle. Both of us played the game at Kandy which began next day, although I struggled on my bung leg. We were bloody lucky.

The one-day innings in Colombo was pretty much the highlight of my tour. I got a couple of 40s in the First Test which we won after Moey Matthews and Warnie had gone through them in the second innings, but I didn't make any sort of great impact on the series. We got out of gaol to an extent in that Test. Kaluwitharana got 100 against us on debut, a terrific innings, but then he dropped a regulation chance off Boonie in our second dig—and David went on to make a crucial 68. Instead of setting them only 50 or so we gave them 180 to chase, and won by 16 runs. Overall we played pretty poorly, but got home 1–0 to take the series.

On our return home, my new-found fitness looked as though it was going to help underpin a good domestic season. When the West Indies hit town, I promptly scored a century against them in Sydney. At that point I was run out by 'bloody' Mark Waugh! That, however, was about as good as it got. I ended up having a shocking series against the Windies—to the extent that, as Australian vice-captain, I was dropped to 12th man for the final Test in Perth, just as Geoff Marsh had been the previous year.

It was, as ever, a highly competitive and fiercely fought series and with more than enough drama, too—particularly in the tension of the Adelaide Test. Overall, it was played in a lot better spirit than our previous campaign in the Windies had been, even though the result ended up the same—2–1 to them. For us it was the one that got away. And very likely that again came down to one word, 'belief'. In Brisbane we had them eight down for 133, chasing 231—and couldn't bowl them out. Then, in Melbourne we won, with Warnie taking 7–52 to confirm his growing status as a super-bowler on the world stage. In Sydney, rain intervened to dampen our chances. After our first-innings 503 we were feeling pretty chuffed about our prospects, but they promptly came out and scored 600, with Brian Lara getting his outstanding 277. However, with two spinners in the team—Warne and Matthews—and them on the defensive early on at 2–31 we were nicely placed. But persistent drizzle turned the ball into a piece of soap and blunted the spinners. Hour by hour the game ploughed on towards the inevitable. A draw.

The Fourth Test, on a most un-Adelaide-like strip, was one of *those* games. The wicket was up and down, favouring the ball more than the bat—and when they set us 186 to win in the fourth innings, it was never going to be easy to get. Tim May had ripped through their second innings, taking 5–9 to give us the chance, though, and we had all day to get the runs. We never looked like getting them. Until . . .

At 7–74 and then 8–102, we were in terrible shape. At 9–144 we had struggled a little closer, but the haul was still a long one. Then Tim May and Craig McDermott united against a West Indian attack that seemed to have lost its bite. Right up to the end, they never looked like getting out as the runs ticked by. Finally, with one to tie and two to win, we were set to bring off a near-miraculous victory.

I can still picture in my mind the two balls before it all ended. Facing Courtney Walsh in what turned out to be the last over, Craig stroked one into the covers, with some space between the fieldsman at point and the one at mid-off. It looked an easy single. But they hesitated . . . yes . . . no . . . maybe. Up in the dressing room we were all going *yes, yes yes*! But they stayed put. Next ball, a very tired-looking Walsh tried a short ball which got up about waist-high. Craig played a sort of half-pull which he hit fairly well—but which cannoned straight into Desmond Haynes at bat-pad. Apart from a mid-on there was no-one else on the leg side and if it had evaded Haynes it would have been a certain single (a tie) and probably two (a famous win). The next ball was short again, but with more bounce. Craig turned away to evade it but it flicked his glove and Junior Murray took the catch behind. The match was over.

For hours AB had been shining a ball in the dressing room as we watched the drama unfold. He often did this—called it his worry ball. He'd get an oldish ball and work away at shining it. On this day he was at it for a couple of hours as we climbed from 8–102 to 9–184. By the end, the ball had a beautiful buff on it—it would have swung a country mile. As the umpire's finger rose in that last awful gesture of the match AB hurled his worry ball—just hammered it into the side of the viewing area . . .

This was a devastating moment for Allan. Deep down he probably realised in that instant that his last chance to beat the West Indies had gone, although Perth remained. Over the seasons, he had copped some serious pastings from them. In a personal sense he had always put his hand up against them and competed brilliantly, often against heavy odds. Here he had been within the width of Desmond Haynes's shin from an historic win.

The tension in the dressing room on such a day is very hard to convey in words. I remember just sitting there for ten minutes afterwards, AB fidgeting beside me, the whole thing just eating away at him. Back at the hotel I rang Jude and told her I didn't believe I'd be playing in Perth. I had scored one and seven in Adelaide, looked and felt pretty awful and failed to contribute, as I had hoped, to an Australian win. I couldn't even say that I was part of the reason we managed to scratch up 184 in the second innings. A Sydney *Daily Telegraph* headline summed it up pretty well: TAYLOR FACING THE AXE.

In Perth for the Fifth Test a few days later, some of the West Indies players really rubbed it in by wearing T-shirts that read 'Form is Temporary, Class is Permanent'. After the events of a series that could so easily have been 2–0 our way, that really got under our skins. It was arrogant and hurtful, rubbed in by a speaker from the West Indian camp at a pre-Test dinner. To make things worse, they then went out and whipped us on a typical Perth track. I carried the drinks. Justin Langer opened with Boonie; within three days we were bowled out for 119 and 178 in our two digs and it was all over. They had come back to win the series 2–1.

The job of drinks waiter held no appeal at all for me—or most other players—although it was a job that had to be done. I have always felt a little sorry for the 12th men of the cricket world; now I knew how they felt. The consolation was that at least I was 12th man. I had had four Test matches to make some runs, and hadn't done my job. I was fortunate to be still part of the outfit.

For me it was a gloomy punchline to a largely gloomy domestic season. Much of the time my footwork was terrible, and I just couldn't get myself going. I had done all the foundation work, yet I had to accept along the way that I still wasn't anywhere near the groove. The message was clear enough: just because you feel physically fit and tuned, there's no guarantee you'll go out there and get runs or take wickets. In fact, in the midst of a bad trot the answer may *not* be to go to the gym for an extra hour a day. My old mate Harpo Marks has a theory. He reckons that when a batsman is struggling he should stick his bat under the bed for a while, drag out the golf clubs and get away from it. There are no guarantees. That season proved to me no matter how much effort you put in physically—and there's no doubt you've got to pay that price—in cricket you've still got to get it right on the night . . . or the day. That year at home in 1992–93, I couldn't.

I was by now installed as NSW captain. Geoff 'Henry' Lawson, very much his own man, was not an easy act to follow. Henry was, and is, a bloke of strong personality. His philosophy as a skipper was more or less: 'This is how we're going to do it . . . if you don't like it, don't bother playing.' He did things his way, and inevitably he trod on a few toes. For a captain, Henry's way is not a bad one— if a bit confronting at times. He was in charge, and he would live or die by the way he got the team to accept his methods. He didn't tolerate too much of what he didn't believe was right. I remember a day when he had a real run-in with Peter Taylor, during a one-day game in Sydney. Peter was playing for Australia at that time, but Henry pretty much told him to get off the field if he didn't like the way things were being run.

Later, when Henry became NSW coach and Greg Matthews was his captain, things got very difficult indeed. The pair of them are so similar in their personalities, with an absolute determination to do things their way. Inevitably there would be, and were, clashes.

I don't remember a lot about being made captain. There wasn't too much fanfare. What I do remember more clearly is how emotional and sad Geoff Lawson had been when he announced his retirement after we lost the Shield final against WA the previous season. It was a game we could have won and to have managed that would have been a great finale for Henry, whose contribution to cricket in his era had been so substantial.

It took a trip across the Tasman to begin to rebuild my form and confidence that struggling season. We played the Kiwis in a couple of Tests that were to be the lead-up to our Ashes campaign. In the First Test in Christchurch, a match we won, I scored 82 on a dark, moist green-top. It wasn't any sort of great innings, but I hung in and started to play some shots towards the end. It was my first 50 in eight Tests, so a welcome respite after one of those 'down' periods that seemed, for reasons I can't explain, to punctuate my life in big-time cricket.

A career of some peaks and some valleys is the reality for most cricketers. Almost inevitably, a bad trot will get you at some time. You start to worry, you get a bad decision or two, people start nagging away. The harder you try, the worse it gets. My own experience was absolutely cyclical, coming like clockwork every four seasons in cricket's equivalent of the seven-year itch: 1987–88, 1992–93, 1996–97. As to 'why' . . . I can't explain that.

The series in New Zealand finished 1–1, plus a washed-out draw in Wellington, and the result was something of a travesty. I don't think there was any doubt we were the better side; we flogged them in Christchurch, then were pushing hard for victory in Wellington when the rains came. In a low-scoring Third Test at Eden Gardens we set them 200 to win and Mark Greatbatch came out and slogged a quick 29 to put them on target. They got the runs, seven-down.

I mean in no way whatsoever to disparage the Kiwis, but the Test series against them, of my experience, were always a few rungs down the ladder compared with playing, say, the West Indies or England. The feeling was that you were sort of playing your next-door neighbours, and that was fine—but that the intensity was less than it is against some of the others. I'm sure fans see it that way, too. I doubt there'd be too many could remember any details of the Australian tour over there in '93. In no way is that to suggest that the Kiwis don't produce good cricketers. They do, of course— with Richard Hadlee and Martin Crowe the stand-outs of the modern era. But New Zealand cricketers play their game in a country in which another sport dominates all else. A bloke I played against in one-day internationals is a good example of that. Jeff Wilson was a very capable player—and New Zealand had hopes for him for years to come. He became instead a winger for the All Blacks. And why not? The dividend reaped was across the board: better money, higher profile, better image. The whole package.

Chapter 11

BACK *to the* OLD DART

E ngland's green fields awaited. I was happy to go back, happy as well to have at least grafted out one innings of some duration in New Zealand, drawing encouragement from it and hope that there would be plenty of runs for the taking in the northern summer.

I was delighted that a touring partner and fellow opening bat this time was another ex-Wagga boy, Michael Slater. We openers have a special bond and I counted myself lucky through my career to have had some fine blokes at the other end, 'Slats' certainly being one of them. I batted with a few 'dashers' over the years. In the NSW side Steve Small and I forged a good partnership of contrasting styles. 'Smallie' was a real tearaway, a bloke who went for it from the word go. If the first ball of the day was there to be hit—then he'd *thump* it. That sort of player seemed to complement my style best of all. And Slats, of course, always was and is that way. Aggressive. If someone serves him up a half-volley in the opening over of a Test, he's quite happy to crash it through the covers. I was always a little more what you could call . . . circumspect. And I'm sure the contrast in style helped our partnership as openers. Apart from the fact that we're left- and right-handers—a perfect balance—the presence of two completely different types of openers poses a real problem for bowlers. With me they would try and bowl a tighter line, realising that I wouldn't play anything that was at all wide (remember 'Helium Bat'?). With Slats they'd bowl a wider line, hoping to tempt him into some sort of indiscretion. It worked just fine for us.

Right through cricket's history, the openers have probably always regarded themselves to an extent as men apart—players charged with special responsibilities. As an opener, when you bat with a bloke often enough you get to know him very well. You accept you're going to have to front up with him to adverse situations on some days: a new innings starting, half an hour to play and the light fading, and you out there in the middle while the rest of the boys are cooling their heels in the dressing room.

Through the shared experience and the shared adversity, close friendship and understanding develop between opening batsmen. I was certainly close mates with Slats, and with Swampy Marsh before him—Swampy, of course, being much closer in style to me as an opener. He wasn't a fast scorer—rather a bloke who would dig in, deflecting the ball for his runs.

There's another thing there which sets openers apart. Unlike all the other specialist batsmen, they are never offered a night-watchman. If the team has twenty minutes to face late in the afternoon, there's no way you'll get an offer to send one of the tailenders out there to see things through. I've never been quite able to work that out.

That's a subject I have mentioned many times during my captaincy career. Nine times out of ten when I have asked guys if they want a night-watchman, the answer has been 'yes'. If batsmen other than openers can avoid batting for three overs late in an afternoon, they'll do it. But whenever the answer to that question has been 'yes', I always get a dig in: 'How come you get one and I don't?' It's a fair call, I reckon. Number three gets a night-watchman, but numbers one and two . . . never! I've never understood it. In a particular team an opener might be the best batsman, yet he never gets the gesture of protection offered to others. This is the reason I have never been a great believer in the night-watchman.

People have often asked me about the talking that goes on out in the middle—those little get-togethers at the end of an over. Well, there's rarely anything too profound—mainly just words of reassurance. It may surprise fans that the bowlers don't get discussed all that much. If a batsman is just out there he might say: 'Is Goughie doing his usual stuff?' The answer will be: 'Yeah, pretty straight—hitting the deck . . . an occasional one swinging away.' Early on in a partnership you'll help each other along: How are you seeing them? How are your feet moving? Playing straight? That will last until you feel comfortable—then you'll talk about anything.

More than anything else it is about building your own little 'island' out there. It's two against eleven and for sure the talk will be going on around you: 'Give him a couple of short ones.' 'That's the line . . . he doesn't like it there.' All that sort of thing. At the end of an over it's just a good break to get down the other end and ask of your batting partner the simple question: 'How's it going?' I don't think you ever learn too much new in words exchanged in the middle, though. If you haven't got it down pat by the time you get out there, you're in trouble.

Occasionally, however, a word of advice can settle a batsman down, particularly when your partner can see you becoming frustrated if you're pinned down by a particular bowler. Then the conversation might go this way: 'Are you thinking about donging him over the top?' 'Yeah, I really want to belt this bloke.' 'Well, look—it's only forty minutes to tea. Why don't we hang around for another fifteen minutes or so, just play 'em as they come. He might start to stray a bit by then.'

With some batsmen, there is barely any talk at all. Mark Waugh is not a big talker. And Boonie was never a talker. He was a guy who was entirely focused on his own role and his own responsibilities. He didn't distract himself with talk.

A funny thing about opening batsmen is that a lot of them get on very well with opening bowlers. Off the field there's often chiacking between the two different breeds. 'Big, dumb quicks', I'd call them and they'd fire back with the not unreasonable response: 'If we're big, dumb quicks, how dumb are you blokes having to go out and face us all the time?' I couldn't really argue with the logic. Deeper down there has always been friendship and mutual respect between those who share the opening of any innings.

I got some runs in the Ashes series of 1993, but I came home from that tour with a feeling of slight nagging disappointment, of potentially greater opportunity lost. I got early runs on the tour, 89 in a one-day match against Northampton and 80 at Surrey. In both digs I threw my innings away, but knew I was hitting the ball well. I got the nod for the one-day series (the Texaco Trophy) this time, opening with Matthew Hayden, and got 79 in the first game at Old Trafford, 26 at Edgbaston and 57 at Lord's. I got to captain the team at Lord's—my first experience of leading an Australian team in England. And what a place to start.

The ultimate personal disappointment of my tour, for which I had the honour of being vice-captain, was that I trailed off—after a great start. Centuries in the first two Tests (Old Trafford and Lord's) gave me the chance of making the series a real runs bonanza. But I bogged down in the middle of that series, before scoring a 70 in the last Test at The Oval.

They sent us in at Old Trafford in the First Test and Slats and I began our campaign together by putting on 128. He got 58 and I scored 124. We ended up winning comfortably on a wicket that progressively took spin. Peter Such took six wickets, and it was in that Test that Shane Warne bowled what was to become known as 'the ball of the century'.

From slip, I had a front-stalls view. Mike Gatting, the unfortunate victim, was regarded as one of the better players of spin in the England team. In the main the Poms really struggled against the spinning ball that tour. 'Gatt' was close to the best of them in that regard. But he just copped a wicked, utterly unplayable ball that day. It was an unbelievable delivery, drifting way across him to leg.

The ball's flight squared Gatting up and he tried to play it with a straight bat. His mistake was that he didn't get far enough forward and the ball's drift carried it outside his bat. The leg-break pitched eight or ten centimetres outside leg-stump, then bit and fizzed, taking the off bail. An amazing ball.

Soon afterwards I caught Robin Smith at slip off Warnie. Smith was probably their best player at that time, but he had no idea against the spinners. He really struggled; 'Maysie' (Tim May) got him a few times, and so did Warnie. The really strange thing about that tour was that the Poms put out spinning wickets for the whole series. I think they must have kept clinging to the belief that they could beat us via Embury and Such and Tuffnell. In fact, Tim May bowled a whole lot better than their off-spinners, with far more variety and aggression. He got twenty-one wickets for the series and Warnie thirty-four.

This was the series that launched Shane Warne to super-stardom. His career was well underway already; the 7–52 he took against the West Indies in Melbourne had made everyone sit up and take notice. Now, in England in '93 he was flying high.

The miracle ball he bowled to Mike Gatting accelerated something that was already under way. The emergence of the flipper and all the other weapons in Shane's armament recreating the wrist-spinning art sparked tremendous interest. With the cricket world watching open-mouthed, Warnie was bowling big leggies, little leggies, wrong'uns, flippers, toppies. Commentators like Richie Benaud (a great leg-spinner himself) picked up the phenomenon and ran with it. Suddenly Shane Warne was the talk of the town . . . the talk of the world!

It was a wonderful breakthrough time in cricket. Suddenly fans were seeing far more overs being bowled in a day and highly eventful cricket. They were seeing good attacking spin bowling—rather than four quicks steaming in trying to knock everyone's heads off. They were seeing overs, they were seeing runs. They were seeing blokes batting in caps rather than helmets. They were seeing a different side of Test cricket, and it was just fantastic for the game.

The comprehensive (4–1) series win we built through the summer wasn't completely due to spin wizardry, though. Merv Hughes did a marvellous job through the campaign, but probably got overlooked to an extent in the euphoria of Warne's domination of the England batsmen. In fact, big Merv took thirty-one wickets to Shane's thirty-four. And Merv Hughes really stepped up to be counted that tour.

It was at Lord's in the Second Test that his bowling partner Craig McDermott was taken ill with the serious bowel problem that was to force him out of the tour. Craig got crook on the first day when we were batting, and never bowled a ball. We beat them with ten men, declaring at 4–632 in the first innings. Slats got 152, I got 111, Mark Waugh got 99 and Boonie got 164 not out. If Mark had scored one more run the top four batsmen would have all scored centuries. We bowled them out twice with only three specialist bowlers—Hughes, May and Warne—with Mark Waugh taking the new ball with Merv. It was a bloody good effort.

Merv did a terrific job right through. I can still see him delivering the final ball of the fourth day in the First Test at Old Trafford— cleaning up Mike Gatting with a big inswinging yorker. It was at Old Trafford, too, that a Hughes delivery produced a cricketing rarity—a handling-the-ball dismissal. Graham Gooch punched the ball away as it headed for his stumps after Merv had bowled him a short one. It was a big wicket. We had set them 512 to win and Goochie, with a fighting 133, was the only one who stood between us and victory. The wicket didn't go on Merv's slate, but it was a vital one for us at the time. It was the only time in first-class cricket that I saw a batsman given out for handling the ball.

As England captain for most of the 1993 series, Graham Gooch took the usual savaging from the British press. He stood down from the captaincy after the Fourth Test and played the last two as one of the troops. We respected Goochie, and I liked him a lot. He's a very decent bloke—maybe not a bundle of fun or one of the great 'characters' of the game, but a bloody nice bloke all the same. I much enjoyed the occasions when I had the chance to sit down and have a beer with him.

I could never really understand what the Poms did with him, either. He was one of the world's best opening batsmen, yet in the mid-'90s they shifted him down the list to prop up the middle order. I talked to him about it during the Ashes series here in 1998–99 and he made it clear that the move down the list was not of his doing, or inclination. It was a poor decision in my view.

Merv Hughes's courage through that series was admirable to behold. Through the late '80s (especially against Pakistan in 1989–90) and into the early '90s he had been a wonderfully aggressive fast bowler for Australia, and a character who added great crowd appeal to cricket. With McDermott gone from the tour, and his own physical health waning, his achievement in 1993 was perhaps the crowning glory of his career. By the end of the tour Merv was out on his feet. His knees were gone. Somehow, he played the last Test at The Oval—and shouldn't have. After it he came home for the necessary reconstruction operations and missed most of the home summer.

Merv was an unlikely package; a big, beefy bloke whose *best* bowling weight was around 100 kilos. A good tooth man and enthusiastic with a beer in his hand, he fought a career-long battle with his weight. When it got the better of him he would have been much heavier than the desirable 100 kilograms. As a fast bowler, he never spared himself and the constant pounding eventually took its toll on his legs. He was great that tour.

He was also the sort of larger-than-life character for whom sport must always be able to cater. It was Allan Border who bestowed on him the nickname of 'The Fruit Fly'—as in Australia's biggest pest. Merv was something else, absolutely hyperactive. If he was awake, he'd bug you. He was like a big kid. Yet he was great to play with. He had the happy knack of finding something funny in even the most serious of situations, and lightening it up for everyone around him. Merv was more mainstream than Greg 'Mo' Matthews, the other great 'character' of cricket's recent years—and because of it he was an easier bloke to work with. Like Mo, Merv was a little eccentric, but his thought processes were pretty much along the same lines as everyone else's. He sailed pretty close to the wind at times, but Merv was a whole lot smarter than some people reckoned him for. He knew how far he could go. Cricket needs the likes of its Merv Hughes, Shane Warne and Greg Matthews—but I suspect that with a probing media, and an (unrealistic) growing insistence that all topline sportsmen and women must be perfect role models, we're going to see fewer characters in the game in the years ahead, and more stereotyping.

In guest-speaking sorties in later years my story about Merv in Bloemfontein, South Africa, in 1994 was always a rough chance of bringing the house down. Merv didn't play much in the summer of 1993–94 because of the aftermath of knee problems he suffered on the '93 Ashes campaign. He made it back late in the summer and won a place on the first tour to South Africa in twenty-four years. The big bloke played the first game and got through okay, but at training a day or two later he did his back in and had to rest up for two weeks to try and get himself right.

The match at Bloemfontein before the First Test was an important one for him, if he was to play in the Test match. Just after lunch on the last day he was bowling to Hansie Cronje.

Merv came steaming in, delivered the ball then stopped in his follow-through and went down on his haunches. Judging by the look on his face he was in considerable pain. Everyone thought the worst. It looked as though his back had gone on him again, or perhaps the knee. So everyone raced up to him, including Hansie Cronje. Just as the scrum of players gathered, Merv rose to his feet . . . and passed wind. It was a Hughes special and I can tell you that if they had such an event in the Olympics he would be a gold medallist for sure.

'Ah,' said Merv. 'That's better!' And turned to head back to his bowling mark. But there was no cricket played for many minutes. Everyone was laughing too much. Hansie Cronje in fact laughed so much he was crying and it was quite a time before he was able to face up again. Merv, meanwhile, stood back at his mark, contemplating the scene.

While we're talking about bowling, and taking wickets, I must relate the following tale from the northern summer of '93.

At a dinner before the tour, I chanced to be in the company of Steve Waugh and journalist Patrick Keane from AAP (Australian Associated Press). The subject of my being vice-captain of the tour came up, and I made the point that as a result I'd probably have the chance to captain the side in a match or two and so have the opportunity to give myself a bowl. Keane sort of laughed: 'Taylor, you can't bowl,' he said. 'I bloody well can,' I said. So he challenged me: 'I'll bet you don't get any wickets on the tour.' After some negotiation, we arrived at a wager. Keane bet me that I couldn't get *two* wickets on the tour; he figured that I might fluke *one*, so it had to be two. It was decided that the wicket(s) could come in any game on tour. He offered me odds of 5/1 and I claimed him for £20. 'Hang on,' said Tugger Waugh. 'I'll have fifty quid on that!' Steve obviously thought I was a better chance than I did.

The first time I bowled myself was in the game against Minor Counties at Stone. They were 8–170, chasing 231 in a one-dayer, and I had Rupert Evans stumped down the leg side by Tim Zoehrer. That was one.

The next chance didn't come for quite some time. We were playing Lancashire in a three-day game at Old Trafford and they were going at a snail's pace. I was pretty browned off with them, so I put myself on to bowl. I was bowling leggies and I sent down an absolute long-hop to Warren Hegg, who was to later tour Australia in 1998–99. Hegg stepped back and smashed the ball in the air, straight to Steve Waugh at cover. And you wouldn't believe it—Steve dropped the catch! Patrick Keane, meanwhile, was putting the pressure on from the grandstand. He had planted a pal up there sporting a big sign which read: MARK TAYLOR CAN'T BOWL!

Next day when play started the bloke with the sign was still there. Next to him was a mate with a second sign: AND STEVE WAUGH CAN'T CATCH! This was getting serious.

I didn't get a wicket that game, and now there was only one real chance left: the first-class game against Canterbury at Kent. Into the last day, on which we had set them 312 to win, we had them at 8–211. I figured it was now or never, and grabbed the ball. My first one didn't come out too well and the batsman, Richard Davis, clobbered it through square leg for four. Next ball was better, of fuller length, and Davis, in trying to take the mickey out of me and sweep it fine for four, missed completely and it snuck around his legs and bowled him. You beauty! Steve Waugh came hurtling in and we exchanged high fives. The way I tell the story these days is that the ball turned even more than Warne's effort against Gatting. Off the field Wayne Holdsworth hot-footed it around to the press box and collected the loot, sprinting out onto the field to hand it over before I bowled the next ball. The scene was beamed back to Australia on TV—money being handed over on the field. In the light of subsequent events in world cricket to do with bookies and betting, I'm not sure how that would have gone down a few years later.

However, it was just some harmless fun and you need that to provide variety and good cheer on a long tour. And there was a bit of it on the 1993 tour. You may remember the prank played at Craig McDermott's expense at Bristol early in the tour. Craig had had a horror start—just couldn't get a wicket. Things got worse, of course, when he got crook and finally had to go home. Craig was known for his rather prominent lugs and before the game against Gloucester one of the guys went out and bought ten sets of big rubber clown ears. I was captaining the side and at tea on this particular day I went to the umpires and explained what we had in mind. They smiled when I told them. 'No problem,' they said. Then I clued up the batsmen: 'It'll only last one ball and that'll be it.' No problems there, either.

And so it happened that as Craig McDermott walked back to his mark to bowl the first ball after tea in the tour match against Gloucester, his ten team-mates whipped ten sets of giant ears from their pockets and put them on. Craig turned at his mark, gazed down field . . . and broke up, so much so that it was minutes before he could bowl again.

The tour itself was very much a case of 'mission accomplished'. To retain the Ashes 4–1 was a pretty emphatic achievement. Early on, we played very well, but towards the end we got a bit lazy.

The Poms had us in trouble in the Third Test at Trent Bridge then beat us in the last at The Oval. They had us six-down at tea, going for the win in the Third Test, but a combination of Steve Waugh and Brendan Julian kept them safely at bay, leaving the Test drawn. Until we took our foot off the pedal we had the wood on them pretty comprehensively. The British media grabbed at England's Sixth Test win as a sign of better times ahead—and it was certainly the sort of positive finish they needed after a fairly one-sided series. My own contribution of 428 runs at 42.8 represented a not-bad series. But I had 244 runs on the board after two Tests and came home with the nagging feeling that to an extent I had let it slide.

Slats and I returned to a terrific weekend back in the old home town of Wagga. The local people put on a tickertape parade for us—and on the same weekend Michael married Stephanie Blackett. The parade was a very pleasant surprise and quite an emotional experience, followed by a civic reception in the Victory Memorial Gardens. I expected just a few people posted down the main street. Instead they were four or five deep and gave us a wonderful reception. It was a great way to come home, and it was really good to be back.

Chapter 12

END *of an* ERA

It's a source of some pride in my career that the centuries I scored were made under varying wicket and climate conditions and on so many different grounds. In a lacklustre home series against New Zealand following the Ashes tour of 1993 I made 142 not out in the second innings of the First Test in Perth after a 64 in the first innings. It was my sixth home Test century—each of them made on one of the six State grounds around the country. It's an unusual statistic, but one which I am quite chuffed about. I also made a Shield century on all those grounds—except for Hobart.

My maiden first-class century was scored at the Sydney Cricket Ground in December 1985, and that was fitting I suppose for a NSW boy. But of all the wickets and grounds of the world my happiest hunting over the seasons came at Brisbane's Woolloongabba—the 'Gabba'. On the hard, flat tracks up there I averaged almost 60 in Tests. It's a wicket that gives something to the quicks, and its general reputation is that early wickets will fall to a new ball. But for me, the Gabba was always just fine.

I think it's one of the great things about Australian cricket that our different States provide such a variety of wickets. On the subcontinent or in England there is a real sameness about the wickets, England's probably offering a little more variety. On the sub-continent you just get hard, flat, turning wickets wherever you go. For that reason visiting teams from that part of the world hitting Perth or Brisbane first-up very often find themselves in deep trouble. They are confronting something completely different.

In my years in Test cricket, Brisbane's was consistently the best wicket I played on. Almost always the Gabba provides a wicket that has something in it for everyone. It plays truly, with the ball coming onto the bat throughout a match. And I've seen Shane Warne take forty or so Test wickets up there, so it obviously gives something to the spinners too. Kevin Mitchell, who looks after it these days, has done an excellent job. In fact, I don't believe you could ask for anything better than the Test wickets he has turned out in the last four or five years.

Sydney has always been a turner in my time. It will probably always be that way, because of the Bulli soil that provides the foundation of the strip. Increasingly curator Tom Parker may choose to leave a little more grass on the wicket. In my experience the SCG has always been a wicket that breaks up and turns. And that's good— cricket needs wickets that provide something for the spinners. But we obviously don't want wickets which turn square on day one and on which the ball is skidding along the ground on day five. The ideal balance is for a wicket that offers *something* later in a game, but with the ball still carrying through to the keeper. The SCG has been a great place for spinners: Matthews, Holland, Bennett, Taylor, Tucker, MacGill, Robertson, Freedman. All of them have had some fun out there.

Melbourne is always an interesting wicket because it provides bounce with the new ball. Someone like Curtly Ambrose was always a nightmare down there because of the bounce he extracted, and the same now goes for Glenn McGrath. Yet it's a wicket that can crumble up quite badly and get nasty on the last day, although that doesn't seem to be happening so much recently. It's generally a wicket that is kinder for bowlers than for batsmen, and for me it always seemed a struggle to get a start there. I did get a couple of Test hundreds at the MCG though—and one of them, I reckon, was among my best. In 1989–90 against Pakistan I scored 101 in the second innings, in a low-scoring game. That was against Wasim Akram and Waqar Younis in full cry on a pretty good bowling wicket.

Adelaide is a quality Test match wicket. Popular belief has it that a Test in Adelaide is a certain draw, but I can't remember too many draws there, though we did manage one in the second Test I played, against the West Indies in 1988–89. But apart from that I have been in a lot of very, very good games of cricket in Adelaide—matches that produced results. If the wicket is right there's generally a little bit in it with the new ball and then it flattens out for the next few days and you have to work hard for your wickets. Towards the end it can get a little uneven, and turn. For good Test cricket I would put it second on my list, just behind Brisbane.

Perth is always guaranteed to be lively, but there have been matches there in the past in which the wickets were apparently absolute 'roads' with WA getting 600 and such like. I can't say I've ever seen it like that, although in the Shield game in 1990–91 when Steve and Mark Waugh each scored double centuries and put on a world-record fifth-wicket partnership of 464 for NSW, I got 57 and was starting to say to myself, 'This is a great wicket', just before I got out. And it really was fine for batting, that game. But generally there is a lot in it for the quick bowlers bowling good line and length with the added bonus of good bounce and assistance from the famous 'Fremantle Doctor' when it blows in from the west around lunchtime or soon after.

The WACA wicket is unique. I can't think of another wicket in the world like it. It's hard and flat and full of life—and if it happens to a be a dry WA summer, the cracks can get very nasty indeed as the match progresses. WACA? Wacky is more like it sometimes! For all that, I subscribe very much to the theory of *vive le difference* when it comes to the different wickets of the cricket world. I'd hate to see them all the same, and the challenge of learning to play on all wickets and in all conditions is one of the big ones of the batting art.

The New Zealand series in 1993 failed to ignite any great passions . . . or cricket. The Kiwis' two class players were Martin Crowe and Chris Cairns and both of them were in trouble with injuries—Crowe to the extent that he went home early to nurse a worsening knee injury. Cairns struggled with a foot injury, and was well below par.

Perth was a pretty ordinary draw and we flogged them in Hobart by an innings and a couple of hundred runs. Again in Brisbane we beat them by an innings and 96 runs, with AB getting 100. They were underpowered with no Cairns and, eventually, no Crowe—and the series was a very tame contest all round.

Moey Matthews and I had a run-in that season, in my early days as captain of the NSW Blues. In fact, he walked off the field after bowling just one delivery on the final day of the four-day match we played against the Kiwis in Newcastle. Greg had a shoulder injury and claimed that I wasn't supporting him. We sorted it out over a few beers, later—and since—but it wasn't a great start.

That match against the New Zealanders also gave me a good lesson in how to handle the media, and what to expect from them. It was a game we lost that we should have won. We led on the first innings and they had to bat last; everything seemed weighted against them. But in our second innings we batted poorly. We made only 109 when we should have got plenty more and ended up setting them 246 to win. After they had reached the target, seven-down, to win the match, the press guys asked me: 'What went wrong, Mark? You had the game in the bag.'

I answered honestly: 'Well, we probably had too many nights out and too many grogs during the game.' The headlines next day were big, and obvious—'Boozy Blues', 'Party Boys get knocked over'. Stuff like that.

It was a swift and sharp early lesson and I gradually learned to choose my words a bit better after that. I remember driving home from Newcastle with Phil Emery after the press conference. 'How'd it go?' he asked. I told him that I'd been dirty at us for losing the game and had probably said a bit too much at the conference. 'I told them we'd had a few late nights and a bit too much grog,' I said. There was a moment's silence. 'They'll make something out of that tomorrow,' said Phil. They did.

I was on a fast-learning curve. My comments after the game had provided big news, and my run-in with Matthews, one of our senior blokes, was fairly public knowledge too. Before we played Queensland in Brisbane next game we had an 'open session'—a frank exchange of views on the couple of subjects at hand and especially about me going a bit far with the press. 'I might have said too much,' I told them. 'But if it was a mistake, I'm going to learn from it—and that's the way we should be as a team, too. If we get things wrong, let's learn from them, and work at getting better.' I told them I wasn't going to try to be an Allan Border or a Geoff Lawson. I was just going to be me—the way I was. We sorted things out in a single session; suddenly we were all on the same track. That match we beat a full-strength Queensland—for the first time in eleven years up there.

The first Australia–South Africa series in twenty-four years, which followed the Kiwi's tour early in 1994, spanned six tests, and two continents—three Tests in each country. It couldn't have been any closer. We finished one-all and a draw in Australia and the same in South Africa. On the occasion of their return from long years in the wilderness we drew the Boxing Day Test in Melbourne, with rain the biggest factor throughout. We then lost a close one in Sydney, chasing 117, and had clearly the better of them in the Third Test in Adelaide, when we made 7–469 and 6–124 and they replied with 273 and 129.

Thanks to the Melbourne weather I had the unusual experience of batting over no less than four days in accumulating 170, picking up an hour's play when the rain eased. We finally declared at tea on the fourth day. I was out in the last over before the break, trying to hit out.

It was an innings that reflected the occasional quirks of the game of cricket. Very early in the match Allan Donald got one through me, and there was a huge appeal for lbw. That's got to be close, I thought. I got the benefit of the doubt—and never looked back for a moment after that.

Sydney was the one that got away, with Australia in the ascendancy all the way until Allan Donald (10) and Jonty Rhodes (76 not out) put on some late runs in their second innings to stretch our chase from about 80 to 117. We lost late wickets on the fourth night, slumping to 4–63 at stumps. The next day we got knocked over for 111, with Fanie de Villiers doing the damage, bowling across-the-seam cutters on a wicket that was giving him something. At about 8–75 we mounted a rearguard action, with Craig McDermott hitting out and Damien Martyn sticking with him. At 8–110 we looked home, but then Damien smashed one to point and was caught by Andrew Hudson. Glenn McGrath was out a few balls later for 1, we were out for 111 and that was it—a loss in a match we should have won. We went to Adelaide hungry for a win after what had been a frustrating start to the series, and beat them convincingly.

The South African 'leg' started about as badly as it possibly could for me. At the team dinner on the eve of the Test in Johannesburg I started to feel bloody awful. I was shivering and my teeth were chattering. Before the meal was even served I walked down to Simmo and AB and said: 'I'm crook; I've got to go.' I spent a dreadful night, much of it in the bathroom. By morning I was diagnosed with having picked up some sort of viral infection. They shifted me out of the room I was sharing with Warnie—and put me on my own, for fear I would pass on the 'bug' to the rest of the team. And so I missed the Test—only one of two Tests that I didn't play in my ten-year international career, the other being the Fifth West Indies Test in 1992–93, when I was 12th man.

It was an unhappy Test match in several ways. For starters we got soundly beaten. And it was the match in which both Shane Warne and Merv Hughes got into strife for sledging, or conduct unbe-coming. Warnie's 'send-off' of Andrew Hudson was headline news everywhere.

It was Warne's first tour to South Africa and I think the pressure of what we ran into got to him. The crowds gave him heaps. South African crowds are very similar to Australian crowds; they're tough and they're passionate and they're more than happy to give the opposition some stick. That tour, they gave it to Warnie from the first game, and by the time we got to the Johannesburg Test he was a player on edge. In that match he struggled, wicketless, for quite a long time, before finally getting one around Hudson's legs and bowling him.

Now Andrew Hudson is a lovely bloke—a quiet, gentle sort of man. They call him 'Moon', Moon Hudson, because they reckon he's up there in the clouds all the time. I doubt he's ever said a bad word to or about anyone, Moon. The funny thing was that when Warnie gave it to him, ripping into him furiously with words and gestures, it had nothing whatsoever to do with Andrew Hudson. Andrew just happened to be in the wrong place at the wrong time as all of Shane's frustrations boiled over. Warnie had been copping plenty from the mob down on the fine-leg boundary, and now he was giving some back. I have spoken to Andrew Hudson since about what happened that day, and he understands and carries no grudge. He could see it all building up, too.

Merv was a bit the same. He had bowled well and got himself back into the team after spending a lot of time out after having a major knee operation. He too had taken some stick from the crowd in that game—and when he got out on the last day, the crowd were really giving it to him when he reached the race. It was there that Merv tried to stick his bat through the fence and clobber some bloke.

Along with Warnie he got hauled before the match referee and the pair of them were fined a trivial amount. Four hundred dollars, I think it was. We all presumed that would be the end of it. But

the problem was that before we left for South Africa Alan Crompton, who was at that time chairman of the ACB, had made some
public observations on sledging—along the lines that it was un-
Australian and unmanly. The Board obviously felt an obligation to
follow through on the chairman's declarations, and added an extra
$4000 to each of the fines. There was some disappointment within
the team at that. The feeling was strong that the matters had been
handled appropriately in the atmosphere of the match over there,
and that that should have shut the lid on it. There is no doubt
that the Board's subsequent stance was prompted by Crompton's
remarks.

The Australians and the South Africans are similar in their
approach to cricket—we are two sides who really go full at it. In
that series there were words exchanged out there, for sure—and I
see nothing wrong with the odd word or two out in the middle as
part of the contest at hand. I believe the focus on so-called 'sledging'
is overplayed by the media. As long as it is kept within reasonable
bounds, it is no great problem for cricket.

Sledging is an over-publicised sidelight of modern cricket—a
reality, sure, but something that gets more headlines than it deserves.
Ask any senior cricketer and he'll tell you that 'chat' has been in
the game for a long, long time. No doubt it will always be there
too. It's a touchy area, but my own view is that in my time it was
never too bad. Sledging is something that should not be allowed to
go unchecked to the point that it becomes a dominant part of the
game, but any attempts to check it should not be too heavy-handed.
The hard reality of this modern era of professionalism in cricket is
that the more the rules of the game are changed, the more they are
likely to be abused as players seek to exploit loopholes in them to
gain an advantage over their opponents.

People are fascinated by sledging, by what goes on 'out there'. In
a game that has been brought by television into the lounge rooms
around the world in intimate detail, it is one 'unknown' area. The
truth is that 90 per cent of the talk out there is simply players geeing

each other up with harmless stuff like: 'Come on Pidgy ... Find that corridor ... Hit the channel ... Great length ... Great delivery ... You've got him worried, Pidge.' It's just part of sport—all sport.

Most of the other 10 per cent might verge on gamesmanship. 'He's scared ... He's backing away ... He hasn't got a clue against you ... He's in trouble' ... coloured by an adjective or two, but still not aimed directly at the batsman. Then there's a remaining one per cent or so of comments aimed directly at a batsman, and using his name—'Hey Mullally, how scared are you?' that are intended to unsettle and fluster an opponent. It's not a regular event and the funny thing is that I've heard far more personal comments of that nature in lower-standard cricket. It's much more prevalent in grade and Shield cricket than it is in the international arena. I have played a number of Shield games in which I have thought: 'Gee, it's getting pretty solid out here'. Across the board Shield cricket is a lot more personal than Test cricket. And it's probably got tougher now that all States are very competitive. The bat-ball contest is often fierce, no matter which States are playing, but so too the 'chat'. By comparison it's a rare thing indeed to hear a real personal attack on a player in a Test or a one-day international.

I honestly can't remember being badly sledged in my career. There were times when someone would have a bit of a chat, or try to reel me in with a comment or two. But I knew they were just trying to put me off, and my policy always was never to hit back. If you ignore it the talk tends to peter out. As Australian captain I was hardly ever the subject of chat out on the field. As a matter of fact if I had been sledged a bit more I might have played better! It can tend to make you grit your teeth and try that little bit harder.

From the 'Demon' Spofforth on, fast bowlers have always been seen as the villains of the cricket field. But I think they've mellowed. I don't think the fast bowlers of today are anywhere near as angry as they once were—or at least seemed to be when I first started watching cricket on television. My memories of the likes of Dennis

Lillee, Jeff Thomson, Andy Roberts, Rodney Hogg, Colin Croft, Lenny Pascoe are that these were raw-boned, *nasty* fast bowlers who hated all batsmen.

Gradual changes in the modern game have demanded a more civilised approach from the quicks. There are laws in place now that dictate that players can't get too carried away. Things that someone like Dennis Lillee may once have done would earn you a suspension for sure these days. A further major influence has been the amount of cricket played. Once the top nations played each other every four years or so and an angry bowler could take the attitude: 'I'm going to *kill* this bloke; I don't like him, and I won't be seeing him for another four years.' Nowadays, we see plenty of each other under the weight of the international program. That too has helped with the mellowing of cricket, although the competition remains fierce—as it should be.

In the to-ing and fro-ing of that Australia–South Africa series of 1993–94, cricket was about as tough as it gets. Johannesburg nudged them ahead 2–1, but we clawed back to win in Cape Town, successfully chasing 90 to win after Steve Waugh had bowled really well in their second innings to take five wickets, and set up the win.

The situation approaching the final Test in Durban was a promoter's dream. It was one-all at home, and one-all away in the series . . . and now it was down to this. Added to the state of play was the growing speculation that Allan Border was close to the end of a long and great career. AB had never been to South Africa and rumours were rife that with that cog now in place, he would give it away after the tour.

The scene was set. But the Durban Test in fact turned out to be one of the real duds of the '90s—and the South African skipper, Kepler Wessels, has to wear much of the responsibility for it. They sent us in on a wicket which contained its fair share of 'juice' and knocked us over for 269. On an increasingly flat and benign batting strip they then spent a painstaking 205 overs making 422, leaving themselves only four sessions to try to bowl us out and then bat again to win the Test. On such a strip they never looked likely and at stumps on the final day we were safe and sound at 4–297. By batting so slowly they had ground us out of the game. They were simply determined to make sure they didn't lose. In the process they turned what could have been a great Test match into one of the dullest draws I ever played in.

Allan Border faced the last ball of the Test from Jonty Rhodes, who was just rolling his arm over, with thoughts of a result long-before gone. It was suspected but not yet confirmed that it was to be the end for AB as a Test player and Australia's captain. How sad that it had to be on such a note, with the life squeezed out of a Test which had promised so much. The game was a shocker.

The one-dayers that followed ended up as a drawn series too, four-all. Late one night after the final game, over more than a few beers, I pulled the skipper aside and said to him: 'AB, I don't know what you're going to do, but if you do decide to retire I just want to say it has been an absolute pleasure playing with you, and under your captaincy.' I meant every word. In my view he was one of the greats of Australian cricket, and it had been my pleasure to be alongside watching how he played, witnessing the enjoyment he got from the game. 'Mate,' he said to me that night, 'between you and me, this will be it for me.'

AB wore the nickname 'Captain Grumpy' yet I can tell you there weren't too many times in the five years I played under his leadership that he was any sort of Captain Grumpy to me. Increasingly, as the seasons went by, he relaxed in the leadership role, and enjoyed it. He was a good captain, and just got better and better as the years went on. AB was tabbed as a 'reluctant' captain early on—taking over as a skipper at a difficult time for the Australian game. But the '89 Ashes tour, when we went away as huge underdogs and came back 4–0 winners, was a big turning point for him, and his team. From that point on he improved as a captain, and the team improved around him. AB was always a guy who just wanted to play cricket—and not to have to worry too much about the peripheral things. He just wanted to get out there and play the very best he could. Every game.

Not long after the conversation I had with Allan in South Africa, it was official, although not yet so when I led the Australian team in an Invitation Cup tournament in Sharjah in the United Arab Emirates, with AB back home in Australia. The ground there, about thirty or forty minutes' drive from neighbouring Dubai, is a truly intriguing corner of cricket's world. On the Persian Gulf, it is an oasis of sorts in the desert country, with huge souks (shopping malls) rising up in the city. The place reeks of wealth, but it is evidenced in the buildings, rather than in beautiful gardens or parks. The cricket ground is bare, in the style of India and Pakistan, and ringed by concrete stands. But it's small, the grass is good, the wicket is good too—and big scores and big hitting can generally be guaranteed. When India beat Australia in the final there in 1998, Tendulkar teed off and got 134.

I went to Sharjah twice, and was actually a financial beneficiary of the last tournament staged there, even though I didn't play. The experience could be summed up as: cricket with a difference . . . in a very different part of the world.

AB's decision to retire—announced via an interview with a mate, Channel 7's Pat Welsh, on a Brisbane golf course—came about a month after the skipper and I had talked in South Africa. He had had time to go home and consider at his leisure exactly what he wanted to do. I really think he would have liked to have stayed on and kept playing, but I know he was not keen on the thought of going back to Pakistan again. He had had a number of tours to the subcontinent and at thirty-eight I don't believe the prospect of that was very attractive for him. I understand what he would have been wrestling with. His philosophy always was that if you play, then you play. You don't skip a tour (Pakistan) to take another (England). If you're going to make yourself available then you play every game and that's that. I think at the end that was one of the reasons he gave it away, although I don't really know the full story.

Almost certainly there was another factor too: about a week before AB made his announcement, Boonie, Heals, Steve Waugh and I were asked to go to Melbourne to meet the ACB. There they talked to us about a number of issues. AB and the captaincy were not among them. The question of whether he should or shouldn't play on as captain was not mentioned. There was one disquieting aspect: that Allan Border didn't get invited to those discussions. I think that was a mistake, and I suspect that he took it very hard. I had the feeling from then on that he had the 'dirts'— whether with us or the Board, I don't know. It was not long afterwards that he rang Pat Welsh and gave his now-famous retirement interview—a conversation that had a bitter edge to it. I don't think there's any doubt that AB had the feeling that everyone was working behind his back. Undoubtedly he was disappointed with the ACB and so made his decision to retire in his own way, via a mate, on a golf course, in his home town.

All of it could have been handled better. In hindsight a far better game plan would have been for the ACB to wait until Allan made his decision and *then* to assemble the senior players for a chat. Instead the perception may have formed of something sinister going on behind the captain's back—even if AB had, as I believe, told Laurie Sawle, chairman of selectors and a Board member, in confidence that he was going to retire (although this was information that Sawle obviously kept to himself). It was all a question of timing. In the light of how things turned out, it was embarrassing for us players in the meeting in Melbourne, even if what was discussed was all perfectly straightforward and above board, which it was.

It all happened about two weeks after we got home from Sharjah, by which time AB had been home a month or so from South Africa. Obviously I knew I was a chance for the captaincy, but as much as anything I needed a holiday. I rang team manager Ian McDonald in Melbourne. 'Macca, I've got a holiday organised,' I said. 'I'll be away for a couple of weeks . . . see you when I get back.' Judi, William and I were heading up to Peter Taylor's cotton farm at Gurley, just south of Moree, 600 kilometres from Sydney. I'd given it some thought and decided I wasn't going to put off holidays pending AB retiring . . . or, perhaps, my becoming captain. That was two ifs away—and I don't live my life on ifs. So Judi and I packed the car and headed off.

Chapter 13

MY COUNTRY'S CAPTAIN

O n the evening of Wednesday, 18 May 1994, I was relaxing after a quiet dinner at Peter Taylor's farm in north-western NSW. Memory suggests that a glass of something cold and frothy may have been close at hand. On ABC radio the talk was of an Australian Cricket Board meeting in Melbourne, at which the subject of the Test captaincy had been high on the agenda for discussion and decision. At about 8.30 p.m. the phone rang.

It was Ian McDonald, on his mobile phone from Mascot Airport. 'I can't say too much,' he said. 'But you're it. I'll ring you when I get home.' Click. Macca had been in Melbourne for the big meeting, and was heading home to Double Bay. Half an hour later the phone rang again. 'Tubby, congratulations,' he said. 'You're the captain— appointed unanimously. Now . . . we need you down here for a press conference at twelve o'clock tomorrow.' He had already booked me on a morning flight from Moree, but in the name of 'Peter Taylor' to try and cover the trail a bit. My appointment was still classified 'Top Secret'.

I'd taken my best suit with me, just in case, and next morning, all dolled up, I hopped onto the metal seat in Peter's 1971 semi trailer. He had thoughtfully wiped the grease off as best he could. Peter was on his way to pick up a feed lot from the other side of Moree, after getting me on the plane. The irony didn't escape either of us—the 'Taylor' Test mix-up back in '87, and now the strange coincidence of our being together again when something major happened was unfolding related to Taylors and cricket. The only difference was that this time it was really me.

At the airport, there was great confusion as we tried to explain that *he* was Peter Taylor and the ticket was in his name, but in fact it was me, *Mark* Taylor, who was flying. It took some sorting out, but finally all was well, and I took my seat in the plane as Peter headed off.

Before long I became aware that a bloke in the terminal who looked like a classic cow cocky was eyeing me off. He had all the gear—the jeans, the braces, the western shirt, the hat. After a while, he came over and spoke up. 'Hey, I know you,' he said. 'You're that Mark Taylor fella, aren't you?' I confirmed I was. 'And you're on the eight o'clock back to Sydney, are you?' he continued. 'Yes, mate, that's correct,' I said. There was a longish silence, and then: 'That Allan Border—he retired the other day, didn't he?' 'Yes, he did,' I agreed. 'And you're the vice-captain, aren't you?' he went on. Another silence. 'Well, you know what?' he said. 'I've been listening to the radio and there's been a lot of talk about an announcement being made in Sydney today on the new Australian captain. I reckon you're heading back to Sydney to become the next captain!' There wasn't much I could say. 'Mate, you've got the news four hours before everyone else in Australia,' I told him. Then he was gone. I have a hunch the news would have crackled around Moree like a grassfire.

This was a real cloak-and-dagger operation. It didn't quite get to the point of me donning a false beard and glasses, but it wasn't too far off. From Sydney airport they hustled me into town and into the NSW Cricket Association offices, through a side door and out into a back room, where I was to wait. At a certain point early in the press conference, Alan Crompton uttered the words: 'Ladies and gentlemen of the media, I would like to introduce you to our new captain, Mark Taylor.' There was some clapping, and in I came.

The impact was enormous. In a single glance I realised that this was *big*. There were cameras everywhere, sixty or seventy journos . . . and me. I thought: Whoa! I honestly hadn't expected anything like that. Thinking about it the night before I had pictured ten or fifteen journos at the conference, a cup of tea and a few questions. I hadn't thought that people would see the appointment as any great news in view of the fact that I was vice-captain, and obviously right in the running. But this was bigger by far than I had imagined, with TV programs waiting for live 'crosses' and radio stations hanging on every word. I said a quiet thanks that I had had a pretty early (and relatively grog-free) night. When Macca had rung me Peter had opened a bottle of champagne to toast the news. But when he reached for a second bottle, I had declined. 'Thanks, mate, but I'm going to bed,' I said. It was a good call.

I went into the conference 'cold', with no briefing. And I think that was good. I was able to speak my mind quite openly. They threw me plenty of questions about sledging, and what I planned to do about it. I told them I was not going to turn the team into a bunch of pussycats or choirboys, because that wasn't how Australians played sport. But I was going to do my best to keep it within reasonable bounds. I got some column centimetres on that subject the next day. Someone asked me how long I reckoned I'd be in the job. I answered that I didn't really know, that cricket was a series-by-series thing, but if I had a choice I would love to say that I could do it for four or five years. It turned out that as Australia's thirty-ninth skipper I was to be in the job for almost five years.

I was happy with the way I handled things, but the conference was essentially the first move along a considerable learning curve for me as Australian captain. I had given no real thought that day to the questions or the issues that might be raised, and I got through okay. But in the future, before any press conference, I would always put myself on the other side of the cameras, and think about the questions I would ask if I happened to be over there behind the lights.

It was an unbelievable day, sweeping by and leaving me with a rush of mixed feelings as I tried to come to terms with the honour that had been landed on me. After all the interviews were done at cricket HQ, I joined reporter Michael Maher in a car to head across to Channel 9, Willoughby and an interview for. 'A Current Affair', followed by another for 'Wide World of Sport'. Then it was back to the SCG for some photos. What had started for me as a press conference around 12.30 p.m. finally finished around 5—at which point I joined Alan Crompton, Graham Halbish and a few others for a beer at the Lord Dudley pub in Woollahra.

I left there, bound for the return flight to Moree, clutching a couple of bottles of French champagne that the ACB had kindly shouted. The champers actually got me into strife. The kind people at Cascades Restaurant in Moree where Judi, Peter and Julie Taylor and I had a celebratory dinner were deeply offended that I had brought my own champagne. They had their own set aside, chilling on ice. They were fantastic—put on this fabulous feed for us, then wouldn't accept any money. 'It's just great that you're here on this day when you've become Australian captain,' they said. 'You are our guests . . . and that's that.' It was a terrific night and a real chance for me to relax after such a hectic and emotional day. At last.

The next day Judi and I drove across country to Glen Innes, to meet up with some of Judi's relatives who lived on a farm outside the town. We had some lunch in the Williams family's Club Hotel in the main street of Glen Innes, and a bit of fun along the way. When it came to my turn to shout, I put in the order at the bar and the bloke serving said to me: 'Mate, I've gotta say this—you look just like that Mark Taylor who has just become Australian captain.' 'You wouldn't believe it,' I said, 'but you're the third bloke who has said that to me today. I keep thinking—surely I'm better looking than that bastard!'

'Yeah . . . yeah, that's true,' he said. 'Not a problem.' But he was still looking.

When Rex Chard, Jude's cousin, got up to order some drinks, the bloke was still wondering. 'Rex, geez that bloke looks like Mark Taylor,' he said. 'You bloody idiot!' Rex said. 'It is!' Next thing the bloke was over at the table, all embarrassed and apologising, but we quickly settled him down and had a laugh and a yarn. Someone tipped off the Glen Innes *Examiner* and then there was an interview to be done, a photo to be taken.

Just about as soon as I became captain and the full realisation came of the demands that would follow, I figured that I was a cricketer in need of a manager. It wasn't so much about money-making opportunities outside the game as a good support system in relation to handling the media, confronting issues that I knew I would have to address, and handling demands made on me from outside the game. For a time while playing for NSW I had linked with a nice guy named Howard Rich. But a Shield cricketer is just a Shield cricketer, pretty hard to sell, and that arrangement had sort of faded out. When I became captain I had a preliminary yarn with Bob Dwyer, the former Australian rugby union coach and a very capable and decent bloke, who was getting into that business and was keen to take me on board. Then one day Ian McDonald said to me: 'I reckon you should have a talk with John Fordham.'

'Who's John Fordham?' I asked. 'Well, you know David Fordham?' Macca said. 'John's his brother. He manages John Laws and Ricky Stuart.' I knew Dave Fordham, the Channel 7 sports-caster, and liked him. It seemed like a good idea to go and see John. We met in the city one day and talked for an hour and a half. I liked him straight away and knew right off he was the right bloke. We talked about how it could work—how it was essential that I had a 'buffer' so I could concentrate on my cricket. John was strong on that angle. By the end of our talk, we had a deal, one that has never been contracted. A handshake was good enough for the two of us. It was pretty much: 'If you don't like me just tell me to shoot through and if I don't like you I will tell you to shoot through.' That's how it's worked ever since.

JOHN FORDHAM, 1999: *I guess we just clicked. We talk the same language and I guess what I have always liked about Mark is his down-to-earth quality. He has no airs. He hasn't forgotten where he came from and he puts the important things such as family and his personal life on a high pedestal. We worked out a strategy: that we would work to supplement his cricket income through judiciously selected associations—quality associations which would enhance his profile. The great thing with Mark is that his exceptional judgment as a player and captain carries across to what he does off the field.*

My association with John Fordham, a wine columnist and renowned as something of a *bon vivant* around town, has led me to many fine lunches and dinners—and very likely played havoc with my cholesterol levels. He is a man who could be said to be 'well connected' in Sydney life. What has grown in the five years (so far), notwithstanding the ongoing threat to my health, has been a wonderfully fruitful partnership, and friendship—with John maximising for me off the field the opportunities I was lucky enough to be able to create because of my role as Test cricketer and captain.

I couldn't possibly imagine having got through my career as well as I did without 'Fordo' alongside to ease the load. People at the top level of high-profile sports are in enormous demand today. Having a good manager to sift through the requests, work with the media and handle the big events is not just important anymore. It's essential. Working with the Fordham company has been both professional and enjoyable, the friendships as important as the business. The easing of the pressure, especially through hard times, was certainly a factor in me getting successfully through the last five years of my career. On the other side of the coin, the progressive links with some good companies helped me set up something worthwhile for the future.

As captain of Australia, it all began for me in Sri Lanka in

September 1994—and there, I did two things. Firstly, I asked the tour manager, Col Egar, if I could take the media guys out for a meal, just to set some sort of basis for our working relationship. Whether they thought AB was a great captain, or whether they didn't, I didn't care. I just wanted to start on the right footing. Over an amiable dinner with guys like Ron Reed, Malcolm Conn and Greg Baum, I got that message across. 'I'm Mark Taylor—and I want to start nought for nought with you guys,' I said. 'If I have bad times, and handle you blokes badly, well, I'll accept the consequences of that. But I want to start with an absolutely clean slate . . . with no handicap.' 'Fair enough,' they said.

Probably the most important thing I did was to have a chat with the senior players, individually. I spoke to Heals, who had been named vice-captain, to Steve Waugh, who had certainly been in the running for the captaincy and was rated unlucky by some, and to David Boon. I had always reckoned that Boonie was a bit unlucky when it came to the leadership roles in the team. He had been vice-captain of the team at one stage under AB, and the blokes certainly looked up to him. Then it had sort of slipped away. I was very keen to make sure that Boonie was happy and comfortable. 'Not a problem,' he said when we talked. 'You have my full support and I'm looking forward to it. I love my cricket, and you and I have been good mates. Let's get out there and win some games.' Heals and Tugger were similarly supportive. I appreciated it greatly. I now felt I was truly ready to assume the captaincy. And considering what lay ahead, with shocking allegations about to rear up of bribery and corruption in cricket, it was never more important that we senior blokes should be on the same track.

In the *Sun-Herald*, John Benaud offered a timely reminder of Sir Donald Bradman's words on the subject of cricket captaincy: 'A good captain will be a fighter: confident but not arrogant, firm but not obstinate, able to take criticism without letting it unduly disturb him, for he is sure to get it—and unjustly too.'

Chapter 14

·····························

CRASH COURSE
in PAKISTAN

ricket got ugly in 1994. Whispers and rumours
that all was not well in the game assaulted us well
before the first ball had been bowled under the
new captaincy of M.A. Taylor. There was a
growing awareness that something was rotten in
the state of international cricket. When we travelled to Sri Lanka in
September 1994 leading Aussie journos like Phil Wilkins quickly
began to dig up details of the increasingly unsavoury allegations,
centred on members of the Pakistan side. Before long they would
write the stories that brought the whole thing—or most of it
anyway—into the public domain.

In Sri Lanka before the playing of the Singer Trophy, there was
daily talk of bribery and the throwing of matches—with the Pakistan
team at the heart of the rumours. I suppose all of us who played in
the one-dayer against the Pakistanis at the Sinhalese Sports Club in
Colombo on 7 September have wondered many times over the years
since whether the win we managed was fair dinkum. Or something
else . . .

I remember that first game well, having spent some time re-
playing it in my head since. We struggled our way to 179, a pretty

ordinary one-day score, and they were seemingly comfortable at 1–77 in reply. We ended up bowling them out for 151 to win the game by a clear margin. We came off feeling very pleased with ourselves; we'd played very good cricket with the ball and we had brought off what seemed to be a quality victory. It was not until later that the thought started to take shape: did we *really* play well enough to win the game . . . or did they throw it? The doubt that even the merest hint of match-fixing casts over an apparently genuine victory is one of the worst aspects of the problem. That day in Colombo we probably won fair and square, and they probably lost fair and square. But I don't really know . . . and I guess I never will.

It was at the end of the First Test in Pakistan which followed the Sri Lankan tournament that the waters got seriously murky. Later in this chapter I will deal with the more positive side of what was really a pretty extraordinary tour. But the whole series was played in the shadow of uncertainty, innuendo and intrigue.

On the afternoon of the last day of the First Test, which we had just lost in a photo-finish, Shane Warne and Tim May came to see me. The essence of what they had to say was this: Mark, we got offered really good money to bowl badly today. To help Pakistan win the game. I had just come from match referee John Reid's room at the ground, where Jo Angel and I had been summoned to discuss the charge that Joey had disputed an umpire's decision. It was something of a storm in a tea cup. Jo had shown his disappointment when a close lbw call against Inzamam-ul-Haq had been turned down near the end of a desperately fought Test match, but there had been no verballing—and the decision to charge him with dissent had finally been made by Reid himself after viewing the incident on TV. I appeared for Jo and told John Reid: 'If a bowler in that situation, with a Test match at stake, *didn't* show some disappointment I wouldn't want him playing for me—and I don't reckon he should be playing for Australia.' Joey got off with a warning.

And now this. Wow, I can do without it! I thought as I listened to the startling story our two spinners were telling me. They claimed that Salim Malik, the Pakistani captain, had offered them no less than $200 000 to bowl below their best.

Subsequently Mark Waugh told me that Malik had offered him money to 'play below his best' in the one-dayer against Pakistan at Rawalpindi. By the following February the allegations against Malik made it into the public arena, bringing furious denials from the Pakistan skipper. From there it just rolled on and on. In November 1998 Saeed Anwar told a court hearing in Lahore that in his view the Singer Cup game was fixed. At the same hearing a Pakistani bookmaker admitted in secret evidence that he offered Salim Malik and Mushtaq Ahmed $US100 000 to throw the match against Australia.

As captain, my choice back in September 1994 was . . . no choice. Some people have asked me: 'Why was such a big fuss made? Why didn't you just forget about it?' Well, increasingly in those difficult days, I knew that there was no other way. What had happened was deeply alarming just in itself—and especially so in the climate existing in cricket at that time. But there was the additional fact that we had *lost* both of the games in question—the Test and the one-dayer. And the Test had slipped away in almost-amazing circumstances with the last pair putting on a world-record winning last wicket partnership 57 to steal the match from our grasp. We had to go public and let cricket officialdom know what had gone on. Not to have done that would have left us wide-open to all sorts of suspicions and insinuations. When the news eventually came out to the wider world, as it inevitably would in the closely scrutinised sphere we operated in, how would we have looked? I can imagine the comments: 'A world record for the last wicket to win a Test match . . . geez, you blokes *must* have taken the money!' The situation was fraught with danger. I did what I had to do and conveyed what Warne, May and Waugh had told us to our manager, Col Egar. ICC chief David Richards was in Pakistan at the time too, so my presumption is that the ICC would have been briefed promptly on what had taken place.

There is one question I can't answer: if we had won the Test, would Warnie and Maysie have revealed that they had been approached in such a way? I honestly don't know. But the fact that we lost the game left them with no choice.

From that point onwards the tour took on a new and darker aspect, for all the good and thrilling cricket that was played. The atmosphere in our dressing room was such that when Wasim Akram and Waqar Younis pulled out late from the third Test we scratched our heads. Were they truly injured ... or was there some hidden agenda slipping into place in the background? With almost everything that happened you started to wonder if there was something more to it than met the eye. There were many more questions than answers. The irony of it is that unlike, say, England's highly visible betting shops and betting tents, there is no overt sign of betting activity on the subcontinent. There it exists in more shadowy reaches, beneath the surface of ordinary life.

Salim Malik's place at the centre of the rumour allegations added to the general unease. He was the opposing captain, after all. The Australian players were upset about what they knew, heard and read, and there was some sledging of Malik, though nothing too dramatic. My own relationship with him, captain to captain, was uneasy. He was a bloke I didn't know too well, and frankly I didn't spend much time talking to him after the things I was told following the First Test. I'll just say this: whatever else he may or may not be, he proved himself a great batsman in that series.

Wasim Akram's name has been mentioned subsequently in relation to match-fixing allegations. I will just say this: to my knowledge Wasim's name was never mentioned in the Australian dressing room concerning any involvement in this sort of thing.

At this stage, on the last day of the First Test, I had no clue of what else had taken place a little earlier, in Sri Lanka. It wasn't until just before the West Indies tour next season (1995) that I learned that Shane Warne and Mark Waugh had been involved in the now-notorious 'bookie scandal'—accepting sums of money in the vicinity of $US5000 each from a bookmaker named 'John' (also called 'Pinky' in some media reports) for giving fairly innocuous information by phone on pitch and weather conditions in the period September 1994–February 1995, the first contact coming in a hotel in Colombo. Shane and Mark were very likely seen as 'easy' targets within the team. Both of them like to have a bet. What they did was very silly, and wrong—and the punishment and publicity they copped later drove it home. The news came to me like a bolt from the blue from Ian McDonald, ACB Media Director and team manager for the Caribbean tour.

It happened when I got a phone call from Macca as departure day for the West Indies neared. 'Mark, what would you think if I told you two of your players have accepted money from a bookie to provide information,' he asked. It stopped me dead. 'You're joking,' I responded. 'No, I'm not,' he said. 'Shane and Mark have done that.' Macca went on to tell me how he had been conducting his own investigations into persistent stories that two members of the Australian team had been involved with a bookmaker on the subcontinent. When he had put it on Shane and Mark—they had come clean. I sensed immediately that this would eventually and inevitably blow up into something bigger, real trouble. Shane Warne and Mark Waugh had never been involved in throwing matches or trying to influence the outcome of matches—apart from trying to win them! The information they passed onto the bookie was trivial. But the potential problem was a wider perception that it was a start . . . and where would it all stop? The innocent phone conversations were Step One. What was Step Two to be?

As captain, I was disappointed that I hadn't been told. I was the one who carried the responsibility of fronting the media and letting people know what was going on, and where we stood on various issues. To be left in the dark on something so serious with the potential of exploding into a huge headache for the game was not pleasing. That's the way I felt then, and feel now. I'm sure the two players saw it then as no big deal—just as something minor that happened that was not worth passing on. They had been offered a fee for providing some harmless information, taken it—and very likely not paused to consider the possible repercussions. In hindsight I'm not absolutely sure what I would have done if they *had* told me at the time. Once the news was out it went straight to the ACB, as it should have. They are, after all, the decision-makers in Australian cricket. The Board hastily convened a meeting and fined the two players approximately $10 000 each. Their decision to keep the fines imposed on Waugh and Warne confidential was the subject of much debate and controversy when it became known three years later. To be honest, I myself always thought the story would come out sooner or later.

In the aftermath of it all, I copped some flak (e.g. from Malcolm Knox in the *Sydney Morning Herald* in February 1999) for allegedly being part of the 'cover-up' of the betting incidents. On reflection, I doubt I could have done more than I did. I passed on what I knew about the approach by Salim Malik to the right people—i.e. officialdom—as soon as I became aware what had happened. In relation to the bookie incident I was privy to that only when the ACB itself became aware of it through Ian McDonald. Once they were disclosed, both matters rightly became the matter of official policy and action. That was not my territory. That the fines imposed on Waugh and Warne were not made public knowledge was strictly a decision of the ACB. I was captain of the side, and like many others I mulled over the whole thing, and was greatly disturbed that cricket had come to this—to dealings with bookmakers and, possibly, bribes. But the fact is I was employed by the ACB. They dealt with the matter the way they felt appropriate in 1995. To be totally honest, I also hoped for the sake of Mark and Shane that the bookmaker story would never become public.

In the Pakistan cities of Rawalpindi and Karachi before the First and Third Tests of the 1998 campaign, I took my own peculiar phone calls—brief and passing moments that I thought little of.

Until later. In Rawalpindi a couple of nights before the First Test, I took a call from a friendly fellow who chatted to me about Pakistan cricket, and told me he didn't like the Pakistanis much. They were all bigheads, he said. The Australians were his favourite team. 'How are you fellows going?' he asked. 'We're going all right . . . yeah, we're in good shape,' I said. 'What do you think is going to happen in this Test?' he enquired. 'Well, mate, I hope we score more runs than they do,' I replied, keeping it polite and light. He pressed on. 'How's the ground . . . how's the wicket looking?' The warning lights flickered just a little, and I cut short the conversation. 'Mate, I'm busy . . . I'm going to have to go.' It was possibly an innocent call, and an innocent question. And in normal cricket conversation I would generally answer such a question without worry: 'Well, it's a typical Pakistani wicket . . . hard and bare and it will probably spin towards the end of the game.' But in the circumstances that prevailed, I cut it short. On reflection, I doubt there was anything sinister. Very likely he was just a keen fan, somewhat chuffed that he had got through to the Australian captain.

He rang me again before the last Test. I don't recall his name, but he was on the line bright and chirpy. 'It's me again,' he said. He chatted on: 'You did well in the First Test . . . and that was a wonderful innings in Peshawar.' On he went. And then: 'What about this Test? How is the wicket looking?' I thought to myself: I'm *definitely* not going down that track again. I thanked him for the call, excused myself—and hung up.

Those stories about dark deeds somewhere in the nether regions of the game emerged during my first match as captain—and were still swirling around five years later. I will just say this: as Australian captain for five years, there was never a single moment that I doubted a single player in my team on the score of commitment and effort towards the task of winning matches. What Shane and Mark did in Sri Lanka in 1994 was unquestionably naive. But never did I have cause to doubt that when they walked out to play for Australia they were giving it their very best shot. I think they have paid many times over for the miscalculation they made, by virtue of the embarrassment they suffered and the battering they took in the media when the news became public property.

I believe the phone calls they received represented the tip of the iceberg. No doubt the bookies, or whoever was the Mr Big behind it, were trying to get a senior Aussie player or two into their grasp until it reached the stage where the player or players involved just couldn't get out. The ultimate plan would be to weave such a web that the question of 'not trying' or 'throwing a game' could be raised. And all of the dealings were guaranteed, by their very nature, to be conducted in secrecy. The bigger the money in sport, the bigger the potential danger.

The story I have told here is not a pretty one for world cricket. The controversy has been going on for five years or so and in different ways has affected some of the biggest names in Australian cricket. My hope is that one good thing will come out of it: that it will stand as a lesson to any young cricketer making his way up the ladder and dying to play for Australia. The message is that the risk is not worth taking, whether it's drugs or cheating or shady dealings that can damage a reputation in a single phone call. What happened in 1994 and after has not done Shane Warne or Mark Waugh one bit of good. And I'm sure that if it happens that Warnie becomes the next captain of Australia, after Steve Waugh, the whole thing will resurface. People will be reminded yet again that as a player in the Australian team he took five grand from a bookie to provide some information. The focus won't be on the trivial nature of what he may have volunteered in return, but on the fact that he took the money at all. The scar is permanent—not a deep gash, but more than a little nick, all the same. And one that won't disappear.

As for the tour itself, despite the seething atmosphere that surrounded it, the 1994 Test series against Pakistan was a classic—although very much a story of lost opportunity for Australian cricket. As captain, I started with a whimper, not a bang, scoring a pair in my first Test as skipper, at Karachi. The two critical moments are imprinted on my mind. In the first innings I spooned a leading-edge catch straight back to Wasim Akram as I tried to turn one around the corner. In the second a slower ball from Waqar Younis bounced more than I anticipated and took an edge. It had just enough puff to carry through to wicketkeeper Rashid Latif.

I paid a price, I think, that captains sometimes pay—and especially new captains. In that match my focus was all on getting the team 'right'. I was concerned that things should be in place exactly the way I wanted them, and with the side running the way I wanted it. I wanted to be a captain in control. People who know me will tell you that I'm not a great delegator. If something has to be done, my inclination is to get in and do it myself.

I came to the Test series in Pakistan as a batsman woefully out of form. I hadn't made a run in Sri Lanka, and I struggled in the lead-up games in Pakistan. My pair in the Test caused me subsequently to take personal stock. 'Hang on—I'm in trouble here,' I said to myself. I started to think about the important element of balance—on matching my important role as a batsman with my captaincy duties.

Notwithstanding my personal struggle, the First Test was among the most thrilling ever played. Our 337 and 232 against their 256 set them 314 to win in a day and a half. At stumps on the fourth day they were 3–150, the match beautifully poised.

The next morning started perfectly for us. We took five wickets in the first session, and even after lunch, at 9–258, we had them, seemingly, dead to the world. The last pair, Mushtaq Ahmed and Inzamam-ul-Haq, still had 57 to get—a mountain of runs at the tail-end of an innings. Somehow, they managed it.

This was cricket of unbelievable tension, with talk of bribery and match-fixing set far, far aside. The last pair dug in with great defiance, while we did our utmost to dislodge them. Not a chance was missed, as they held us out.

Before what proved to be the last ball of the Test, with the Pakistanis needing two to win, I spoke to Shane Warne, the man with the ball in his hand. 'Righto, Warnie, what are we gonna do?' I asked. Our problem was that the accomplished batsman Inzamam was on strike, with Mushtaq Ahmed down the other end. That was the most frustrating thing about losing that Test—that Mushie, a real 'rabbit', managed to get 20 runs. In the next Test he scored a pair. He's not a batsman, but that day, we just couldn't get him out.

Warnie and I worked out a plan to leave a gap at mid-wicket for Inzamam, as it was too late now to give him a single and try to get Mushie. To win the game, we had to get Inzamam. Shane would tempt him with the gap at mid-wicket, toss one up and hope for a leading edge.

It worked almost perfectly. Warnie bowled the right ball, and Inzamam danced down to whip it through mid-wicket. The delivery drifted on him and crept through between bat and pad, with the batsman a metre out of his crease. But, unfortunately it kept low—shooting beneath Ian Healy's gloves and on to the boundary for the winning runs, four byes. We reacted with anguish and disbelief, in equal measure. A five-day Test match had come down to one brute of a bounce—and it had gone against us.

For Ian Healy, it was absolutely devastating. If he had managed to snare that low shooter and whip the bails off, he would have been an Aussie hero. Inzamam was gone, stranded well down the wicket. But Heals missed it—and in the eyes of some was unfairly seen as the villain of the piece. I can still remember him an hour after the match slumped in his chair, head down, pads still on, a picture of dejection. We all felt for him in his agony.

There could be no 'blame'. The ball just decided it wasn't going to bounce. For all the enormous amount of hard work Heals has put into his wicketkeeping job, it was one that he just couldn't get to. I believe it was a ball that would have beaten any keeper.

The win that we should have had in the Second Test in Rawalpindi got away from us too—and for that one, I blame myself. I went to the game under some pressure after the First Test loss, and my own personal double-failure. They stuck us in on a wicket that looked as if it was going to do a bit. Early on I pushed one from Wasim Akram past the bloke at bat pad and scampered off for a single. 'Beauty!' I thought. 'I'm off the mark . . . I've scored my first run as captain!' The very next over I got a wide one from Waqar Younis and played a big, wild drive, which was never my game, and nicked it. It didn't carry. Phew. I went on to make 69, with my feet moving better by the minute, and reckoned I was a bit unlucky to be out lbw at that point. We made 521, with Slats getting a great hundred and Steve Waugh 98. When we knocked them over for 260, we were in terrific shape to win the game.

I put them back in and at stumps on the third night, they were 0–28. Late in the day Aamir Sohail was batting and I asked Joey Angel to bowl a few bouncers at him. Almost immediately Sohail swung at one and sent it looping straight to Warnie, out on the fence. Warnie has a good, safe pair of hands, and normally he would 'swallow' a catch like that. But he put it down . . .

We picked up one more wicket next morning, but at lunch they were 1–111 and we desperately needed a breakthrough. Salim Malik, who had come in at 1–79 with Sohail retired hurt, was at the crease and I called the bowlers in as we were walking off the field. 'We're bowling okay,' I said. 'But I'm asking you for some more fire and venom after lunch.' Over lunch, I spoke to Jo Angel. 'Malik is obviously their key man.' I said. 'Why don't you go around the wicket to him. I'll put two out on the hook, and a bat-pad in. Let's bowl him a good round of short ones and see how he handles them.'

Immediately after lunch Joey bowled Malik a short rising ball, just outside off-stump. The Pakistan captain went onto the back foot to drive and nicked it straight to me at first slip. I dropped it cold. I couldn't believe it. It was part of the plan, something we had talked about, and I had put it down. I got both hands to the ball—a catch that I would have backed myself to make nine times out of ten.

Malik was 20 at the time. He went on to make 237. It was long hours later before Damien Fleming finally got him, in the third leg of a hat trick which provided a spectacular end to the innings. But by that stage they had scored 537 and our chance of winning was gone.

Even my own personal highlight was a hollow one in such a game. On the last day, with any chance of a result down the drain, I picked up my only wicket in Test cricket. I'll give you the true version first . . . and then the one that I prefer. Bowling my leg-spinners to Rashid Latif, I sent down a long-hop which Rashid crashed to mid-wicket—straight into Michael Bevan's hands.

My other version of the story is of how the ball came beautifully out of the front of my hand, skidded on the batsman and cramped him up. With a desperate fend he managed to get it away—but straight to mid-wicket, victim of a ball that was just too good for him.

Remarkably, Michael Slater got *his* only Test wicket in that match too—Waqar Younis lbw for ten. He finished with 1–4 and so has a Test average of four. I finished with 1–11, but owing to other brief appearances at the bowling crease, my Test average is 26. There are those who suggest that the wicket at Rawalpindi was one more than I deserve. I'll take it anyway.

By the time of the Third Test at Lahore, the atmosphere was tense. The bribery stories were now huge news, attracting daily attention, and it was impossible to work out where the truth started and the speculation ended.

Coming into the match there were rumours that Wasim Akram was in some doubt because of a back problem. As we walked out into the middle for the toss, Salim Malik confirmed: 'By the way, Wasim is out,' he said. 'Yeah, mate, I'd heard he might be,' I said. 'And Waqar is out as well,' said Malik. What the bloody hell is going on? I thought. There was talk about who was in whose camp . . . and who wanted whom to win the game. The change room was full of speculation about what might be going on in *their* change room.

Their two strike bowlers were gone and the wicket looked beautiful. It was shaping as a great toss to win. But I lost the damned thing and they batted first and scored 373. We got 82 in front, scoring 455 with Bevan leading the way with 91. And when we had them 5–107—effectively 5–25—this surely was the Test we were going to win. But Salim Malik got in the way again. He scored 75 in the first innings, 143 in the second, and for the second Test in a row stopped us from winning, just when the match seemed to be ours.

Malik was the difference in that series—he made 557 runs, and we just couldn't get him out. But we let ourselves down too. The statistics of the three games showed eleven dropped catches, a huge tally for an Australian side which worked harder on its fielding than any other team in the business. It was a terrific series, but an absolute frustration too. We got beaten by a whisker in the First Test, were beautifully placed to win the next two, and came home with nothing . . . except regrets about what might have been.

None of us would forget the game at Gujranwala, however, a place about an hour and a half from Lahore. A straightforward one-day match there turned into a potential time-bomb, thanks to the weather. We had to leave Lahore at 6 a.m. for the trek up there and before we headed off word came through of heavy rain in the region. In my experience rain is not something that interferes too much with the cricket in Pakistan, but this particular morning they'd obviously had quite a storm. The roads that took us into the rural area where we were to play were just bogs.

When they pulled the covers off at the ground, one end was completely saturated. It was almost at precisely that moment that they started letting the crowds in. People with tickets and people with no tickets and fake tickets came rushing into the ground. So great was the swell that a fence collapsed and fans were in real danger of being crushed. It was terrible, but they just kept letting people in, 40–50,000 of them. Gujranwala is a small place and for the people of the district to have an international cricket match there was obviously the highlight of the year, if not the decade.

It was an enormous dilemma. The wicket was absolutely unplay-able, with no possibility that a one-day international could be played on it. I was out in the middle talking to one of our press guys when one of the Pakistan officials walked up, somewhat flus-tered. 'Mark. What do you think is going to happen?' he asked. 'Well, I honestly can't see us getting on that wicket today,' I told him. 'I don't care if you get a helicopter here to help out but the wicket is wet a foot down and you won't get it dry. I can't see us playing.' 'Oh Mark,' he said dejectedly. 'If we don't play the game, they will kill us'. As soon as he said it, I thought, 'You shouldn't have said that.'

This was obviously a huge story for the media, and I could already picture the headlines back home: PLAY OR THEY WILL KILL US. Looking at the crowd, we realised we had to do *something*. So we ended up putting on a sort of fun game, fifteen overs a side, bowling just from the wet end.

It became a slog-a-thon and some huge sixes sailed into the now-placated crowd. The mob took it well and seemed to go home happy enough. But it was pretty edgy out there for a while, I can tell you.

In the course of Pakistan's ever-colourful pageant we ran into an earthquake as well on that tour—at Peshawar. We'd played the South Africans there—they were the third side in a tri-series tour-nament—and early the next morning, I was fast asleep in my hotel room after a latish night. Suddenly I woke from what I thought was a dream—to the sight and sound of the paintings in the room banging against the walls. I jumped out of bed and headed for the door; David Boon was already half-way down the stairs, wearing just his sleep-shorts. Boonie and Hansie Cronje spent a long time in the garden out front. They didn't want to come back in. But the locals were quite nonchalant. 'Just another tremor,' they said. 'We get a lot of those.'

When I look back on that trip, my first as captain, I realise what a crash course it was for me. If you were to look for things that could make life tough for an international cricket captain, you'd find just about all of them along the course of that campaign. It was a very steep learning curve. The whole tour was conducted in the shadow of bribery and match-fixing allegations, the rumours ever-present. I had to deal with match referees over an incident or two involving our blokes, such as Joey Angel being up for disputing an umpire's decision in the First Test. We had injuries like you couldn't believe, and some sickness. Later I calculated that every one of our seven bowlers was out through injury at some stage during the tour. We lost a Test match we should have won (and I scored a pair), then failed to nail down two more that we were in a great position to win. We contended with a potential riot and an actual earthquake. We lost the Test series by a hair's breadth but won the one-day final (over Pakistan). My own form was a struggle, although I gathered steam as the tour went on and the 56 I made in the one-day final at Lahore was a positive ending.

Really, there wasn't too much more that could have gone wrong through the eleven weeks. Yet, when I look back on it my overwhelming thought is that it was a really great tour. And whatever I became as an Australian captain subsequently—that being something for others to conclude, not me—there is no doubt that the initiation of the Pakistan experience in 1994 played its part.

People have often asked me in the years since whether the responsibility of the captaincy inevitably impacts on personal achievement in cricket. My answer is that I think it does. As I mentioned, I have never been happy about delegating too much to others. When I became skipper, people now and then said to me: 'You should shed some of the responsibility, ease the pressure on yourself, get someone else to do some of the media stuff.' But it wasn't my way. During the time I led the side if there was an issue to do with the captaincy, then I felt it was my responsibility to deal with it.

The statistics of my career as a Test batsman back up my personal theory that a full, hands-on captaincy role has an effect on individual performance. Someone showed me the figures recently: I played fifty-four Tests just as a 'batsman' and averaged a shade under 47. I then went on to play fifty Tests as captain, averaging a shade under 40, Overall, I averaged 43.5. So the difference between 'batsman' and 'batsman-captain' sits at about seven runs an innings. People might say that the captaincy came later in my career, and perhaps I wasn't quite as good a player then. But the fact is that most batsman have their best years between the ages of twenty–nine and thirty-four. Yes, I believe the captaincy cost me some runs. But I wouldn't have changed a thing. To have captained my country was to me a great and significant honour. If I gave up a run or two, I was compensated mightily by the pleasure of the captaincy, some great results . . . and some wonderful times.

PETER ROEBUCK, *Sydney Morning Herald: Only those who toss a coin to decide an innings can appreciate the draining effect of captaining a professional cricket team. It is a unique experience in sport. A cricket captain is an isolated figure working within a team at the closest quarters, yet also duty bound to provide direction and morale. It is exhausting. A captain cannot relax.*

Chapter 15

SWEET SMELL
of SUCCESS

After the near-misses of Pakistan, I was pumped up for the Poms when Mike Atherton brought his team here for the Ashes summer of 1994–95. In Newcastle, Phil De Freitas—'Daffy'—and I clashed robustly, nothing earth-shattering but a sign of the keenness of cricket's two oldest rivals to get at each other's throats. The brush took place in a match between NSW and England in which I had been especially keen to (a) play and (b) do well. The disappointment of Pakistan—so near to a series victory, yet so far— had left me determined to get on the front foot straightaway in the battle to preserve the Ashes, in this my first series as captain against England.

We had been back from Pakistan only a week when the NSW– England game came around. For me it proved a resounding beginning to the quest at hand—a knock of 150 in the first innings, plus 47 in the second, which was a great psychological 'kick' for me, and hopefully a worrying sign for them too.

The Poms were keen to get at us up there. They picked a good side and blokes like Devon Malcolm and De Freitas were steaming in. My little 'debate' with Daffy came half an hour into the NSW innings. He had been bowling tight, and swung one back into me which I hit sweetly out through wide mid-on. 'Aaaahhhh!' went Daffy, adding something else about luck; he obviously figured the ball was almost through me. Before that, there had been a close lbw call that had not pleased the bowler. As I ran past him at the other end I commented: 'That was right off the middle!' Daffy came back at me, then the ump jumped in. It was lively stuff—an indication of two teams keen to get down to serious business.

We ended up winning that game, chasing 208 in the second innings, and I picked up another 47. The pressure was on me that first summer at the helm, but I felt it in a positive way and was determined to respond. We had lost in Pakistan, and now I was captain against England—a side we had beaten in the last three series 4–0, 3–0 and 4–1. To lose to them, as skipper, would have set up a great hue and cry. 'Maybe he's not the bloke for the job', they would have been saying.

My first Test against England as captain produced a 'controversial' decision which gave the pundits something to talk and write about. After we led by 259 on the first innings, I decided that we would not enforce the follow-on but would bat again. I had talked it over with some of the guys at stumps on the second day, when they were 6–133, way behind our 426. The Brisbane wicket was beautiful, a perfect batting track, and my inclination was strongly for us to bat again and make use of what was there. There were differing opinions. Billy McDermott was bowling superbly, and some of the team felt that we should stick them straight back in again once we knocked them over in the first innings.

The next morning we got the final wickets in about half an hour—bang, bang, bang, bang—finishing them off for 167. I was starting to have second thoughts. It had happened so quickly and easily; maybe we should put them back in after all? Anyhow, I stuck to Plan A—to the annoyance of a few commentators, and we ended up setting them 508 to get in five sessions. At stumps on the fourth night they were 2–211. Their batting fightback, via Graeme Hick and Graham Thorpe, vindicated the decision I had made. The other way, the chance would have been there for them to put some pressure on us on a tricky last day.

England needed another 297 to win the game, and from the start of the final day it was obvious they were not in that market and were just going to try to hang on for the draw. Hick and Thorpe played very defensively, and our main strike force, Warnie, was grunting and groaning in frustration at not being able to get the breakthrough. I ran down the wicket to chat with Warnie, saying 'Don't worry about it. Just keep hanging in there ... we only need to get one wicket.' Warnie figured he had the left-handed Thorpe's measure but couldn't quite get him. The first delivery after our conversation Shane got a full-pitched leg-break—an off-break to Thorpe—past his defensive prod, the ball biting in the rough beyond the popping crease before scattering his stumps. Next over he had Hick caught behind by Heals off the gloves ... and we were on our way to a decisive win. Shane finished with the brilliant figures of 8–71.

Afterwards, I had some fun with the media guys. They asked me what I had said to Warnie the instant before he skittled Thorpe. With tongue in cheek, but face straight, I told them: 'Bowl him a full-toss. That'll get him.' I think there was actually some serious reporting of the 'tactic'—which was in fact a lighthearted throw-away line.

That Test, starting our campaign so well, was highlighted by some fine bowling, particularly from McDermott and Warne, but more especially by Michael Slater's dashing 176 in our first innings. Slats really smashed them, then sacrificed his wicket late in the day, caught at mid-off trying to hit Graham Gooch over the top. Slats's innings came up when we were chatting after my 334 in Pakistan in 1998. He's an emotional sort of guy and he was really thrilled to be there when I made my score. 'Well, mate, I've given you a mark to get past,' I said to him. He laughed. But I talked to him seriously about that 176 in Brisbane—how the Poms were absolutely gone that day, and didn't look like getting him out. And how late in the day, he had given his wicket away more cheaply than he should have with what was an arrogant shot. By rights he should have been 200 not out overnight, with every chance of going on to another 100 the next day, so dominant he was. Slats put his stamp on the Test match from the opening over in Brisbane, crashing two fours off De Freitas and virtually saying to the Poms: This is what I'm here for.

So, in my fourth Test as Australian captain, I was a winner at last. It felt good. We then made it two-straight in Melbourne, a Test with a Christmas Day hiccup in the middle of it. This time we set them 388 to get in four sessions, and had them 4–79 overnight coming into the last day. Early next morning Mike Gatting, on 25, nicked one off McDermott and I took the catch at first slip. It was pretty much a procession from there.

But for the fans who had come along, there was a great thrill at the end of it—something that is a rare bird in Test match cricket. Warnie, a real demon that day, put the icing on the cake with a hat-trick near the close of the match. He got Phil De Freitas lbw with a skidder, and then Darren Gough with a regulation leg-break that turned sharply and flicked the glove for Heals to grab the catch.

Warnie was not short of advice on what to do next. A popular vote was for the flipper, with the theory being that Devon Malcolm would never pick that. The wrong one got a mention, too. 'What will I bowl?' Warnie asked me. 'Just bowl a leggie,' I said. So with the entire team clustered around the bat, Warne came in and bowled . . . a bloody top-spinner.

It was a beauty, pitching on middle-stump and bouncing sharply. To be honest Devon didn't do a lot wrong. He pushed forward in textbook fashion, but the ball caught the glove and then the front pad and flew low to David Boon's right side. Somehow, Boonie took a screamer of a catch to complete one of those special events— and, incidentally, to celebrate his thirty-fourth birthday.

It was over before lunch and after beers and showers we headed back to the team hotel in downtown Melbourne. Channel 9 were showing the day's highlights, so we gathered in the bar and watched the build-up to the hat-trick. It was a great way to finish a Test match.

I played in three 'hat-trick' Tests: Warne's in 1994, Damien Fleming's against Pakistan earlier that year in which the third leg was Salim Malik on 237, and Darren Gough's in the Sydney Test of the 1998–99 series. Not one of the nine dismissals was 'dodgy'; each one of them was absolutely clear-cut.

What a bowler Shane Warne was, and is. I rate him the most influential cricketer of my time in the game. He was the player who did more than anyone else to bring the art of spin bowling back into cricket. Largely because of him, spin bowling became no longer something young guys did just because they couldn't bowl quick. Instead it was something they set out to do in their cricket careers from the word go. Warnie made it fashionable again, and that will be his legacy to the game.

The combination of Warnie's profile and prowess have drawn unending attention to him in recent seasons. He grew into such a superstar, re-enforced by the nicknames (e.g. 'Hollywood') that he was (and is) forever in the news—sometimes for the wrong reasons. In some ways, he has been unlucky. In reality Shane is just a normal bloke who happens to love cricket, Aussie Rules—and bowl a bit of leg spin. The shame of it is that the side of him that always seems to be portrayed is the bad side. Yet you know, there's not much of a bad side at all to Shane Warne. In fact he's a bloody good bloke, a nice bloke. His dilemma is the dilemma of all 'superstars' of sport—expectations that are simply sky high. People sometimes expect them to be things they cannot be—to be people they are not. Expectations for our top sportsmen and women these days often simply aren't realistic.

Apart from the drizzling rain which always seemed to be lurking not far away, the Sydney Test of the 1994–95 Ashes series, on a lively wicket, was a compelling game. After being 3–20 and then 3–194, with Atherton (88) and Crawley (72) getting the runs,

England's 309 was a pretty fair score. I then had the unusual experience of batting for all but one ball of our innings—and scoring 49! Reeling at 8–65 at one stage, we scrambled 116 with the unlikely partnership of McDermott–Taylor adding 51. Finally I sent a leading-edge off a slower ball from Goughie straight back to the bowler, as I tried to work one around the corner to keep the strike. Damien Fleming was out next ball, and our innings was all over before I got the pads off. We had at least avoided the follow-on.

The Poms then set us 449 to get in four-and-a-half sessions, with great controversy surrounding Mike Atherton's decision to declare with Graeme Hick 98 not out. I think Atherton was totally justified in what he did, notwithstanding everyone saying what a terrible thing it was to do to Hick. My reading of it was that 'Athers' had given Hick plenty of time to get the runs and that Hick had forced his captain's hand by fiddling around in the 90s, taking an inordinately long time to get from 90 to 98.

The haul was a long one for us, but at tea on the second last day we had hurried to 0–41, with me on 29 and Michael Slater on 7. 'What are you trying to do—embarrass me?' Slats commented as we walked off. I had decided out there that I'd die with my boots on, rather than stonewall. Malcolm was bowling very quick and I made myself a promise: 'If I'm going to get out I'm at least going to fall going for them.' So I just teed off. By stumps that night we were 0–139, with Slats on 65 and me 64. This was turning into quite a game.

At lunch the next day we were still none-for, at 206, adding only 67 runs in the morning session against an England attack that was tight and well marshalled—but with ten wickets still in hand the chance to win the game was with us almost as much as with them. There was only one question at lunch: 'What are we going to do?' And only one answer: 'Go for it . . . yeah, we'll go for it.' We had a minimum of sixty overs to get 243 on a non-typical Sydney wicket that wasn't turning much at all. We thought we were a big show.

But as can sometimes happen in cricket, it wasn't a player who had the final word on the game, but a far more powerful hand: Mother Nature. Rain trimmed an hour-and-a-half of what followed, although under match rules we could make up an hour of it. It was enough to change the balance of the game slightly. Slats was out hooking not long after lunch for 103 at 208 and I fell to Malcolm, shouldering arms to one that came back late and took off-stump. I scored 113, and we were 2–239.

With the drizzle it was a different match. I ordered the team to change tack. 'We're not going for it now. We're going to defend.' With the second new ball on a wicket that was juicing up because of the drizzle, batting became difficult, the ball starting to do a fair bit more than it had been. Amid growing tension we battled on until early evening. The final ball was bowled around 7.21 p.m. with Tim May (10) and Shane Warne (36) toughing it out late in the day under considerable pressure—which included their being called back from the dressing-room gates to face one more over— for 7–344 and a draw.

This was a terrific Test match, with the intensifying drama of the final day drawing a crowd of 25,766—the best last-day crowd at a Sydney Test for many years. It was yet another example of how great an entertainment Test cricket can be, and how the longer format can build to truly spine-tingling finishes. It was just a shame about the rain, that was all. We reckoned that without it we would have gone close to winning the game.

The Adelaide Test was almost as good in its crowd appeal, even if the result was not what the home fans (or the Australian team) had hoped for. We led by 66 on the first innings, with Greg Blewett getting a century on debut, much to the delight of the home crowd, and we had the Poms two down by the time they passed our score in the second innings. With our record of knocking over their tail we were in great shape to kill the Test. Then Phil De Freitas teed off and made 88, and instead of a gimme score we ended up chasing 263, in two sessions.

By then, the Ashes were safe, at 2–0. 'Let's go for it,' I said to the guys. We struggled from ball one. I was out early, trying to drive off the back foot, and Slats fell to the hook again. Others followed in a steady stream, and far too soon we were 8–83 and way out of it. Late in the day we almost hung on for the draw, but they knocked us over finally with thirty-five balls to go. It was a Test match in which we 'led' on days two, three and four. Day five is the one that counts in Test cricket, however, and on that day we were outplayed, and beaten. As Geoff Lawson put it in the *Sydney Morning Herald* next morning: 'Catastrophe! Shame! Humiliation! The Poms have beaten us at cricket.'

For me, the Test was played under a happy cloud of anticipation, with my thoughts straying back to Sydney, and home, where Judi was waiting to give birth to our second child. I flew back straight after the press conference which followed the match and was there when Jack Anthony Taylor made his first appearance in the world at the Seventh Day Adventist Hospital in Wahroonga, early on the morning of 31 January 1995. I drove from there into town to register Jack's arrival, to ensure we could get a passport for him to travel to New Zealand, where we were bound after the England series, then back to the hospital to spend some time with Jude. Then it was home to East Ryde, some packing, and a cab to the airport for the long haul to Perth and the Fifth Test. I was knackered when I finally got there, I can tell you, after the long flight and all the emotion and excitement of becoming a dad again.

Fortunately I had a couple of days in Perth to recover from such things. Subsequently, in a Test match which offered them the prospect of an honorable draw in the series, the Poms performed shakily, dropping a number of chances and letting the game gradually slip away. Slats scored 100 in the first innings, and was dropped three or four times. Then just when it looked like they might have us in a spot of bother in the second, Greg Blewett smashed them, collecting his second successive century. Chasing 442, they crumbled for 123 on a Perth wicket that had a bit in it and we ended up winning easily, for a 3–1 series win and a very satisfying retention of the Ashes trophy—especially for the new captain.

It was a good series for the Australian openers. I got 471 at 47 and Slats finished with 623 at 62.3. In contrast their openers generally struggled, although Mike Atherton had a fair series with 407 runs.

It was the summer in which I had some terse things to say about the 'Australia A' concept in the one-day series. Fundamentally, I didn't agree with it—an experiment to bolster the one-dayers with what were virtually Australia's 'Seconds'. It pitched Aussies against Aussies in a fairly uneasy situation. Australians being the way they are, they will always go for the underdogs in sporting contests where they don't really care *who* wins. When we beat the 'A' team in Adelaide in a close call by six runs, it was a funny feeling. I sensed that most of the crowd were disappointed with the result.

I finished up on the front pages when I told the media: 'I don't like playing against my own players and I don't like it when the crowd does not support us when we're playing at home.'

I am certainly not against the 'A' concept in every respect—it's a fine way of developing players for the future—but to pitch them against the national side there can only be one winner, the 'A' side. If you go out there and belt them everyone says, well, that's the way it should be. So you're not really a winner—and you're certainly not a winner if they happen to upset you.

As it turned out we played the 'As' in the one-day finals that year, and they won the tosses in both Sydney and Melbourne—a considerable advantage at that time when the wickets were slowish in both places. We chased them both times, and won two hard-fought games to make it four out of four against them.

I didn't think much of the concept or enjoy the matches themselves and I made my feelings known. That caused quite a stir, with calls for me to be censured by the ACB because I was speaking out against a matter that was Board policy. The Board was sympathetic. 'We understand your position,' they said, 'but it's a concept we at least wanted to try to see how it worked, and how the public took to it.' Having evaluated the idea in the course of the season the Board met again and dropped it and have never raised it since.

The Taylor family travelled *en masse* to New Zealand for the short campaign that would lead us back to the West Indies and no doubt into furious battle. I was going to be away for the best part of three months, so I was keen to spend time with Judi, William and the newly arrived Jack, sporting his first passport at twelve days of age. The night before we played the Kiwis at Eden Park was a bad one. Little Jack was off-colour and hollered and screamed all night in our hotel room. I got hardly any sleep—but next day went out and scored 97 and won the Man of the Match trophy. I was filthy at not getting my 100, which would have been my first in one-day cricket. The innings still had eight overs to go when Chris Pringle bowled me his slower ball and I leading-edged it straight back to him. I was knackered at the time after the night I had spent, but shortly beforehand had promised myself: 'I'm going to get this hundred . . . get this bloody monkey off my back.' We won that game easily, and the final of the four-cornered series (New Zealand, South Africa, India and us) just as comfortably against the Kiwis. It was a handy lead-in to the West Indies challenge. I knew though that far tougher days lay just ahead.

Chapter 16

WINNING *in* the WINDIES

We made the long trek to the West Indies in 1995 via London—confident we were in great shape to win the one-day series that opened the tour, but even surer the Tests would be a war zone. At first, however, things did not go as planned. We got belted in the one-dayers, 4–1, lost our two main strike bowlers along the way, and were left looking at a mountain to climb if we were going to take any element of glory and success out of the tour.

Australia hadn't won a series in the West Indies for twenty-two years, and hadn't beaten them at all in a series since 1975–76. And when Craig McDermott jumped off a sea wall in Guyana and ended up writhing in pain on the ground with a badly damaged ankle, after Damien Fleming had torn his bowling shoulder rotator cuff in Trinidad, we were seemingly in dire straits. Our opening attack from the Ashes series at home was no more.

But there's an old saying about opportunity producing the man, and so it proved. Or in our case in the exciting weeks that followed, the men. With Craig and Damien both off home before a ball had been bowled in the Tests it was down to Glenn McGrath and Paul Reiffel to do the job.

And do it they did . . . mightily. I recall a conversation with Glenn soon after the double blow of losing McDermott and Fleming had hit us. 'Mate, you'll be taking the new ball—this is your big opportunity,' I said. Glenn didn't say much in reply, but it wasn't really what he said so much as how he said it. 'I'm really looking forward to it,' he said in his quiet way. 'I want the new ball for Australia.' In a single bound he had gone from 12th man or third seamer to strike bowler.

That tour was the making of Glenn McGrath—until then a young bowler of great potential, but troubled somewhat by injury. And Paul Reiffel stood at his shoulder, the pair of them finding an extra yard in pace and bowling aggressively and intelligently throughout the series that unfolded. The pair of them were hungry. Then Brendon Julian chipped in too, and he wasn't even in our original squad. Yet there he was in the First Test as first-change bowler, contributing a terrific spell of 4–29 and 30 valuable runs. It's funny how opportunity works. You can have people pigeon-holed a certain way, then suddenly they're doing far more than anyone ever expected of them.

It was a tour that changed almost in a single moment. In the diary I kept of the tour, subsequently published as *Taylor Made*, I noted a particular training session on a particular day as the First Test neared. It was as if someone had flicked a switch. The one-dayers were gone and we were into fresh territory. Suddenly everything felt different and better. In a blink of an eye the team's whole attitude had changed. No longer were we just going through the motions at training. I remember watching it happen and thinking, 'Something real is taking place here'. The switch was back to 'on'.

At the training session that day we took the back of the nets down. We decided that practice from now was going to be full-on, mimicking match conditions as closely as possible. There would be no bowling no-balls—a general practice in the nets. That apart, it was anything goes. If the quicks wanted to bowl bumpers, then they could bowl them. The message was roughly this: Don't worry about this business of keeping the ball up. Bowl flat out, bowl what you want to bowl. We had some great sessions at the nets after that—batsmen ducking and weaving and getting the chance to play the hook. We knew what we were going to cop from the West Indies pacemen. This was our way of getting ready to confront the 'devil'. We turned training into fun—although 'fun' with a slightly dangerous edge to it. Practice sessions grew closer to real game time. There would be acclaim for a ball 'well evaded' as a steepling bumper soared past. We talked about looking ahead, not looking back.

It was a very different approach from that taken in 1991. On that tour, Craig McDermott got cut above the eye in one match, and there was a lot of talk about the short-pitched stuff . . . *sort of* joking. 'That's it,' Bob Simpson, who was coaching us this time as well, said one morning. 'No more talk about short-pitched bowling on the tour.' Frankly, I think that's about the worst approach you can take when it comes to the short stuff. My view is that if you're going to get it—and you're sure going to get it on a West Indies tour—then you might as well talk about it. It's better to have it up-front, discussed and dealt with, rather than lurking at the back of players' minds, where there are things unsaid that would be better out in the open.

The Test match at Barbados was just a great game, one of the greatest I have played in. It was preceded by something of a kerfuffle in the press. After the Windies had given us a towelling in the one-day series, I was asked to comment on how we were shaping up. 'Well, I think we're getting stale in one-day cricket,' I said. 'We've played a lot of it.' The papers made more of it than they should have: 'Australian team stale, says Taylor', was the theme. I had a subsequent quiet word with some of the press guys, telling them we *weren't* stale at all, just that we'd had enough of the one-day game, having played three series of it in succession. 'The guys are really looking forward to playing some Test cricket,' I told them. And we were.

An incident involving Brian Lara—and there have been one or two of those over the years—partly soured a spectacular start for us in Barbados, a place where Australia hadn't ever won a Test in six attempts. When the Windies were 5–156 on the first day after winning the toss, Steve Waugh took an awkward juggling catch from Lara at backward point, in which the ball got somehow tangled up in his arms. Steve had no doubt he had caught it and held the ball up. Umpire Venkataraghavan agreed, and Lara walked off, with no hint of disagreement.

It was only later that the incident blew up into something major, with claims the next day that the ball had hit the ground and that Waugh hadn't made a fair catch. The slow-motion replays were inconclusive, but as far as we were concerned Steve genuinely believed he had caught the ball, the umpire had agreed and that was that. But after we had cleaned them up in three days, all hell broke lose. Viv Richards came out in the press, calling us cheats and declaring the victory a hollow one. We copped some unwarranted flak. In their second innings I have no doubt we had Brian Lara out for nought, caught at bat-pad off Warnie. He was given not out, and that's the way cricket is. Sometimes it bounces your way, sometimes it doesn't.

Significantly, the 1995 series was played in good spirit despite the Waugh–Lara 'incident'. Viv Richards's criticism was more representative of a past era when everything was fury and confrontation. Richards really tried to put the boot in, labelling us an 'ordinary' team. There was no doubt in my mind he was trying to whip up the old hatreds that supposedly existed between Australian and West Indian teams. But the game had moved on. We had our run-ins in '95, but they were no more than in Test series against any country. Things had changed—and Viv Richards' voice was no more than a cry from the past.

The Barbados win was a stunner, with just about everyone

chipping in for a victory that was sealed within three days, an extraordinary result considering that we were rank outsiders.

That gave us the rest day and two full additional days free of cricket. 'When are we going to train, Mark?' Bob Simpson asked. 'I reckon if you win a game in three days you shouldn't have to train on the free days you have earned,' I answered. The coach nodded his agreement. So instead of cricket for a day or two we went game fishing and touring around. A few of the pubs around Barbados saw a bit of the Aussies in those days too.

Simmo was in trouble at the time—yet another casualty of a troubled tour. Stricken by a worrying leg problem, the development of a thrombosis, he was in hospital on the day we won the First Test. On the way back from the ground late that afternoon we asked the driver to head down past the hospital. Out front we pulled up and roared out the windows: 'Simmo . . . we've done 'em!' He reckoned he heard us, too. On the night of the third day, we joined the West Indian players aboard the *Bajan Queen* on a dinner cruise around Barbados Harbour, something that had become a tradition during Test matches there. The getting-together of the two teams that night helped to further ease any lingering friction that might have existed between us. If it had been, say, 1991 and Australia had won the Barbados Test, I doubt there would have been any fraternising on the *Bajan Queen*. One team would have been at the pointy end of the boat and the other down the back.

Rain intervened to kill off the Test in Antigua after a great struggle that ebbed and flowed and looked set for decision on the last day. A big highlight was the way we got rid of Brian Lara—by now the chosen one of West Indian cricket—in their first innings. Bowling around the wicket, Steve Waugh nagged away at him outside off-stump, with seven men on the off-side. Brian kept hitting them sweetly, but couldn't get the ball through. Finally in some frustration, he moved across and worked one on the leg side. David Boon, posted at a sort of 'nothing' position at straight short mid-on, took a screamer of a catch, left-handed.

The removal of the covers at Trinidad for the Third Test revealed one of the worst big-match wickets I ever saw in my career. To be fair to the groundsmen there had been a lot of rain, but when they pulled the covers off, the grass was about three centimetres long! We presumed they would cut it—but they didn't, merely running the roller up and down. If I ever needed to win a toss, this was it. I called tails, as I always did, and lost it.

The wicket dominated everything, producing more tricks than a nightclub magician. It was flying and it was seaming. If a ball hit the seam it was a chance of going anywhere. We got 128, they made 136 and then we crumbled again, after being 0–20 at the end of the second day, to be all out for 105. At the warm-ups before day three, I called the guys in. We were really pumped up. 'Righto, this is a big opportunity to nail these blokes and win the series,' I told them. 'I want you to be positive in everything you do out there today. If we can set them anything over 200, we'll win this game.' The talk was terrific, the performance a little less so. They knocked us over for 105 and got the required 98 for only one-down. We had lost the Test in three days.

It came down to Jamaica for the Fourth Test, the pressure on and the anticipation high. I lost the toss again, and just before lunch when they were 1–100, I was thinking: 'This is not good. We looked like winning the series, now they're going to make a huge score here.' Then Warnie struck, getting Lara bat-pad just before lunch, with Heals haring around from behind the stumps to take the catch. Richie Richardson made 100, but we soldiered on very well after the Lara breakthrough and knocked them over for 265 at the end of the first day.

Waugh-power has rarely been better glimpsed than it was on day two of that Test. It was 3–73 when the brothers got together, and 4–321 at stumps, with Steve still there on 110. These were two innings that pretty much summed up the diverse talents of Mark and Steve. Junior's innings was an absolute beauty; probably he batted better than Steve. But as happens with Mark, he was out just when he looked set enough to get 500, caught at bat-pad to Carl Hooper. Dropped at 42 by Courtney Browne, Steve just batted and batted—a super performance of application and concentration, never veering from his game plan. It was the way the brothers have always been, I suppose.

Greg Blewett's partnership with Steve was decisive. 'Blewie' got 63 in a session and really whacked them to ram home our advantage. As Steve ground down the Windies attack, Blewie hopped into them. His was a mini-masterpiece of an innings. Steve's 200 (last man out at 531) was the sort of championship performance on which Test matches are won. The bowlers promptly picked up the baton, and ran with it.

By stumps on day three we had them 3–63—Lara and Richardson both gone—with a rest day to follow. The series win that all of us had dreamed of was within tantalising reach, but still an elusive forty hours away. On the rest day it rained like mad as we took a bus trip to Ocho Rios, three hours north of Kingston. Weather-wise, the day was a shocker; for sure no cricket would have been possible, if any had been scheduled. Through the night that followed I woke several times, listening for the sound of rain. There was none.

Next day we knocked them over for 213—and so became the first Australian side since Ian Chappell's team of 1973 to beat the West Indies in a series at home. Warnie took 4–70 on that last day and the Test was never going to be anything but ours. I had the pleasure of snaring the last catch, Kenneth Benjamin off Shane, to lock it up.

The significance of what we had achieved—beating the unbeatables on their home turf—began to sink in at the long and enthusiastic press conference that followed the game. Being in Kingston, an edgy place, we had our celebrations 'in', dressing up one of the big rooms at the top of the Pegasus Hotel where we were staying. At about 9.30 p.m. a TV film crew turned up, dispatched from Miami to get an interview with the team. I politely refused them entry. 'You had the chance after the game,' I told them. 'For us the work has finished . . . we're celebrating now.' They were disappointed, and possibly in strife with their network back home. But the fact was that anyone could see we were in a position to win the game on that fourth day and they should have been there for that and for the press call afterwards like everyone else.

It was regrettable that Richie Richardson chose to end the series by introducing a sour note. At his final press conference after the match he described us as probably the weakest Australian side he had played against, and suggested that the West Indians had just 'batted badly'. Knowing Richie, who is a pretty decent bloke, I don't think he was trying to have any sort of big go at us; I guess he was just trying to explain away something that was pretty painful for West Indian cricket—that they had lost. He copped a huge serve in the Aussie press for his ungracious words.

I believe that the freshness in our side was a winning factor. We had a number of young blokes who carried no baggage of previous defeats at the hands of the Windies. They just wanted to get in there and win the series. Perhaps on paper we didn't compare with the 1991 outfit. But this squad of 1995 was a team on the upside of the hill. We weren't too bothered about what anyone said about us. We had gone there, jumped some very difficult hurdles that chance had thrown up, and won.

The tour finished with a dreamy eight days in Bermuda where we played some relaxed one-dayers and mainly just enjoyed a place which has the second- or third-highest living standard in the world. It reeks of wealth. Mansions as pretty as big dolls' houses are all over the place. We stayed at a place called Elbow Beach Resort which was just fabulous. The water was crystal clear and a beautiful blue-green.

However, as I have already said about the 1991 tour, visiting the West Indies is not all like that. The island-hopping that is involved takes you to a great mixture of cultures, living standards and scenery. Often the true holiday beauty spots are away from the cricket centres—such as Montego Bay and Ocho Rios in Jamaica.

The facilities are rougher than Australia, with grandstands and change rooms being much more basic. The crowds are boisterous and fiercely loyal and every island is a different country, while the travel between them is slow and arduous, made more trying by the need for immigration and customs checks. There are many things, though, that stay in your mind about touring the Caribbean. I can still picture the beautiful little ground at St Vincent where we played a one-dayer, overlooked by a spectacular tree-covered tropical mountain.

We came home from balmy days in Bermuda to a much appreciated motorcade through Sydney streets—and we fathers in the team to littlies who had changed quite a bit in the months since we had left. For me, the long tours became harder to take as the boys grew older. Going to New Zealand—albeit with the family—and then straight on to the West Indies ate up the best part of four months. Yet I didn't find that as much a wrench as I did the Pakistan tour of 1998 when William was six and Jack nearly four, and the boys realised that I was heading off for quite a while. Those early minutes on the plane after you've said your goodbyes are very quiet and reflective ones. Invariably, there is a lump in more than one throat.

In 1995, Judi had a really tough time as she so often did. I was away with the team and she was back here alone with two tiny kids. It was harder on her than it was on me. So when I was named NSW Father of the Year in late 1995, people were probably thinking: 'How could *he* be father of the year? He's away half the time.' Which wasn't a bad call. When I received the award at a function at a downtown Sydney hotel, I didn't really know what I was going to say in my speech. So I got up there and said: 'Well, I like to think of myself as a *quality* father rather than a quantity father.'

The positive side of touring from a family point of view lay in the free time that followed a trip away—three months off, for example, after the Windies tour of 1995. Nine-to-five workers get weekends off. Cricketing fathers like me got their time in blocks.

For me in '95 it was a chance to say howdy to a new son, to play some backyard cricket with my fast-growing No. 1 and for Judi and me to have a break and grab some holiday time before it all started again.

Unbeknown to any of us, Bob Simpson was then nearing the end of his reign as Australian coach. The role that he played—and Geoff Marsh carried on—are undoubtedly worthy of attention in profiling the decade of Australian cricket.

Bob Simpson had his admirers and his detractors in his ten years as Australian coach (1986–96). He was certainly off-side with more than a few when his reign came to an end and Geoff Marsh took over in 1996. But, looking back, I know that I worked very well with both of them. Bob was a 'hands-on' coach and there was a feeling around that he was running the whole show during the period of Allan Border's captaincy. There was some truth in that— but for reasons mainly to do with the fact that both of them were happy with it that way.

When AB tore a hamstring in the 1992–93 season and I took over the captaincy for a few one-day games we had a good yarn about how it should work. 'Get out there and do it the way you want to do it,' AB said. 'You're the captain now, you run the show.' Allan went on to talk about the way it worked with him and Simmo. AB really just wanted to play the game—he never wanted to do all the other stuff. So he was happy to leave a fair lump of that, including some of the media obligations, with the coach. Simmo liked it that way too.

Before I took the side to Pakistan as captain in 1994 Simmo and I got together. I told him then that I was keen to have a bit more of a hands-on role, and was happy to attend to the media duties and so on. There were no problems. Some people drew the conclusion that Simmo would object to taking a backward step. In fact, he didn't have a problem with it—and our working relationship then, and later, was good.

The only thing which I disagreed with was his being a selector. I felt it was better all round for him not to be in that role. And from a year or so after I became captain, he wasn't. Simmo and I were in disagreement on the principle of that, but it wasn't a major issue. He accepted the way it turned out and we continued to work well together.

When he finished up in 1996, I thought it was time for him to go, although Bob no doubt didn't see it that way. In fact there were indications he blamed me to an extent for his demise. That wasn't the case—I would have been happy to work on with him if he had been reappointed. Bob had had some physical problems; his knee wasn't great and he had some screws in his back. And Simmo was a hard bastard who would push himself to the limit. He was sixty then and had had ten years as coach, a pretty fair innings, and maybe the Board did him a favour when they decided on the change. But whether he had continued on as coach or whether he didn't wouldn't have worried me in the slightest.

My view of the Simpson era is that he was very good for the side. He took over a young side in the 1980s at a tough time for the Australian game. In the early '80s when it had looked a much better side on paper—essentially, they just went out and played. Simmo took his new young side back to basics, began the teaching of how they should play at an international level, imposed a strong work ethic in practice sessions. He and I never had a problem.

In 1996 the Board sought my views on who would be a good replacement. Geoff Marsh was already on their list and Steve Rixon had rung me and asked if I reckoned he should throw his hat into the ring. I said yes; I had worked well with 'Stumper' for years within the NSW team. Swampy, Stumper or Simmo—there honestly wouldn't have been any drama at my end with the selection of any one of the three of them. And when my old opening partner Swampy Marsh got the call, I was pleased for him and knew we would work comfortably as a 'team'.

I felt as captain I didn't need a domineering coach. I was keen to work in partnership with someone who would time the nets and do all the other bits needed to make the picture complete. When Swampy came in as coach it was in more of a behind-the-scenes role in comparison to Simpson's higher-profile approach. It was interesting how Swamp's role increased with the two-captains policy. Suddenly he was the key link between the two sides.

Swamp has done a first-class job. He picked up a lot from Simmo in the physical drills of practice sessions, an area in which Bob was at his very best. The best drills in cricket are the ones in which you use the ball. Simmo's fifty-minute fielding sessions were physically strenuous—you were running all the time—but interesting as well, because the ball would be in play the whole time. Much better than a fifty minutes' run. Geoff picked up a lot of Simmo's methods and, when he came in as coach, brought his own fresh drills too.

There is a lot of Simpson in the Marsh methods, but differences too. Simmo was the guy who brought a brand new work ethic into the side, and Swampy has kept the hard-work side of it going. But Simmo, especially in the earlier years, was pretty much the 'all-purpose' coach—physio, media advisor, coach, trainer, spokesman, manager. Geoff has taken the game another step forward with his readiness to bring in experts to help the team's preparation—in the areas of physical fitness, nutrition, sports psychology, etc. The teams now have a full-time manager and full-time physical fitness guy (Dave Misson), with other areas of expertise available when needed.

I think the game has to be careful about not surrounding the players with too many experts though. The more people are involved, the more people have to justify what they do. It can get a bit cluttered, and I subscribe to the Simpson view of keeping it pretty lean. But tapping intelligently into experts in the high-pressure, high-profile world that top-level cricket has become of course makes sense. It's just that blokes playing ten or eleven months of the year don't need to be loaded with extra stuff all the time.

I was certainly greatly in favour of having a year-round fitness trainer associated with the team—someone who can provide an unobtrusive program in the brief off-season to keep you going, as well as keeping the team sharp and fit in the playing season. Along with blokes like Merv Hughes and Shane Warne I waged a career-long struggle in the physical area, and to have an expert on hand to keep you going is a real bonus for the 'tubbies' of cricket.

Chapter 17

Sri Lankan
Strife

In 1994, the focus of cricket had been on bribery and corruption and the fixing of matches. In late 1995, when the Sri Lankans came to play in Australia, it was ball-tampering and then chucking that captured the headlines. It was hard not to think that the game once regarded as the pastime of English gentlemen was going through one of the stormiest periods of its existence.

The three-Test Pakistan tour here which preceded the arrival of the Sri Lankans was whisper-quiet by comparison. The Pakistan side looked strong on paper, but seemed under-prepared for a short campaign which demanded good early form. We flogged them in Brisbane, then beat them in Hobart to take the series, this latter Test being a much better game than the first. We won under difficulties after a Waqar Younis yorker had left Shane Warne with a broken toe and out of the firing line. I believe that the 120 I made in the second innings down there was one of my best knocks as captain of Australia. It helped provide the springboard for us to take the match, although a bowler short. In the Third Test in Sydney, the Pakistanis were much closer to peak form, and beat us on a typical SCG turner on which Mushtaq Ahmed had a field day, taking nine wickets and also the

Man of the Match award. As an indication of what sort of wicket it was, Warnie got eight wickets, on a still-tender toe which he iced at the end of each day. He was named Man of the Series, a mark of the quality of his form at that time, considering that he only bowled in two of the three games.

The three-Test Sri Lankan series that followed proved to be a far more explosive event. The touring side arrived with a positive message, skipper Arjuna Ranatunga declaring that his team was on a mission to make Sri Lanka one of the best Test-playing nations by the year 2000. But the tour was a prickly one, almost from the start. A ball-tampering drama that was to rumble for months blew up in Perth, when the international umpire for the first Test, Khizar Hayat, decided in the seventeenth over he didn't like the way the Sri Lankans were picking away at the pill. But he and his partner Peter Parker failed to take the next step and as a result the exact details of what was being done—or might have been done—were clouded and uncertain. Instead of confiscating the ball in question and replacing it with one of similar quality, they decided to continue with the same ball. When they did finally replace it, it was too late. Match referee Graham Dowling subsequently received a report from the umpires and issued a reprimand to the Sri Lankans—a mild measure which was nonetheless overturned by the ICC in late December when they dismissed the charges of ball-tampering and rebuked the two umpires instead.

Ball-tampering is a contentious matter in cricket—much discussed, hard to prove and inevitably leading to allegations of deliberate cheating when raised in a serious way, as it was in that Perth Test match. It's a fact of cricket life that every team does what it can to get the most out of the ball, to try to gain some advantage. One ploy is to pack sweat on one side, to get it to swing. Then there's Irish (reverse) swing, achieved by letting one side of an old ball get as rough as possible and vigorously shining the other. For reasons that are beyond me an old ball will swing *towards* the shiny side, while a new one will swing *away* from the shine.

Irish swing is quite a mystery. The Pakistanis are experts at it on their hard, dry wickets on which the ball gets very roughed up. They invented the art. The problem surrounding Irish swing has always been the suggestion that no matter how dry and dusty the ground may be, the ball needs some help by scraping and picking at it to make it rough enough to swing as desired. Sometimes on TV you'll see blokes picking things out of the ball. The rules are that you can remove grass from the seam but not tamper with the rest of the ball in any way. In Perth in 1995, there were allegations that the Sri Lankans were scratching away illegally at the ball. However true that may have been, it didn't seem to matter. We gave them a real belting, as so often happens when visiting teams shape up to the challenges posed by the WACA.

Then, on Boxing Day in Melbourne, the second big controversy of the summer arrived when the Sri Lankan off-spinner Muttiah Muralitharan was called seven times for throwing by umpire Darrell Hair, from the bowler's end.

Hair was standing back from the stumps to get a clear look at Muralitharan's action. When the Sri Lankan captain, Arjuna Rana-tunga, switched Muralitharan to the other end, however, Hair's fellow umpire, New Zealander Steve Dunne, failed to call him. I understand that Hair then asked Dunne to move back and watch the bowler's action from behind. Dunne declined. He said later that it wasn't a question of his not supporting Hair, but that he was reacting in accordance with how he saw things from his end. It was a shame. I don't think umpires should ever 'gang up' on a player, but Murali-tharan had already caused headaches for a lot of umpires around the world with his unorthodox action. I very much agree that it has to be an umpire's personal decision whether he acts against a bowler, but to have Muralitharan called from one end and not the other created a perplexing situation.

I can still remember Hair making his first call out in the middle of the MCG. Suddenly everyone in the players' room was looking around saying, 'What's that for?' Then Ranatunga walked up to Hair gesticulating, and we could see Hair clearly demonstrating that in his view Muralitharan was throwing the ball. Straightaway the Sri Lankan captain switched him to the other end. But at the tea break, the drama came to a head. Hair told Ranatunga that if he kept bowling Muralitharan, he would have no option but to call him from square leg. Left with no choice, Ranatunga took the spinner out of the attack.

The blow-up was big news in the media, but no great surprise. It was fairly well known that on a number of occasions in the past match referees had written to the ICC on the subject of Muralitharin's bowling action. It's worth noting that his being no-balled was not and is not 'an Australian thing', or caused by the opinions of the Australian team. It was just that the controversy surrounding him began in about 1992, yet here we were in 1995–96 still confronting the question of whether or not he was a thrower, rather than a bowler. In the one-dayers in Australia in early 1999, the issue was still dragging on.

Whether Muralitharan is a chucker or not is almost irrelevant. The problem lies in an administrative system which gives no clear guidance. After the 1995 incidents the ICC appointed an independent panel representing various countries, charged with the looking at any suspect bowlers and making appropriate recommendations about them. But the process has proved largely a waste of time. The panel does not make decisions. It makes *assessments* by studying videos of players with questionable actions, and then recommends that they work with someone like Fred Titmus or Bruce Yardley for three months to try to straighten out the problem. The panel then passes all information on to the player's home body, effectively leaving the decision in the hands of the individual countries. As Muralitharan has been his country's best bowler since about 1994, naturally the Sri Lankans were and are going to keep picking him. He hasn't been banned—and they can consequently infer, without drawing too long a bow, that he has been 'officially' cleared.

In fact he hasn't been cleared at all. He's been noted as a player with a suspect action and put through a bit of remedial work, with the question of his future left to his home selectors to decide. Of course they're going to keep picking him.

The ICC guidelines obviously need to be tightened. My own view is that if a bowler is called and subsequently found on formal investigation (by an independent board) to be a thrower, a penalty should be imposed—say, three months out of the game first time around. That would give him three months to work on his problem. If when he is selected again and an umpire still believes he is throwing, rather than creating embarrassment out in the middle, the umpire should express his opinion to the independent ICC board via the match referee. A second 'guilty' verdict on a throwing charge would see the player out for a further fixed period—say, six months or a year. In my opinion the ICC needs such a formal, fixed penalty structure to handle the issue, rather than the vague system now in place. There is no question that the ICC has tried to be as fair as it can and give the players in question as much benefit of the doubt as possible.

Even without such changes, the ICC panel needs to be ever-vigilant. Often where there's smoke there's fire when it comes to throwing. In assessing a bowler the panel does not have to find that he is actually throwing, and does not have to be unanimous. But if enough of them are not happy with a bowler's action, they can decide there's sufficient doubt about it and the need for further steps. The obligation is then on the player to prove that he *is* bowling— and not chucking, as the rules of cricket suggest.

It is such a difficult area. A bowler *can* straighten out his action under the guidance of a Titmus, Yardley or Ashley Mallett but then drift back to his old ways in the pressure of a match.

Over the seasons there has been a lot of talk about this bowler or that being a 'chucker'. I recall another Sri Lankan—Kumara Dharmasena—whose action looked a lot worse than Muralitharan's. But he has since faded out of the picture. In Australia in recent years we've had players like Greg Rowell and Geoff Foley from Queensland and NSW's Brad McNamara questioned at various times over their actions. Straightaway the problem has been addressed and the players have had to do some remedial work, being watched like hawks from that point on. Unlike the situation with Muralitharan there are no racial overtones or undertones with these locally based players and the issue is straightened in a very direct way: get it sorted out or you don't play! There have been other suspect cases elsewhere. Now and then I have heard people question Courtney Walsh's action, although personally I could never see anything wrong with it. Almost inevitably, if someone bowls a really quick bumper, talk starts that he throws that particular ball.

The saddest thing about the whole Muttiah Muralitharan case is that he's a very nice bloke—and that when he gets called there are inevitably suggestions of 'racism' . . . which are just not true, or I truly hope they're not. The fact is that there are a lot of people in world cricket—not just Darrell Hair and Ross Emerson, the umpire who also called him in 1999—who believe that Muralitharan throws the ball. The Sri Lankans point out, correctly, that Australia is the only country in which he has been called. That has lead to the ugly claim: 'You blokes hate him. You're racists!' But I know for a fact that there are other umpires and referees around the world who feel exactly the same way as Hair and Emerson, but who have done nothing about it.

I don't want to see any bowler thrown out of the game. But if there are bowlers with unusual actions coming through, the game has to make sure they're okay. After all, there are lots of kids out there watching the game on TV, who will inevitably mimic their heroes.

There were people who criticised Ross Emerson for calling Muralitharan in a one-day match against England in Adelaide in 1999. Muttiah had started bowling some leg-breaks and Emerson called him for chucking. Some people will try to tell you that you can't throw leggies. Well, you can. I've seen Warnie do it in the nets. But the off-spinning art is the one considered most susceptible to temptation. Offies don't have the range of deliveries that a leg-spinner has and to bend the elbow allows an off-spinner to vary the amount of pace and spin on the ball. The Adelaide incident blew up nastily, to cricket's detriment. Sri Lankan captain Arjuna Ranatunga argued heatedly with Emerson and then led his team towards the gate, holding up play for fifteen minutes. Match referee Peter van der Merwe was subsequently unable to enforce a decision to suspend Ranatunga when the Sri Lankan's lawyers threatened court action. Ranatunga was fined about $150 and given a six-match suspended ban. It had all dragged on for so long. The media came to me for comment and I told them: 'I think it is an unfortunate moment for the game. I've always been a great believer that the umpire makes the decision and you accept the umpire's decision.'

The tension of the 1995–96 Test series, which we won 3–0, spilled over into the one-dayers—and how. There was speculation that there was some sort of push to 'nail' Muralitharan coming from the Australian dressing room. It was absolute rubbish. The fact was that Muttiah wasn't bowling well. In the First Test in Perth, for example he took 2–224, in our only innings. It wasn't as if he was ripping through us. To be honest, we didn't care whether he was there or not. The ball-tampering controversy was still fresh in the air, too. There had been verbal sniping on the field in the Tests, and some spiteful dressing room talk; the air needed clearing. Towards the conclusion of the one-day series (with the West Indians the third side), the Sri Lankans needed to beat us in Melbourne to qualify for the finals, against Australia.

Before the game there was a meeting of the team leaders, along with the ICC match referee, New Zealander Graham Dowling. The big disappointment was that Ranatunga didn't come along, sending Aravinda de Silva in his place. That gesture didn't help. But we all had a chat anyway and decided to work hard at getting on a bit better and playing the game in good spirit. It was a useful meeting, and after the match, in which they beat us to advance to the finals, we went to their dressing room to have a yarn and clear the air a bit.

We beat them in the first final, in Melbourne, scoring only 201 but then bowling them out in a good, competitive game in which there was no real drama. In Sydney we made 273, batting first—a score good enough to be nigh-ungettable. But then it rained—just poured down—and their innings was reduced to twenty-five overs, with the chase total being 168. The fact that we had to have everyone 'up' for the first fifteen overs really turned things their way. And for a time, they looked to be on target.

A real edge came into the game with the arrival of Ranatunga at the batting crease—followed before long by his request for a runner on the grounds that he was suffering from cramp. Ranatunga is portly and slow, and we just knew that the runner would be Jayasuriya, who is athletic and fast. That was naturally something we didn't want and there were some pretty tough things said to Arjuna when he made his request. The 'chat' was on for sure.

With Jayasuriya on the field the match became something of a time-bomb. A collision between Jayasuriya and Glenn McGrath gained huge media attention subsequently. I have watched the incident a few times since on video and think they were pretty well equally to blame. McGrath was certainly looking for it, and Jayasuriya no doubt took a step in his direction. Both players were at fault in what was now a match at white heat.

The manner of Ranatunga's dismissal in the first final added to the drama. McGrath tried to bowl him a yorker and it ended up a full-toss which Ranatunga mishit as he tried to smash it away. The ball popped up in the air, and he was out bowled. The Sri Lankan captain stood there for quite a while evidently thinking it could have been above waist-high and therefore a no-ball. Anyhow, we went on to win the game, and the series. But when I headed over to shake hands with the Sri Lankan players afterwards, they wouldn't shake. The whole thing had spun nastily out of control. Something that had started with an international umpire raising an early question about ball-tampering had grown so much that by the end of the season it had driven a wedge between two cricket-playing countries.

People often ask me about Ranatunga. What's he like? Well, he's an interesting man, projecting the image of a very genteel and cuddly sort of bloke. But when he gets out there in the middle he's as fierce a competitor as there is in world cricket. He knows every rule—and he knows how to get the most out of every rule. He is not a cheat, but if he can find a way of getting the best for his team out of any rule or any situation, he'll do it. I think a lot of people are fooled by him—by the fact that he's a tubby bloke like myself, with a lovely smile. Wouldn't hurt a fly, you'd think. He is, in fact, one of the toughest opponents I ever played against. He plays it hard, and he gets people off-side. I have no problem with that. He's in there fighting for his blokes . . . and that is never in doubt.

In the Adelaide Test that followed the one-dayers, I made a small personal decision which, I suppose, was my way of trying to break down the tension between the two teams. It was something that I didn't make a habit of, although I did it a couple of times in my career, and something that no-one in international cricket does any more. I walked.

I got a feather touch to one down the leg side off Vaas and was caught by Kaluwitharana. I didn't wait for the umpire's finger. By this time, following the one-dayers, the two sides were really at each other's throats, and I thought that maybe this was a chance to begin settling things down. We were up 2–0 in the series, so this was a dead-rubber Test. I thought we'd had enough controversy and, what's more, I knew I had gloved the ball. I don't think it was any big deal, or any great gesture. The umpire was probably going to give me out anyway. I just figured it was a fair move for me to get off and not stand my ground.

The Adelaide Test, David Boon's last at the end of a wonderful career, became something of a healing operation in that regard. Again it was preceded by a chat between representatives of the two teams. And during the Test our players made a point of going to their dressing room at the end of each day's play. In those few days the distance between the two sides narrowed. I specifically asked

Glenn McGrath to go and try to sort things out with Jayasuriya; the pair of them had been having real problems on the field. Glenn did that, and reported back that it had gone well and they had made up some ground. I had a long talk with Arjuna, and we seemed to be getting on all right. But then, far from the cricket field in Sri Lanka, other forces intervened—and Australian and Sri Lankan cricket was again at loggerheads, separated by a widening gulf.

Chapter 18

WORLD CUP
BLUES

T he fallout of the bomb that exploded in downtown Colombo on 31 January 1996, killing eighty people, reached all the way to Australia—and deep into the heart of Australian cricket. Sport is inconsequential, of course, when such tragedies occur, but the after-effect was real enough for cricket all the same. In the sporting sense nerves were jangling here anyway, after the edgy summer of cricket against the Sri Lankans. The fact of an upcoming World Cup match against them in Colombo was a worrying prospect in itself, without the shock of the terrible blast that ripped through the Sri Lankan capital.

In Brisbane one afternoon Craig McDermott received a message from a man claiming to be a Sri Lankan. 'We have planted a bomb in your house,' Craig was told. It's true that crazy threats are an occasional part of a high-profile life in sport. I've had them myself. But because of the situation that existed both here and over there, this was far more serious. Craig rightly took the threat seriously and the bomb squad checked it out, going right through his house. It helped to put our scheduled visit to Sri Lanka further in jeopardy.

I had letters myself. One in particular said very strongly that as the captain of the side, I had to bear much of the responsibility for the (subsequent) decision not to go to Colombo. The letter continued that I had let Sri Lanka down. 'You never know what might happen when you get over there,' it read.

The news from Colombo and from Brisbane was unsettling, to say the least. The public perception was that the Australian and Sri Lankan cricket teams were at each other's throats, though in fact it was a little better than that after the attempt to patch things up in Adelaide. But the reality was that many Sri Lankans were unhappy with what had taken place in Australia in the summer of 1995–96. There was great unrest in their country about the far more important problem of the war in the north of the island against the Tamil guerilla movement, but it was impossible not to think that the arrival of an Australian team perceived as 'villains' could be a further source of potential trouble. From the moment the bomb went off, it was always likely that we would not be going to Colombo for the first game of the World Cup.

It never got to a vote of the players, although a number of the guys rang me to express their private concerns. The matter was settled at higher levels, as it should have been. Graham Halbish rang me one morning to say that the ACB had decided that we wouldn't be going to Sri Lanka, thus forfeiting our first game in the World Cup and beginning our campaign in India. The decision had been taken on the advice of the Department of Foreign Affairs, who were warning all Australians to avoid Sri Lanka during that period of internal turmoil. I have always believed that a game like cricket can be a considerable bridge-builder between nations. But I agreed that the dual factors of the troubled series against the Sri Lankans and then the bomb blast were reasons enough for us to say no. The West Indies had also decided that their team would not play in Sri Lanka. In retrospect, I don't believe we would have gone at that time even if the preceding on-field series against the Sri Lankans had been trouble-free. We made a request for the game to be played elsewhere but, as suspected, that went straight through to the keeper.

On 5 February the ACB formally announced that 'for reasons of safety and security, Australia was not prepared to tour Sri Lanka for the 1996 World Cup'. Not surprisingly, it proved to be a highly controversial decision. We were effectively snubbing one of the three host nations of the World Cup (Sri Lanka, India, Pakistan). I knew we were doing a terrible thing to them—and it was not something that any of us were entirely comfortable with or wanted to do. Personally, I had never knocked back a tour or a cricket commitment in my life. It caused such resentment over there that there were calls not only for the Sri Lankans to be given the two points for the game, but that we should be docked two points as well! What were we to do? Foreign Affairs had advised us not to go. That in itself was reason enough.

The two weeks that followed in India at the start of the tournament were the worst of my life in cricket. Our decision not to go to Colombo had not gone down well anywhere on the subcontinent, and with feelings running high, the organisers took special steps to keep us safe . . . me especially. They obviously felt that if there was going to be a target for dissatisfaction with the Australian cricket team, it would be the skipper. For two weeks I had two guards carrying Italian submachine guns accompanying me everywhere and posted outside my hotel room in Calcutta. The organisers had put me in a room of my own, on a different floor to the rest of the team. If I went down to the pool the guards came too. When I went to an ICC captains' meeting, they travelled with me. I can tell you I didn't sleep very well for those two weeks.

As a team we felt badly out of step with local sentiment. We were unwanted and off-side. But we pressed on, getting ready for what lay ahead. A guy named Gene Swinstead, formerly with News Ltd and head of Star TV over there, organised some accommodation and training facilities for us in Bombay. We had a week to kill, thanks to the aborted Sri Lankan match. With Swinstead's help we managed to make it a pretty productive time.

We beat Kenya, and then played a terrific match against India in

Bombay, snuffing them out after we got rid of Tendulkar for 90 as they chased our 258. Mark Waugh got 126 and I got 59, and we did the job really well considering the sort of build-up we had had.

There was some fun at the press conference that followed the game against Kenya. With the next match against India, there were many questions about how we thought we would go and what our tactics would be against them. The questions were endless, or seemed to be. Finally, just as it seemed all over, a guy who must have arrived late threw his hand up. 'Yes, mate?' I said. 'Mark Taylor, what will be your strategy against India?' he asked. Somewhat exasperated, I stuck my tongue in my cheek and said: 'Well, our strategy will be to score more runs than they do.' At this, there was some laughter from the Aussie journos, but I noticed there was some serious pencilling going on, too. Next day one of the Indian papers reported: 'Mark Taylor, the cagey Australian cricket captain, says his strategy is to score more runs than India in today's World Cup game.' Well, that's it, I thought. Mark Taylor, Master Tactician. It's not a bad theory actually . . . it works in most forms of the game, I find.

We were in the tougher group for sure in the Cup, along with Sri Lanka, India, West Indies and Zimbabwe, as well as Kenya, but we ended up with three wins and two losses—a good effort considering we had started with a 'loss' due to the forfeited game in Colombo—and second on the ladder to the Sri Lankans. In the quarter-finals the top four sides from our Group A knocked over the top four sides from Group B, a mark of the respective strength of the two groups.

We went in hot favourites against the New Zealanders in Madras, but the Kiwis smashed us in their innings, getting 286 with Chris Harris playing an innings the likes of which we had never seen a hint of before, for 130 off 125 balls. It was a huge chase, but we got 'em with an over to go, the Waugh brothers and Stuart Law playing really well.

So it was us and the West Indies in the semi-final, at Chandigarh—and what a game that turned out to be. We were never out of trouble in our innings, being 3–8 and 4–15, but somehow scraped together 207, with Stuart Law getting 72 and Michael Bevan (69) staying with him to get us somewhere near to respectability.

At 2–160 with ten overs to go the West Indians were home. Or so it seemed. But unaccountably they panicked, just when the match was in their grasp. Richie Richardson was out there doing it easy, but at the other end blokes were flinging their wickets away. The drama level was unbelievably high and climbing further still as the wickets tumbled. On a dewy field Shane Warne could barely hold the ball, but he kept sending down these flippers—and the Windies kept slogging across the line and getting out. When Damien Fleming skittled Courtney Walsh with the fourth-last ball of the match we had won by five runs. It was a fantastic night. Mike Coward summed it up well in the *Weekend Australian*, I thought. 'This was not just another game of cricket,' he wrote. 'This was a human drama played out before a raucously impartial audience of 45 000 at a cricket ground that is a shrine to flannelled gods.'

In the other semi at Eden Park, the Indian crowd had the final word, rioting when the Sri Lankans, with 251, had India done to a dinner at 8–120. The match referee, Clive Lloyd, awarded the game to Sri Lanka.

Looking back, I'm sure that the way we won against the Windies worked against us in the final, played in Lahore in Pakistan and watched by a world-wide audience of 800 million people. We came to that match still exhausted from the semi. We weren't quite ready. What an odd twist of fate that was—that after the season we had all been through the showdown turned out to be against Sri Lanka. And what happened was that they outplayed us . . .

I thought it was strange when they won the toss and put us in. Generally over there the wickets get slower as the match progresses—and to bat first is usually the way to go. But they had trained under the lights at Lahore and had some local knowledge. They were aware of just how heavy the dew is at that time of the year as night comes in. Bucketing rain the night before did its best to chip in and spoil things too. I woke about three o'clock on the morning of the match and it was absolutely hammering down. Generally on the grounds of the subcontinent the drainage is not as good as in Australia and the water gathers in pools. At breakfast I suggested to the guys that there wasn't much point heading down to the ground early, because we were going to be lucky to get on at all. It was a day-nighter and when I finally wandered down there about midday the ground wasn't anywhere near as bad as I thought. I rang the hotel. 'You'd better get down here, now,' I told them. We had to snap from being fairly relaxed to match-mode, in quick time.

There was a stage in the final when we were going great guns. I batted as well as I had at any other time in the tournament and scored 74 as we got to 3–150 off thirty overs and were looking strong. We then fell in a hole, limping to 241, with only 90 coming off the last twenty overs. As the innings closed down I had the feeling that we were at least 30 runs short.

They beat us, the bat eventually having the better of a ball that progressively resembled a piece of soap, so wet did it become. Warnie just couldn't hang onto it and finished with 0–58 off his ten overs. But the manner of the Sri Lankan victory was not without some irony. The commentators had been raving about the way the Sri Lankan openers Kaluwitharana and Jayasuriya had 'revolutionised' the one-day game by slogging from the start on the fairly benevolent subcontinental wickets. Not this time they didn't—and we had them 2–23 early.

Something happened when Arjuna Ranatunga came in at 3–148 that I will never forget. In the event of anyone asking me whether I had any regrets about my captaincy career and if there was anything I would do differently, I would say no—apart from one ball bowled in that match. It was the only time on the field I can recall *not* doing something I intended to do. I had been fielding at mid-off and we had been a bit 'down'—a couple of chances had been missed. When the third wicket fell I called all the guys in and we gathered in a huddle. The message was: 'C'mon, we've put down a couple of catches, but we're still right in this. C'mon, let's go!' I had been intending to go into first slip for the new batsman, but I didn't. In thinking about the state of the match and the team I forgot momentarily what I meant to do. With Glenn McGrath running in to bowl I suddenly thought, 'I should be at slip', but not wanting to stop the game, I stayed where I was. The very first ball from McGrath to Ranatunga caught the edge and flew low, but catchable, through where first slip should have been—and down to the fence for four. Ranatunga was still there at the end, on 47, when they won the match . . .

Ultimately they beat us by playing the way we play, with Aravinda de Silva contributing a controlled and masterly 107 not out. The Sri Lankan rip 'n' tear approach is still regarded with some awe by a few commentators, despite the lessons of that match. I listen to them talking about how this is the way to play one-day cricket. It's rubbish. Explosive opening batting does work under certain circumstances, particularly on low, flat wickets. But it is *not* the be-all and end-all. Sri Lanka won the World Cup by reverting to a considerably more traditional approach. Because of the rain and the wear-down effect of such a season, the match somehow didn't feel like a World Cup Final—although there was a huge crush of fans at the end of it, with people racing everywhere.

After all that had gone on, the match was played in a highly competitive but good spirit. At the end of it I would have loved to have held up the World Cup—yet to be honest I wasn't too disappointed about not winning. Relief was the main emotion. The Sri Lankans had had a tough time of it too and we had beaten them in the other arenas in Australia, but now they had come through for a win they deserved. Mainly, I was just glad the whole thing was over. When I look back on my career, the World Cup was the only thing I didn't get to achieve, yet on that night I was tremendously proud of my team—the way they had battled through the immense pressure of the previous weeks and still played darned good cricket. The dramas had been enormous and ongoing; it was nice to be going home.

I had one last whack at the press conference following the final, calling on the ICC to get on top of all the controversies dogging the game—the throwing, the bribery issue, the ball-tampering. I felt as though I'd been dealing with one or other of the controversies right through the summer. The handling of it all had been wishy-washy and inadequate, with the issues seeming to drag on endlessly, passed from one set of hands to another. I felt that the game needed to be tougher at its highest administrative levels, to act decisively on the things that were pulling it down. I had a chance to say those things to the cricket world's media in Lahore—so I said them.

Four months later we were back in India, facing some tough cricket for which we were significantly under-prepared. And when it came to physical fitness, the captain was further behind than anyone. Lifting weights in the gymnasium at the Olympic Aquatic Centre, Homebush in July I 'did' my back—and quite badly. Eventually doctors performed a partial dissectomy on my back in St Luke's Hospital, King's Cross, to remove an errant piece of disc. In the midst of a full-scale rehabilitation program I decided I would make myself available for the tour, even though I knew I wasn't yet right. I reckon I was only about 65 per cent fit, and when Errol Alcott put us through sprints on an early day in Bombay, I was so far behind I was almost out of sight. I persevered.

Before the scheduled one-off Test against India we requested at least two lead-up games, but we couldn't get them. We headed away with no cricket under our belts, just net-work, and all we got one three-dayer at Patiala, north of Delhi, supposedly a three-and-a-half-hour train trip. Instead it took us six hours to get there—and then it rained hard the night before the game. We didn't get on until after tea on the first day, and so managed only two days and a session to prepare for a Test match.

We got belted, with Kumble taking nine wickets in a match in which we trailed by almost 200 on the first innings (182 to 361) and never looked like winning. Steve Waugh was the only one of our batsman to get above 50, with 67 not out in the second innings, and my own batting contribution was middle-of-the-road—27 and 37, getting starts in both innings but failing to push on. In the end they won by seven wickets. The Indians were far more wound-up for Test cricket than we were, and the result was no surprise.

We subsequently gathered momentum in the three-cornered one-day series for the Titan Cup that followed, involving India, South Africa and us, but kept losing games that we seemed in shape to win. After the Test and our first loss in the one-day tournament I called the players into my hotel room in Bangalore and gave them (and myself) a bit of a rev-up. 'We're playing ordinary,' I said. 'We owe it to ourselves to lift our game, lift our effort.'

Next day I went out against India and scored my first one-day hundred! We made only 215, my contribution being 105, though it wasn't a bad score on the slow Bangalore wicket—and then had them 8–164. It came down to them needing 50 off the last eight overs—and they bloody-well got them. Srinath made 30 not out and smashed us everywhere. It was an extraordinary effort from a player who barely got a run against Australia, before or since. It was hard to believe we lost. Tendulkar scored 88, after we had picked up Azharuddin cheaply lbw—at which point the crowd rioted, thanks to Azharuddin's decision to stand his ground and show very obvious disagreement with the umpire's call.

Jason Gillespie trapped him plumb in front, but he just stood there and held up his bat, leaving no-one in any doubt that he believed he had hit the ball. In a highly-charged atmosphere it was enough to send the crowd into a frenzy—and bottles and fruit started raining down on the field.

Play was held up for half an hour or so. To his credit Azharuddin eventually came back out and helped settle the crowd down. I stayed out in the middle doing my best with gestures to indicate that if they wanted us to resume the game then they were going to have to stop throwing things. The crowd, in fact, almost cost their team the game. The score stood at 3–42 when the trouble broke out and if we had been forced off, and the game abandoned, the match would have been ours.

My first one-day hundred was gratifying. Shame I didn't get a few more of 'em, and thus prise a few people off my back on the score of whether M. Taylor should have been playing one-day cricket or not. My one-day statistics in fact are quite reasonable: 3500 runs at 33—strike rate about 60. They are not legendary figures, but they are not bad either. The drawback was that I made only one 100 in 113 games. I made a lot of scores over 50: a 97 at Eden Gardens, 94 in Sri Lanka after battling the worst heat I ever confronted, 74 in the World Cup final—and 50s, 60s, 70s and 80s elsewhere. The campaign in India sort of summed up my one-day life. We didn't win a match, but I scored 302 runs in five innings. But only one hundred.

The funny thing about that Titan Cup competition was that we could have made the final, even though we ended up not winning a single game. South Africa were clearly dominant, and won all six of their preliminary matches. But after the Indians had beaten us in Bangalore, our next match against them, scheduled for Cuttack, was washed out—on my thirty-second birthday, as it happened. So when we came to the last game in Chandigarh with no wins and four losses (plus one abandoned), we still had a chance of getting through to the final, if we could come up with a comprehensive win.

We got close. India made 289 and then a few of us got among the runs, with Michael Slater making 52, at number six, Bevan 40 and myself 78, and it came down to us needing around 20 off the last three overs. We didn't get 'em—and so it was the Indians who went on to the final. Confirming the glorious uncertainty of cricket, they then went on and won it, against an apparently dominant side.

We had played seven games on tour, and lost six with one washout. We knew we had to get moving.

Chapter 19

THE BIG SLUMP

Though unfortunately I couldn't say the same about myself, Australian cricket got back on the rails in the summer of 1996–97. To lose six out of six in India had caused some serious bruising to personal pride, along with the damage done to a team reputation that meant so much to all of us who pulled on the baggy green. When the West Indies came to play, we were ready.

We got them on the last day of the First Test in Brisbane after a good match—one in which I didn't enforce the follow-on, prompting some debate and disagreement. We led them by 202 on the first innings, then set them 420 to win on the final day and a bit. At 1–89 at stumps on the fourth day with Brian Lara at the crease, the match was nicely poised. But when Paul Reiffel got Lara early the next morning, snared by Mark Waugh with a great catch at second slip, the match steadily swung our way, despite the fact of a batting track that was still in good shape.

It was a good start, although with the Sydney Test to follow almost immediately, I spoiled any celebratory fun by insisting after the win we should hop on the plane south that night and start getting ready for the second game. As is often the way in Sydney, it was a match full of incident. For starters, Glenn McGrath scored 24 in our first innings as we battled back to 300. To keen students of Glenn's batting this was a momentous event, claiming justified newspaper space the next day. Glenn's rearguard action preceded a tragic event, that showed how unexpectedly physical cricket can be at times. The collision between Matthew Elliott and Mark Waugh in the course of taking a run in the second innings was a brutal moment which left Matthew in agony with a serious knee injury—bound for an operation and a long time out of cricket. It was a cruel blow. 'Matty' had batted superbly for his 78.

Again, we set the Windies a tantalising last-day run chase—340 in three sessions, plus twelve overs at the end of the fourth day. And again we bowled them out, although Chanderpaul and Hooper caused us a flutter or two with a fine partnership after we had had them 3–35 and then 4–152. I can still see Warnie skittling Chanderpaul with the last ball before lunch—an absolute ripper of a delivery that fizzed out of the rough wide of the off-stump and cleaned him up, to prove that Warnie was indeed back in business after the finger surgery he had had a few months before.

This was a highly dramatic day's cricket, with action on and off the field. Ian Healy's dismissal of Brian Lara off McGrath was discussed for days afterwards. Glenn had been troubling Lara and when a short one flicked off the bottom edge, Heals lunged forward and claimed the catch. It was one of those moments that happen in cricket. Did he get it in time, or didn't he? Ian genuinely believed he had taken a fair catch and the umpire agreed. Brian Lara did not. Back in the old SCG Members' Stand he touched base briefly in the West Indies' room, then strode through the Members' Bar to our room and told Geoff Marsh and our manager Ian McDonald in no uncertain terms that we were all cheats and that Heals would no longer be welcome in their change room. Lara was bitterly disappointed at the way he got out; I was just as disappointed at the action he chose to take. In my view the replay showed that Lara was correctly given out, caught behind. Both umpires saw it that way too.

West Indies manager Clive Lloyd subsequently wrote a letter of apology to Macca and me concerning Lara's appearance in the Australian dressing room. We appreciated that. Clive was looking for a harmonious and fair-spirited series, as were we.

In the SCG incident there may have been the remnant of an earlier brush between Lara and Healy, four seasons previously. Healy's stumping of Lara off Greg Matthews in Brisbane was another one of those touch-and-go decisions—the stumps broken, the ball either in or just out of Heals's hand. Again it was a tough call. Established practice is, and should be, that if there is a doubt the batsman should be given the benefit of it. In both the Lara–Healy incidents the umpires involved obviously felt sure enough to give the call. I could understand Lara's disappointment—but not his petulance.

It was in Sydney too that I took my 'Moscow Circus' catch to get rid of Carl Hooper. There are those who reckon the catch, off Michael Bevan, took half an hour to complete. I doubt it was quite that long. But it was certainly an episodic event, the ball finally coming to rest in my mitt as I lay horizontal on the ground—via Healy's leg, my rib, hands, hat and finally foot. I can confirm that the final kick which lobbed the ball fortuitously back into my hands was quite deliberate, although I admit I had no idea where the ball was going to end up. With Hooper gone, we rammed home our advantage and finished up closing them down for 215 to win by 124 runs.

This was a series in which there was some chopping and changing in the Australian team—something out of step with the old belief that it has always been just as hard to get out of the Test team as it has to get into it. At different stages Michael Slater, Ricky Ponting and Michael Bevan lost their spots. It was one of only a few times I didn't agree with some of the selection decisions. Slats lost his spot before the Brisbane Test. He had been struggling a bit, having copped some flak for the manner of his dismissal in the Delhi Test—a wild slash at a wide ball, leading to a great catch by Azharuddin at first slip. Slats hadn't had a great twelve months and I think the selectors were increasingly worried about the way he was getting out. They dropped him, I'm sure to push home the message that he should go back and learn a bit more about shot selection. He was very disappointed—and I was disappointed for him. It really cuts deep with an opener when his partner gets the chop. I believe there is a 'partnership' factor between openers that is not matched anywhere else in the order. When good teams pick openers they try to put together a *combination*—rather than just the two best individual openers at a particular time. I missed having Slats up the other end—and he was gone for quite a time.

It was very likely no coincidence that my own personal struggle to find form began with the Slater change, although it's not fair to blame it on that to any major degree. Matthew Elliott came in, suffered his freakish injury in Sydney and was replaced by Matthew Hayden, who celebrated with an excellent 100 in the Adelaide Test. My own series was a battle—getting starts in Brisbane (43 and 36) and Sydney (27 and 16), then a gradual decline into a worrying slump. In fact it was the start of 'The Slump'. I missed out in Melbourne, and missed out in the one-dayers too.

Our wins in Brisbane and Sydney had us in the box seat in the series. They then came back at us in the Boxing Day Test in Melbourne, courtesy of some vintage Curtly Ambrose strike power—nine wickets in the match—to make it 2–1. In the Fourth Test in Adelaide I lost the toss, which was the last thing I wanted to do on a belter of a wicket. We had picked two spinners (Warne and Bevan) and only two quicks (Bichel and McGrath)—and the plan worked. The Windies played poorly, crumbling for 130 in the first innings and never being in the match. With Bevan at seven, Heals at eight and Warne at nine we had lots of batting and our 517—with everyone getting runs except me (11)—left them with an impossible job. We cleaned them up again, although Brian Lara made his first score of the series with 78.

Michael Bevan played rather an off-beat role during my time as captain. He was and is obviously a batsman first and foremost, but at about this time he seemed to be evolving into a front-line bowler too. 'Bevo' was pretty much unique, although I always liked to use the part-timers. My approach with the strike bowlers was not to bowl them for too long—a policy that admittedly had to be ditched at times when blokes like Warne and McGrath were all over an opposing team. The rule of thumb was that if they didn't come up with wickets in five or six overs, I would start to think about a change. I was always happy to try a Bevan or a Mark Waugh or a Ricky Ponting for two or three overs. The worst scenario might be no wickets and 15 or 20 runs. Meanwhile the 'guns'—Warne and McGrath, etc—would be freshening up, thinking about what they'd been doing and how they could go about getting the batsmen out next time around. Bowling can be like batting: you can easily get yourself into a rut.

Often in my experience the part-timers would jag a wicket. The relaxation factor would have clicked in, the batsman thinking: 'I've seen Warnie off . . . geez, he was bowling well.' The same applied with Glenn McGrath. A batsman relaxing just a fraction in such circumstances is then very vulnerable—particularly against a bowler like Michael Bevan, a bloke capable of bowling some unbelievable balls. Bevan doesn't always land them, but he can bowl a really good wrong 'un, a good quicker ball and a chinaman (the left-armer's off-break to a right-handed batsman). And when he does land them he's bloody hard to play. The left-arm wrist-spinners are a pretty rare breed. David Freedman is another of them, although he's slower and more conventional than Bevan, who fires them in with that strange action of his.

At the time of the Adelaide Test he was bowling really well, which was precisely the reason he was picked as a front-line bowler. It was an inspired move, considering Bevan's haul of ten wickets. Warnie picked up more of the top order, but Michael did a terrific job of cleaning up the tail to add to the prime scalps of Campbell, Chanderpaul and Adams.

The win in Adelaide wrapped up the series, 3–1—but as usual

they beat us in Perth. The statistics show that our performances in dead-rubber games in recent years has not been great. Here was another one—and once again in Perth, always a tough task for us against the West Indies. They love the place, especially the bounce of the wicket. And with dead-rubber matches I think no matter how hard you try you can't help but switch off a bit. The motivation of the other side is much greater, as they seize the chance to regain some self-respect and make the series look a bit better than it actually was, whereas the team that has already wrapped up the trophy often loses that slight edge they need to spur them on to further victory.

By the end of that series I was batting poorly. And it was not an easy summer to regain touch as I slid into the doldrums through January. The visiting sides that year were the West Indies (Ambrose, Walsh and co) and Pakistan for the one-dayers (Wasim and Waqar). For an opening batsman the question posed match after match was about as tough as it gets. There are no easy runs at the top of an innings against that sort of company. There is no respite.

People kept saying to me: 'You should go back and play State cricket and get a bit of a hit.' But I never wanted to do that. I have always felt that if you're captain of a side, then you have to lead that side until someone in authority decides that someone else is going to do it. I never wanted to step down—I believe to have done so would have established a poor precedent. In Perth I was run out for 2 and caught behind for 1 and was by now really struggling. During a month of cricket I hadn't made a score above 20.

Physically, I felt fine, but the harder I tried on the field, the worse it got. I probably reached the point where I needed a break from the game. I could have done with getting away from it all. Neil Marks's advice on cricket 'slumps', offered long ago—about pulling out the golf clubs and forgetting about cricket for a while—buzzed in my mind. Unfortunately, for all the commonsense of the advice, it's not that easy when you're Australian captain. I would dearly loved to have finished off against the West Indies and had a break to get myself back on the rails. Unfortunately, there was barely even a breather. South Africa awaited.

So I headed off with the team, with sections of the media now howling for blood. Mine. I didn't get that feeling from within the team, and the support from the Board and the selectors was terrific. But I needed runs . . . badly. And when I managed to put together 85 in the first game against Western Province at Cape Town, I was greatly heartened. 'Phew, I really needed that,' I said to myself, even though it was no classic innings. And when another 50 followed in a one-dayer against Boland and I hit them all right, I allowed myself the thought: 'I'm okay. I'm back.'

Unfortunately for me, the pressure on a captain out of form is more intense than on any other player in the team. It's a double-edged sword: firstly, because you're the captain and, secondly, because you're the bloke who has to keep fronting the media all the time. My duties included talking to the media four or five times a week, and if you happen to be out of form, then you're going to be asked the same questions, time and again. Any other team member struggling for form is at least free of that sort of direct pressure.

After my personal struggle against the Windies there was certainly no shortage of advice. It seemed that everyone was suddenly an expert on what I should, or shouldn't do. Some of the advice came from respected figures in the game—and it was a fact of my career that now and then in the bad times I took some stick via newspaper columns from the likes of Greg Chappell, Jeff Thomson and Neil Harvey—all former Test greats.

I had no problem with most ex-senior players and ex-captains having their say. In fact, I respect their right to do so and the ideas they express. They are thoroughly entitled to their opinions, even if some of them have added unnecessarily to the burden of criticism I and others like me have had to cope with at difficult times. And as for the 'usual suspects'—Harvey and Thomson—well, there were no great dramas there either. I'm sure the pair of them are on automatic dial with some journos whenever it's thought some stirring needs to be done or something controversial to be said. I'm not sure if either of them suspects they are being 'used' by the media. But that's the way it very often seemed to me. It was a case of: 'Let's ring Thommo (or Harv)—we'll get a bit of rip 'n' tear out of him.' To me the two ex-Test men became akin to the boy who cried wolf. The value of their words diminished in direct proportion to each outburst. In the end people thought: 'Oh, it's only Harv (or Thommo) having a whack again.'

I understand fully that ex-players who become commentators, whether occasional or full-time, have a very different job to do once their playing careers end. Some of the things said will not always be to the liking of current players. That's just the way it is. As my struggle intensified in South Africa, Greg Chappell had some tough things to say in a Sunday paper—although the headline was stronger than the story, which often seems to be the way. Greg suggested 'technical' reasons for my problems—that I was too open-chested, the weight was on my back foot, my footwork was negative, etc. There was merit in what he wrote and at Centurion Park he came down to the nets and we chatted about my problems, and his thoughts on a possible solution. He was strong in his view that I hadn't 'lost it' . . . and that I *had* to keep believing that.

In June 1997, when I was in England, Chappell got stuck in harder. 'Mark Taylor is in no fit state to be captain of the Australian cricket team,' he wrote. He suggested I was caught in a mental whirlpool—and could only keep going down.

One of my problems back then was my constant prominence in the media. As captain and opening bat, there was absolutely nowhere to hide. As opening batsman, you are under scrutiny at all times, with the unchanging task being to blunt the new ball. You don't get a night-watchman if an innings happens to start late in the day. You are a man alone with your partner at the start of every innings. And as captain—win, lose, succeed, fail—you must keep the lines open with the media. Those factors made the task tougher as I tried to find the way out of my slump in '97.

The media were not convinced by my early glimpses of form in South Africa. They were onto me without let-up about making some runs in the big-time. At Johannesburg in the First Test, I was feeling great on a beautiful batting wicket. I had hit Allan Donald for a couple of fours and had seen him off. Then I got a ball off Shaun Pollock that just didn't bounce—a real shooter. It caught the very bottom of the bat and kept going to nudge the off-stump. I had scored 16, and was feeling totally in control—better than I had for quite a while, both physically and mentally.

I had come to South Africa very confident of our chances, even though the betting was against us. I honestly believed we had a better Test side than they did. They had some very good quick bowlers, but not too much else in the bowling department, and while they batted pretty-well all the way down the list, I felt they lacked real stars. Their batsmen all the way down the list to Pat Symcox at ten averaged between 37 and 22. They didn't have a bunny, but they didn't have an outstanding player who could really hurt us either. I believed we would win.

We smashed them in the First Test at the Wanderers Ground, a place where they are always hard to beat, with Greg Blewett getting 214 and Steve Waugh 160 in our innings of 628. Warne and Bevan did a great job there, both of them bowling beautifully—Warnie getting the big wickets and Bevo backing him all the way as we knocked them over twice, for 302 and 130. At the end of the Test, I felt calm and confident, and back on top of things after the struggle of my summer. Then fate intervened.

At a practice session before the provincial game against Border I did my back in. A simple thing. We were doing some running-between-wickets drills and I just felt something 'go'. Suddenly, I couldn't bend. In the dressing room, I lay on a bench, resting the injury, and told Ian Healy, the vice-captain, that I couldn't play the next game.

I was on my back for a week, with no practice sessions, let alone match play, the momentum of my 85, 50 and unlucky 16 gradually ebbing away. The match at East London against a fairly weak side would have been a chance to keep the roll going. Instead I had to climb from a week of largely horizontal living to face a juiced-up Port Elizabeth wicket for the Second Test. They left it green, obviously scared about Bevan and Warne ripping into them again as they had in the First Test. Port Elizabeth is supposed to be a turner, a spinners' delight, but for this Test they left the grass two or three centimetres long. I failed there, and struggled for the rest of the campaign, a 38 in the last Test the only real glimpse of light at the end of a longish tunnel.

Nonetheless, Port Elizabeth provided a marvellous match—and a truly outstanding Australian victory, one the greatest of my time without doubt. We bowled them out for 209 on an under-prepared wicket after having them 7–95 and then got knocked over for 108 ourselves. At stumps in the second innings they were 0–83—in real terms 0–184—with three days to go. That night we met at the hotel and pledged that although the situation was difficult, we would not concede we were looking at a lost cause. A team promise was made that we would fight back and at least salvage a draw out of it.

The next day we blitzed them, with Bevo and Warnie again getting among the wickets, supported by a wonderfully committed team effort in the field. From 0–87 we bowled them out for 168, leaving us with 270 to win a Test match that the previous night had looked to be in the realm of the impossible. At stumps on day three we were 3–145. I had missed out and Matthew Elliott had gone for 44, but Mark Waugh was still there.

On the final day Mark Waugh played one of the great innings of his life. I rank it close to the top as it was an innings carved out under the enormous pressure of a difficult run-chase. Junior scored 116—brilliantly. In a near-flawless and ultimately match-winning performance, the only thing he didn't do was finish it off. This was not Mark Waugh the dasher. It was, rather, a subdued, elegant innings—befitting the occasion. It was more the Mark Waugh of later times. These days he still plays beautiful shots all around the wicket, but he's not quite as dashing as he used to be.

At 5–258, chasing 270, I was sitting next to Steve Waugh, still nervous—and giving my nails quite a chomping. 'Tub, what are you doing?' Steve said, looking me over. 'We're home!' Next ball, his brother was out, bowled by Jacques Kallis. Then Bevan, who had stayed there for 24 as a tiring Waugh guided us towards the win, fell next over. Now it was 7–258. Heals was out there, joined by Warnie who did his best to settle it quickly with a couple of hefty swipes, before falling lbw to Kallis. It was down to 'Dizzy' Gillespie, followed by Glenn McGrath, to stick with Heals. Now *everyone* was into the nail-biting as Gillespie played out an over from Kallis. Then Cronje bowled to Healy and—bang!—the ball was over the fence for six on the leg side and we had won the Test.

It was an unbelievable finish to a fabulous game. At the end of the second day we were at odds of 10–1 or so to even draw the game, let alone win it. The party that followed was long, and late. I didn't get to bed until the sun was peeking over the horizon next morning.

Positive faxes from home, often from people I didn't know, helped keep me going at the depths of my own dilemma. One, signed by 'an old pensioner who admires your guts', urged me: 'Hang in there! Don't you dare be affected by the insinuations of our idiotic media. The essence of being a captain is to offer leadership and inspiration, and you are doing that in an eminent way. The runs will come by themselves one of these days.'

There was one too from Ian McDonald which I particularly valued: 'Congratulations on another series win. It was a tremendous fightback. On a personal note—hang in there. Don't take any notice of media talk—it's important you keep leading the side and winning series. Winning series is what it's all about.'

South Africa won the toss and sent us in at Centurion Park in the Third test and we got bowled out for 227, my 38 over some three hours being something of a struggle, but a sign perhaps of better days ahead. On the second day came a milestone—Ian Healy's catching of Gary Kirsten, giving him his 300th Test match dismissal, a fabulous achievement by a great keeper. Eventually, however, we got rolled comprehensively, by eight wickets after our disappointing totals of 227 and 185. But we had taken the series 2–1. Looking back, with the momentum we had gained from the great second Test victory coupled with the fact that they had been struggling with the bat, it was a shame our bowlers didn't have the first crack at them.

The one-dayers proved a happy surprise packet. I had been confident about the Tests, not nearly so confident about winning the limited-overs series. But we did it, 4–3, to complete a highly successful tour. As the days passed, the media focus was increasingly on me, as much as on the team. People were now writing that I had had a bad trot for eighteen months, which was crap. In fact, the doldrums, which became the obsession of the cricketing media, lasted from around Christmas 1996 through to the century I scored at Edgbaston in mid-1997. Six months.

At the point pretty close to the lowest ebb of my career, during my struggle to find some form in South Africa, William, then almost five, provided me with some wonderful encouragement. He used to send me faxes, containing such messages as 'Have a nis [nice] day at South Africa' and the like. He was also very concerned with my battle to get among the runs. As I scratched around, he worked on a declining scale. First it was: 'Dad, I hope you make 100', then, 'Dad, I hope you make 90', then, 'Dad, I hope you make 80.' Finally, it got down to: 'Dad, I hope you make 20.'

I remember him ringing me up and saying, 'Dad, how did you go?' And I answered: 'We won.' 'No . . . how did *you* go?' 'I made 15.' There was a pause, then: 'Oh, how did Mark Waugh go?' 'Well, he made 120.' Another pause, then: 'Dad, do you think he could share a few of his runs with you?'

When I think back on that difficult time, I reflect on the truth of the old theory that when things aren't going too well, good luck goes walkabout too. My back played up, just at the time I didn't need it. Any snick seemed to lodge in remarkably safe hands. When you're at the other end of the graph, on a high, the opposite happens. Catches are dropped, run-out throws miss the stumps and you sail blithely on. No worries.

MALCOLM KNOX, *Sydney Morning Herald: I saw, and spoke with, Taylor most days during the worst of it, in South Africa, when he simply looked like every run was a fluke and he spoke of himself, humiliatingly, as a 'free wicket'. Only in the mildest ways did his demeanour change. He was candid, diplomatic, and absolutely focused on the job of winning. Every day his batting got worse and every day his behaviour emphasised to everyone why he was worth keeping.*

Before the one-day series Trevor Hohns, the chairman of selectors, and I had a talk. Trevor told me that the selectors wanted me to captain the side to England—something which was the subject of vast media speculation late in the tour. Along with many others, Trevor was very sympathetic to the struggle I was having. 'Would you like to fly home and have a month off before you go to England?' he asked me. I appreciated the offer, but I told Trevor: 'I don't believe it's the right thing to do. I think as captain I should stay on—even if I don't play.' There was some later criticism of the fact that I had stayed on, while the likes of Justin Langer, Matthew Elliott and Matthew Hayden flew home.

I had not intended to play the one-dayers, but when the team vice-captain, Ian Healy, got into a spot of bother in the final Test and copped a two-match suspension, it was decided I would play the first two games. Heals got a pretty rough deal. He was given out caught down the leg side, off a ball that clipped his boot. Walking back into the dressing room he threw his bat in from about two metres outside the door. There wasn't really a lot in it, but he was suspended. Mainly in the interest of reducing the chopping and changing in the team leadership I played the first two games—at East London, where we lost, and Port Elizabeth, where we won—stepping down then to let Heals take over the captaincy for the last five games. That event, allied to Australia's failure to make the finals of the World Series Cup back home in the summer of 1996–97, was the beginning of the end of my somewhat chequered career as a one-day player.

During the campaign in South Africa a couple of stories appeared in the papers back home that disappointed me a good deal. At different stages I had one on one talks with Malcolm Conn of the *Sydney Morning Herald* and News Ltd's Robert Craddock about stories they had written which I believed had gone beyond the bounds of fairness and accuracy. Malcolm Conn wrote a piece suggesting there was unrest within the Australian side, centred on my role in the team in the midst of my batting slump. Malcolm told me that he had heard whispers to that effect in the bar and had based his story on them. 'Look, mate,' I said, 'I don't believe there is any problem in the side at all—apart from me not making runs. And I think our record during the period you are talking about supports that strongly as well.'

Robert Craddock wrote a piece which was published back home under a headline along the lines of 'Gilchrist ends Taylor's one-day career' after Adam Gilchrist had scored an impressive 77, batting number six in a one-dayer at Durban. The article suggested that Gilchrist had saved Australia in the match—which, effectively, he had—and had thus pushed me out of the one-day team. I confronted him, pointing out that Adam had come in at 4–50 and with a different slant the article could have been 'Australia needs Taylor in form and in the top order' or even more significantly 'Gilchrist shortens *Healy's* career'. Craddock is very good mates with Heals, having co-authored his book, and there was no chance the story was ever going to get written that way. I just made the points as firmly as I could, and Craddock agreed they were fair enough. It was a reasonable discussion.

The relationship between Craddock and me ebbed and flowed a bit. The following season—1997–98—I ended up barring him from my press conferences for a couple of weeks. It happened when I had just made 70 for NSW in a one-day game against Queensland and was then told by Trevor Hohns and Steve Bernard that I was out of the Australian one-day side for a match against the Cricket Academy in Adelaide. I was pretty angry; I was coming out of my 1997 slump and starting to make some runs and I felt the decision was poorly timed and only added to the pressure that was on me.

Next day at training I got asked a lot of questions about what I thought of the decision. I did my best to answer honestly and certainly didn't hide my disappointment. Afterwards Craddock asked if he could send a photographer around to the team hotel to get a picture. Not wanting to be seen as evading the issue, I agreed. The photographer wanted me to look 'sad'—but I wouldn't be in that and ended up having my photo taken looking 'nonplused'. Next day the photograph appeared alongside a personal attack on me by Craddock. They toned it down a bit in the Sydney *Daily Telegraph* but in the Brisbane *Courier-Mail* he really gave it to me. I was not impressed.

Before the press conference which followed the ensuing Shield game against Queensland I called Craddock into the room and told him he was not allowed to attend it. 'You can't be serious,' he said. 'Mate, I can tell you I'm *very* serious,' I replied. 'I am very, very disappointed with the stuff you wrote before this game.' Craddock accused me of being 'childish'. His article questioned my selection in the one-day team over a number of years, not just the six months of my slump. He also suggested that some players had lost respect for me. As a cricketer you have to expect criticism, particularly when you're playing badly, as I had been. However, I believe the extent of his criticism was unfair and unjustified and, as a person rather than a player, I felt I had the right to tell him.

Apart from this unpleasant episode involving Craddock I didn't experience any major problems with the media. Only when I felt that certain published comments were clearly biased or seriously wrong did I seek out individuals to debate the matter. I knew they had a job to do and the right to express their opinions, and I respected that. Generally we operated pretty harmoniously, with the lines of communication just as open during the difficult times as during better days. My job as Australian captain was to talk to the media. I really liked a lot of the guys, especially old hands like Phil Wilkins and Mike Coward. I understood what they had to do and accepted there would be some bad with the good.

My relationship with the British media over the years was really good—notwithstanding the reputation of the tabloids. Ian Mc-Donald, an ex-journo himself, gave me a thorough briefing before the '97 Ashes tour, setting out in some detail who the fair dinkum cricket writers were, and who liked to dig the dirt. I found that the ones who were inclined to have a go at you, churn out the sensational stuff, were not the ones who went to press conferences. The others were just fine—real lovers of the game who would sit around talking cricket for hours if the opportunity was there. In Brisbane before the start of the 1998-99 series I had a press conference just for the visiting media guys, and it was a very relaxed event which dragged way past schedule, and covered a lot more than just cricket.

It's fair to say, I think, that today's cricketers are wary of the media—a situation that I'm sure exists in other sports too. I think there was more of a 'them and us' attitude in the mid '80s than there is now—although there is still very much a line in the sand. Tours these days are so packed with cricket, cricket and more cricket that there's not a lot of time to mingle and socialise with anyone, let alone the media.

Off-the-record chats are pretty much a thing of the past. The players are well aware that these days the media are there to report on a lot more than just the scores which are beamed instantaneously around the world, and are old news within the hour. They are there to write comment, to provide insightful background material. Something offered off-the-record can be filed away and used further down the track. Or information offered off-the-record can be produced later in open forum at a press conference.

Criticism goes with the territory, and the sooner professional sportspeople accept that, the better. It's like going to the dentist—no-one likes it, but it's a fact of life in the sporting spotlight. No matter how good or how unblemished a career there will be glitches now and then, and criticism. Sometimes it can grate though—and now and then I have thought how much easier it is for the bloke writing the cutting words than the sportsman he is criticising. The journo can sit in the privacy of a warm study, and if he writes a bad sentence, he can just hit the erase button, and start again. How different it is for a Glenn McGrath who makes a single spur-of-the-moment gesture after bowling a ball, and perhaps regrets it. The thing is then shown from 16 different angles, and 100 commentators and writers have their say on it, dissecting it, and blasting the bloke who strayed.

McGrath copped a tremendous shellacking from the media after the spitting incident which took place during the last Test of the 1999 West Indies tour. To be fair and honest, he deserved some of it, and I'm sure in retrospect that Glenn would wish he hadn't done what he did. It was a heat of the moment thing which deserved, and received, some punishment. But the media pounding he took was way over the top. Suddenly Glenn McGrath was un-manly, un-Australian and such a poor specimen that he should be kicked off the team. It was a furious reaction. My view is that he deserved a rap on the knuckles, because he stepped over the mark. But he didn't deserve what he got. Glenn McGrath is a fierce competitor and a tremendously decent young man who has done a mighty job for Australian cricket. He is one of the best-liked blokes in world cricket. Yet he has a 'hate' inside him for batsmen that all the great fast bowlers seem to have. His problem has been that his intensity when he has the ball in his hand sometimes nudges him across the line of reasonable behaviour. He has been working very hard on that for a couple of years. But he is no Superman—and like all of us, makes some mistakes.

I shared meals and drinks with the media guys over the years and was thoroughly aware that it was better for us all to work in some harmony, rather than not. In fact I started my tenure as Australian captain with a media dinner I hosted in Pakistan in 1994—an event at which I requested that we start our 'innings' together with a clean slate . . . at none for none. On the tours there's a tradition of occasional get-togethers—the press putting on drinks or whatever—something that Ian McDonald fostered during his time with the team. An ex-journo, Macca had a clear view of both sides of the fence, and knew that a good working relationship was of considerable benefit to players and press alike.

Players of the future have to learn to live with the reality that they will be dealing with a much more probing media than ever before in the game's past. Incidents that years ago would have been swept under the carpet now have every chance of appearing in lights, and headlines. Ricky Ponting found that out to his great pain and discomfort after a drinking session that turned nasty at Sydney's Bourbon & Beefsteak in early 1999. In the major games (cricket and rugby league in particular) there now seem to be sections of the media obsessed with goings-on away from the field. The Warne–Waugh bookie matter in cricket and league's multiple agonies seem forever in the headlines. Call some of it gutter journalism . . . call it whatever you like. I call it reality, the way it is.

We talked about it a lot within the Australian team in recent seasons: that stumps are no longer drawn at 6 o'clock as far as the players are concerned. It goes with the territory when you are an international cricketer. You're public property from midnight to midnight—so be careful. It's life in a fishbowl, and frankly a bit hard to take at times. Do something away from the playing field that is a bit newsworthy and you're gonna get a headline, that's for sure.

In South Africa that season the strain on the relationship between me and the media was about as intense as it got. Never though, did it reach breaking point. For all that, I was glad to get out of there and back home to the brief calm, before the storm of another Ashes tour.

SYDNEY MORNING HERALD, 12 May 1997: *So quickly does one Test series follow another that the first question Australia will have to confront in England is also the last question they hedged around in South Africa barely a month ago: what is to be done with Mark Taylor?*

Chapter 20

BACK *in* the GROOVE

The place is called Shimlar Pinks, a comfortable Indian restaurant in Edgbaston, a suburb of Birmingham, where they do a not-half-bad curry—something of which I am rather fond. It was there that I went to dinner with my Mum and Dad on the second night of the First Test on 6 June 1997. At dinner we talked of things I shared with no-one else at the time (apart from my wife) and have felt no real reason to share since, until I sat down to begin this reflection of my life in cricket. Over dinner that night I said to my folks: 'If I don't make runs in the second innings here, I am thinking very seriously of standing down.' 'Do you think that's the right thing to do?' Dad asked. 'Well, I'm starting to believe it,' I said. 'Dad, you know that I have always believed in the principle that the captain should see it through, but I honestly feel that my form is starting to affect the team.' I told them it was the first time I had started to think that way. In South Africa I had been struggling, but there had still been a relaxed feel within the team, a beer and a joke shared. 'Yeah, poor old Tub's still struggling but he'll be right . . . '—that sort of thing. Now, it was different. We were in desperate straits in the Test after only six sessions. Taylor had failed again in the first innings—and the media were again sharpening their pens.

> JUDY TAYLOR: *It got us down—the media attention day after day. It wasn't so much what they were saying, it was just that they wouldn't let it go for a moment. We got to the point where we just wanted a day when there was no Mark Taylor in the paper.*

I had come to England in good heart, rested by a period at home during which I did not even pick up a bat. Not until we got to Lord's for our first practice session of the tour did I wield a bat in any meaningful way. And my start to the tour was mildly promising.

Right from our arrival at Heathrow, however, I had been reminded of the unrelenting pressure I was under. At the Immigration gateway at the airport, I handed over my passport. 'Oh . . . Mark Taylor, eh?' said the bloke behind the desk. 'The Australian captain?' I agreed. 'Ahhh . . . but for how long?' he asked. Welcome to England!

I made 45 in the tour opener against an Invitation XI captained by John Embury, at Arundel Castle, a battling innings with a couple of good shots towards the end. I followed with 76 against Northants. It was a false dawn. I played the first two one-dayers in the Texaco Trophy series—we lost all three—to no great effect. As the First Test approached, I was back in the doldrums, starting to get out to 'nothing' balls again. The match against Derbyshire, then being captained by Dean Jones, was a case in point—a real chance for some good runs on a docile wicket. On six, Phil De Freitas bowled me what was near enough to a long-hop and I caught it on the toe of the bat—straight into the hands of the bloke at mid-wicket who had been shifted out there only a ball or two before. Ninety-nine times out of a hundred, I would have hit that ball for four. This time, I duffed the shot and found the only fieldsman in the vicinity, with radar-like precision.

Before the Derbyshire game sections of the English media—the

Daily Mirror to be exact—had done their best to make a goose of me. They tried to get me to pose with a bat a metre wide. I declined firmly, but at the ground as I headed to the change rooms a bloke jumped in front of me again with the bat and they snapped a photo. Steve Waugh and our manager Alan Crompton intervened, and the film was eventually handed over, followed by an official complaint from Alan to the newspaper.

None of it helped. By the second innings in Derby the cry for the captain's head in the media was becoming a shout again. On one, I chased a wide delivery from Daffy, getting no more than a thin edge. The ball flew hard and true to Dean Jones at first slip— and Deano, to my everlasting gratitude, dropped it cold. The conversation I had with Justin Langer at the end of the over has been well reported. 'That's bloody it, mate,' I said to him in my frustration. 'I just can't f—— play!' The young bull consoled the old bull. 'Mark, that's bloody rubbish,' he said. 'Of course you can play. You know that. Just watch the bloody ball really close, stick in here— and it will come.'

The words were timely, and right. I started watching them a bit closer and half an hour or so later I hit a straight drive for four. I hadn't hit a straight drive for six months! This is getting better, I thought, my confidence growing. All of a sudden my feet were moving better, and the ball was hitting the middle of the bat. By stumps I was 59 not out. I had hit some good shots, and felt comfortable against an attack that was not great, but fairly persistent all the same.

Next morning for the first time in ages, I felt I was going to go on and score 100. Instead, after cracking a boundary early on, I chased one that decked away—and was caught behind. That had been my story; I had even lost the art of playing and missing! Inevitably if I chased one I got a nick.

Dean Jones and I have had a yarn once or twice since about the catch he missed and had a good laugh about it. It went low but straight to him, heading between his legs only a few centimetres off the ground. Bang! It hit his hands and was gone.

The innings which followed that let-off represented a wider reprieve—in some ways, anyhow. I felt better within myself. I had hit some shots and moved my feet well. It was, at least, one small step. I probably would have played in the First Test anyway, even if the catch to Deano had stuck. Yes, the few runs at Derby gave me a greater reason for being in the team. But, as the press had been pointing out, Michael Slater hadn't had much of an opportunity on tour and I think it would have been a bit unfair to throw him in cold then. Another Taylor failure, in the Test, would, of course, have represented a very different situation. Back home, as I grafted out my 63 against Derby, one section of the press was just as busy, burying me.

On that day I took a call from my manager John Fordham, in Sydney. 'Mark, I've had contact from the *Daily Telegraph*,' he said. 'They're going to run a story that you've told a close circle of friends you're going to drop yourself from the team because of your form.' My first response, as reported later back home was succinct: 'That's wrong ... it's bullshit! John, you're in my close circle of friends, aren't you? And I haven't told you that, have I?' 'No mate,' Fordham answered. 'Well, the story is not true,' I reiterated. 'I haven't told you, I haven't told my wife, I haven't told anyone ... because it's not true. I am going to play in the First Test'. 'That's great, mate,' said Fordo, and dashed off to inform the *Telegraph*.

It made no difference—they ran the story anyway, under a huge front-page headline: HE'S OUT! I wasn't, as was proved almost as soon as the story hit the streets.

Back home, it must have seemed that M. Taylor's struggle with a wooden bat against a leather ball on a small strip of mown turf was the only story in the world. The Adelaide *Advertiser* had a write-in 'Donate runs for Mark Taylor' promotion and in Sydney FM station Triple-M called their promotion 'Donate runs to Tubby'. Ex-Australian captains like Ian Chappell and Bob Simpson—by now replaced as our coach by Geoff Marsh—were entering the fray, offering advice in strong terms. It was impossible for me to avoid the news. I wouldn't necessarily see a particular story but then, sure enough, it would be brandished at the next press conference. 'Mark what have you got to say about what Simmo wrote?' 'Well, to tell you the truth, I haven't seen it,' I'd reply. In a flash, there it would be.

In the run-up to Edgbaston the papers back home recorded in large type 'Taylor's Run of Outs', tracing my Test slump back to the 7 I had scored in the Melbourne Test against Sri Lanka in December, completely disregarding my 96 in the first Test. It did not make happy reading, for me, or anyone: 25 not out, 21, 10, 27, 37, 43, 36, 27, 16, 7, 10, 11, 2, 1, 16, 8, 13, 38, 5. Three hundred and seventeen runs at an average of 17.61.

TONY TAYLOR: *It was just a barrage of publicity. I don't know how he stood up to it. But he did. It was on the day we were due to fly to England for the Edgbaston Test that the* Daily Telegraph *ran its front-page story:* HE'S OUT! *Jude and I were just getting on the plane. I just threw the paper in the rubbish tin and I said: 'He'll play.' We were never so pleased as we were to have been there on that day.*

My future in cricket came down to the old ground which stands in a pleasant suburb of Birmingham. Edgbaston is nothing flash, pretty much unchanging over the years with its old grandstands, its short squarish sides and funny angles. It's a strange sort of ground; you get the feeling that it is a place that just grew—that they had a basic outline for it, then tacked a few stands on. It is not one of the prettier grounds of the world. One of its distinctive features is the big plastic cover the groundsmen pull from one side to the other when it rains (which it does now and then in Birmingham) and which covers around 80 per cent of the ground. I remember in '89, when we ran into torrential rain there, people running out and doing big swan dives and slides across the wet plastic.

The first two days at Edgbaston provided a horror opening to the Test campaign. They cleaned us up for 118 after having us 8–54

('Taylor fails again'; I scored seven, caught at second slip off Devon Malcolm) and England then made 478, on the same wicket. The end of the second day was the low spot of the entire tour. The Poms had beaten us convincingly in the one-day series. Now at 6–449, with Nasser Hussain having made 207 and Graham Thorpe 138, they gave every indication they had us done to an absolute turn in the Test opener. It was that night I went out for dinner with my folks.

And you know, the more I opened up about my feelings to my Mum and Dad, the better I felt. I think the word is 'cathartic'. I said to Dad: 'Look, even if it does end now I've played eighty-two Test matches—and eighty-two is not bad for a bloke who didn't think he'd even play one.' In my own mind, I had come to terms with the fact that if it had to end like this then that was just the way it was. I felt pretty good at the end of the dinner. The curry had been okay, too.

JUDY TAYLOR: *At that dinner with Mark on the night before he scored his 100, it was so typical of him that in the midst of his own struggle, his concern was to put the team first. That was one of his lovely characteristics as Australian captain. His concern was not knowing what to do from the team's point of view. Whether to stand down—that was the big question. He felt the media coverage was upsetting not just him but everybody. As you can imagine on the night he scored the century, we had a great celebration . . .*

We started our second innings on the third day, 360 runs behind. That's quite a mountain. To start, I didn't play that well, but at least I managed to hang around. A few things went my way. I played a couple of pull shots that I didn't quite get onto, but they fell safe. I got a couple off my pads which went for some runs, and I squir- relled a couple through slips—not in the air, but thick edges. I played and missed a few times. My feet weren't moving that well, but things were happening—or not happening—in different ways to what they had been in the previous six months. There was a ball from Andy Caddick that reared and hit me in the chest, off the bat—then fell safe. On all those other days it would have popped up for someone.

I reached 50 in sixty-five balls—and couldn't believe I had got there that fast. That was quick going in Test cricket—or for me, anyway. The funny thing was that at 50, I *knew* I was going to get 100. That's one of the few times that ever happened to me—that I had that sort of certainty. My concentration was good; I hadn't had to waste too much energy in that department in the months before. Then Andy Caddick bowled a ball short of a good length and I pushed it into the covers for a single. I was 100.

My feelings right then could be summed up in three words: You little beauty! I hadn't looked like making a twenty in all those innings before; now it had turned around on a single day. Amazingly. I had the feeling out there in the middle that some of the English players were genuinely delighted for me, even though they were doing their best to grind us into the turf. Mike Atherton walked up and shook my hand. Like me, Athers had borne some pressure over the years. He knew about it, about how I felt.

TONY TAYLOR: *We arrived a few days before the Test and stayed at a bed-and-breakfast place in Birmingham. There we met an English couple who had been the scorers for Essex for twenty years or so and told them why we were there. The morning after Mark scored his century we got a standing ovation at breakfast. The people staying there were so happy for us—they came rushing over and kissed us. They were delighted he had done well.*

It was hard-going, watching Mark's innings. It wasn't that hot, but the perspiration was running down my back. He grafted away—it was a painful century—but a beautiful one all the same, even though England ended up winning. I can tell you I had a few large ales that night. After the match was over Mike Atherton's parents came to see us. 'We're so pleased for you,' they said. 'We know what you've been through'. The English couple we had met at the B&B sent us a booklet, listing the scores of the match—and with photos they had taken during the game. They were lovely people.

We finished the day at 1–256 with me on 108 and Greg Blewett on 61. Afterwards there was a blur of congratulations, a general sense of happy relief, encompassing a lot more people than just me. There was still work to be done, but I had a couple of beers at the bar with the boys. Then I had dinner at the hotel with Mum and Dad, the atmosphere a lot different to what it had been the previous night, I can tell you.

I dodged the phone, apart from a call to my wife in Sydney, who had been taking calls herself all night. But the faxes started rolling in almost as soon as I got back to the hotel—and I greatly appreciated the supportive messages they carried. But I had to stay focused. We were still a mile behind in the game, although I thought if we could give them 200 to chase we were still in with a chance.

The message that perhaps meant most to me was one that arrived on the day that I scored my 100, from Kieren Perkins. In wishing me well, Kieren wrote of the 'FUD Factor'—the temptation to succumb to the fear, uncertainty and doubt caused by critics and detractors. 'I know you will ignore the distractions,' he wrote. 'You can do it, and I know you will.' Coming from Kieren Perkins, who had been through it all in the Atlanta Olympic Games, the message was timely and very greatly appreciated.

KIEREN PERKINS, 'This is Your Life', 1998: *Mark was copping a lot of flack from the press . . . and there's been times when I've been through a troubled patch in swimming. I saw what he was going through and understood it—and felt that if I could just send a few words of encouragement, then maybe it would help him along.*

SUNDAY SUN, London, 8 June 1997: *Can you bloody believe it! Just as England looked like destroying the Aussies blunder boy Mark Taylor turns into wonder boy overnight. Tubby has taken a bigger thrashing than one of Miss Whiplash's clients. But the Oz skipper's fairy-Tayl unbeaten ton has brought his side back from the dead and restored shattered pride.*

SUNDAY MERCURY, Hobart, 8 June 1997: *The Qantas 747 which was taxiing on a Heathrow engine to take Australia's beleaguered captain Mark Taylor back to the Antipodes can switch off the engine.*

Next day, when Blewie and I got comfortably through the first hour, there was hope. But at 1–327 I played a bloody awful shot, dollying a catch back to Robert Croft, and was out for 129. Greg went for 125 at 354, but on a wicket that was variable in its bounce we lost our last eight wickets for 123 runs—leaving them 119 to get. They did it easily, Stewart and Atherton steering them through in only 21.3 overs.

Throughout England there was great rejoicing and many large and glowing newspaper headlines. The England win set up the series that followed. But in different ways the Test had been good for us too. We had got rid of our one big problem—me. The 100 I scored changed the dynamics in the entire team, it took the pressure off everyone. Talking to the guys, it gave them as big a thrill as it gave me. The major trouble spot had been dealt with.

The day after the Test we had a centre-wicket session and it was as if a cloud had lifted. Now there was the chance to address the other problem in the team—the fact that we were bowling very poorly. Suddenly there seemed more time to look at the bigger picture. I realised there were things I hadn't been doing leading up to the First Test. All of us had been too preoccupied with me. Now we were back on the rails—and I was out there doing what a captain should do, and talking to the bowlers about what we had to do as a team, about line and length, about the way we had to bowl if we were to beat the Poms. That training session, following my own breakthrough, was one of the big turning points of the campaign.

One-down when we went to Lord's, we quickly had the Poms on the rack. But there was an opponent we couldn't beat—the weather. Weeping skies over London looked like settling the issue for most of the five days of the Test and they did, even though we managed to rumble England out for 77. The weather kept the Test down to 180 overs in total, and although we reckoned we had a chance on the last day, they held on strongly to finish at 4–266, with Atherton getting 77 and Mark Butcher 87 after I had dropped him on 2. My own contribution was disappointing—one run in our innings, dragging a wide ball from Darren Gough back onto the stumps. I would dearly loved to have kicked on with another score after the watershed innings at Edgbaston, but it wasn't to be.

Old Trafford and the Third Test were no better for me—2 and 1. This Test featured a great debate before the toss . . . featuring me. The decision was one of the toughest I had to make in my years as captain. The wicket was damp, and I had no doubt the Poms' preference would be to bowl. Most of our blokes thought we should bowl too. But always at the back of my mind was the thought that this would be a good wicket for Warnie to have the last crack at them. So when a watery sun broke through at the toss, and I called it right, I decided on the spot that we would bat.

It proved the right call, preceding a hard-fought Test in which Steve Waugh recorded the rare feat of a century in each innings— a beautifully timed contribution. We set them 469 to win in six sessions or so, and they were never in the hunt. Glenn McGrath took seven wickets for the match, and Shane Warne nine. The series was all-square. But for me the individual pressure was starting to pick up steam again. People were starting to ask the question: 'Was Edgbaston a fluke . . . a lucky hundred?'

I was still having my troubles. By the Fourth Test at Headingley we were starting to gain the ascendancy in the series, but after we had knocked them over for 172, I fluffed another chance—losing my wicket early as I tried to dodge a Gough bouncer. The ball

In 1996 I joined the famous cricket broadcaster Alan McGilvray for this posed shot (below) at the SCG. (Photo courtesy of News Limited)

Discretion being the better part of valour, I'm ducking for cover (above) as Sri Lankan 'keeper Romesh Kaluwitharana leaps for a wayward return during a one-dayer in the 1995–96 series. (Photo courtesy of the Sydney Morning Herald*)*

Press-ganged in Vishakhapatnam as our 1996 World Cup campaign kicked off, against Kenya. (Photo courtesy of Allsport)

'No, this is how you do it.' With Shane Warne (below) during the match against Kenya, World Cup 1996. (Photo courtesy of Allsport)

With Mark Waugh (above), heading out to open the batting for Australia against Kenya at Vishakhapatnam, India—the first game we played in the World Cup of 1996. (Photo courtesy of Allsport)

A man alone. Waiting for a partner in the 1996 World Cup final against Sri Lanka, played in Lahore. My 74 that day was the highest score by an Australian in a World Cup match—to that time. (Photo courtesy of Allsport)

I start the long walk, and the Sri Lankan celebrations begin at the end of the 1996 World Cup final in Lahore—a win to the Sri Lankans by seven wickets. (Photo courtesy of Allsport)

A diving catch to dismiss Shivnarine Chanderpaul off Michael Bevan in the fourth Australia–West Indies Test of the 1996–97 series. Bevan finished with 6–82. (Photo courtesy of News Limited)

Dean Jones and I shared a fateful moment (left) in the Derbyshire–Australia match on the 1997 Ashes tour— when Deano dropped me in slips, the lucky break I needed in the depths of my slump. Here we share a lighter moment off the field during that game. (Photo courtesy of Allsport)

Edgbaston, June 1997 (below). Once I got to 50 I knew I was going to get 100. It was one of the few times in my career that ever happened to me. (Photo courtesy of Allsport)

It was a huge relief and a wonderful thrill when I reached my 100 at Edgbaston (above). On a single emotional day I had turned my career around. I knew I was back. (Photo courtesy of Allsport)

Driving—Fifth Test at Nottingham, 1997. Alec Stewart ('keeper) and Adam Hollioake are the other players in frame. (Photo courtesy of Allsport)

Leading the Aussie team on for a charity match at a place forever etched in the Australian consciousness—Port Arthur, Tasmania, January 1997. (Photo courtesy of News Limited)

The Taylor family reunited at Sydney Airport, April 1997 on my return from the South African tour. In the background Steve Waugh chats to the media. (Photo courtesy of the Sydney Morning Herald)

A meaty cover drive v New Zealand in the November Test of 1997. My 112 was my highest score in Australia for two years. (Photo courtesy of News Limited)

Christmas 1997, Melbourne—and Jack and I exchange gifts with Steve Waugh and Steve's daughter Rosalie. (Photo courtesy of the Sydney Morning Herald*)*

A handshake with South Africa's Shaun Pollock after I had carried my bat (for 169 not out) in the Adelaide Test, February 1998. (Photo courtesy of News Limited)

Golfing in India, March 1998. (Photo courtesy of Allsport)

A show of aggression during my 102 not out v India in the third Test in Bangalore, March 1998—on our way to winning the match. (Photo courtesy of Allsport)

Doing my best to deal with a fast bowler—yet again. Working out with Glenn McGrath at pre-season training in the winter of 1998. (Photo courtesy of the Sydney Morning Herald)

The day I had a yarn to the Sydney Swans in 1998. Their season had been going well up to that point ... That's 'Plugger' Lockett, looking pensive, on the right. (Photo courtesy of News Limited)

Unforgettable days in the sun ... getting hold of one during the 334 not out in Peshawar, October 1998. (Photo courtesy of Allsport)

In Peshawar's sticky October heat you needed to keep the fluids up. (Photo courtesy of Allsport)

The impromptu guard of honour that awaited me at the gate—Peshawar, second Test, 1998. An extra 'buzz' provided by my team-mates as I came in at stumps, Day 2, with my score on 334. (Photo courtesy of Allsport)

The morning after. A brilliant blue sky, a scoreboard telling the story and a batsman a little fresher than he had been the previous night. (Photo courtesy of Allsport)

Sweeping—on the last day of a Test match I would never forget, against Pakistan in Peshawar, October 1998. A photo snapped during my second innings 92. The wicket-keeper is Moin Khan. (Photo courtesy of Allsport)

With Prime Minister John Howard at a tribute lunch in Sydney, which followed the homecoming from Pakistan in 1998. (Photo courtesy of News Limited)

A handshake, an award and kind words from Australian Cricket Board chairman Denis Rogers on the occasion of my 100th Test—v England, Brisbane, November 1998. (Photo courtesy of Allsport)

With Mike Munro after the huge surprise landed on me by 'This is Your Life' in Brisbane, November 1998. (Photo courtesy of Nine Network)

Test catch No. 157—and the record. Thankfully a Mark Ramprakash edge off Glenn McGrath is about to land safely, as Mark Waugh (left) and Ian Healy shout their encouragement. Fifth Ashes Test, SCG, January 5, 1999. (Photo courtesy of Allsport)

With Steve Waugh (centre), Ian Healy and the rest of the team as the Ashes celebrations begin after the Fifth Test at the SCG, January 1999. (Photo courtesy of Allsport)

Looking suitably serious on the cover of Time, *November 1998. (Photo courtesy of* Time Australia)

With Judi, William (behind) and Jack on the day I was named Australian of the Year, January 1999. (Photo courtesy of News Limited)

Meeting the press— and how! The scene at my retirement press conference at the Sheraton on the Park, Sydney, Tuesday, 2 February 1999. (Photo courtesy of the Sydney Morning Herald*)*

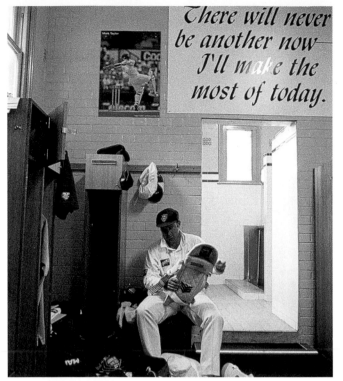

Everything has to end. Packing my gear in the SCG dressing room for the last time after the final home Shield game of the 1998–99 season, v South Australia. My last game at a famous ground. (Photo courtesy of Allsport)

Time for a beer and a yarn and some memories shared with an old mate, David Boon. This shot from the Bellerive dressing room after the NSW–Tasmania game in March 1999 is an historic one. It was Boonie's last Shield game ... and as it turned out, mine, too. (Photo courtesy of Allsport)

didn't get up quite as much as I expected and flicked my glove, sailing through for Alec Stewart to take the catch. I was gone for a duck. There was little other news on the downside for us there in Leeds, however. With Matty Elliott getting 199—after Graham Thorpe had put down a sitter from him at slip when we were 4–50 and in trouble—and Ricky Ponting 127, we took the game way out of their reach at 9–501. A century by Nasser Hussain in the second innings delayed the inevitable for a time, but we ended up winning by an innings and 61 runs.

Another decisive win in the Fifth Test at Trent Bridge wrapped up the Ashes—and provided confirmation, at last, that I was working my way back into the 'zone'. I scored 76 and 45 and we beat them by a wide space, Warne and McGrath getting seven wickets each, and just about all the batsmen getting among the runs. It was a great 'team' performance. Warnie subsequently hit the headlines with some celebratory antics on the balcony after we had won the Ashes. His shirt-twirling and champagne-spraying gained big space in the English papers. It was just exuberance; I had no problem with it. But I was disappointed with some of the reaction . . . some people just seem to look for negatives. Shane was just enjoying the moment. If there had been anything offensive in it I would have stepped in.

The Sixth Test provided one of those Australian below-par dead-rubber efforts. In a low-scoring game at The Oval, we needed only 124 to win, but we struggled all the way, and fell 20 runs short—much to the absolute delight of an entire nation, which relished every victory that came along in a struggling period for the game over there. I scored 38 and 18—nothing great, but runs made with much more confidence than in the 'bad' days.

At the end of August, we came home with the Ashes trophy, or a replica of it anyway. Mission accomplished. But it had been a positive few months for cricket generally, with England's First and Sixth Test wins being good for the game and our series victory confirmation that we were a bloody good cricket team.

Personally, I felt a great sense of relief. I had endured a long drag through some pretty dry country, and survived. I was ready to get on with life.

But before I continue, here is a story I have never told publicly. It happened during that 1997 Ashes tour. And it chills me, still, to the bone . . .

Later in the tour, Judi flew over with the boys, joining me for what turned out to be the celebration of the winning of the Ashes. They stayed for much of the time at a fine house in Bury, owned by Phil Neville, a great pal from my days playing with Greenmount in the Bolton League back in 1988.

The Nevilles are quite a family. I met them through Phil's father, Neville Neville (Neville-squared, or double-Neville as we called him), who was secretary of the Greenmount club. The three Neville kids—Gary, Phillip and Tracey, have all represented their country at sport—Gary and Phillip at soccer, and Tracey at netball. They are a real sporting family.

With Phil away much of the time, he let us have the house at Bury, a lovely big place with a big backyard. Perfect for kids— except for the pond . . .

Unbeknown to Jude, there was this small pond tucked away in one of the gardens. When she gazed out over the yard it just looked like a landscape of green and a great place for the kids to play. The pond was completely covered by a green reed of some sort, obscuring any sign of the water.

JUDI TAYLOR: *It happened the first day we arrived. I suppose we were all pretty much on edge after the months before, and weary after the long trip. Some friends of the Nevilles showed us over the house, which was brand-new. The plastic was still on the dishwasher! There was a huge backyard, with a practice golf net. It was terrific. But I didn't notice the pond.*

The boys were out the back and as I learned later Will had noticed

*the 'grass' move on the pond. 'Look at the bouncy grass,' he said—
and little Jack thought he'd better try it and stepped in and went
straight to the bottom. Will came running inside and said, 'Mum,
Jack has fallen in some water.' It being England, with rain always
around, my first thought was that he had stepped in a puddle. But
when I went out, there he was in the pond, his little head and face
all covered with the green stuff and kicking himself off the bottom.
The pond was deep and Jack was way out of his depth. I thought
later, thank God we had taken him for swimming lessons. Because of
that he was able to stay afloat and keep his head up until I was able
to get there. And what a mess he was, covered in green . . . and he
smelt something awful.*

*The Nevilles and their friends were just devastated when they
learned what had happened. They had the pond drained as soon as
possible.*

Thankfully Jack was quite okay, just wet and cold and scared. As
you can imagine Judi was a mess when she rang me to tell me
about what had happened. And so was I when I got off the phone.

It's a story with a happy ending. But it still shakes me when I
think about it. This came at a tough time for Jude—and obviously
there could never be a 'right' time for something like that. Her
policy during my time in Test cricket was pretty much to maintain
her privacy and the private lives of the kids, to shield them as much
as possible from media demands, although of course there were
times when we were all out in the spotlight, when I came home
from tours and such like. But 1997 had been an especially hard
time, with me in the headlines every day and struggling to find
form. She had to handle it alone and keep her spirits up, and those
of two little boys as well. It was a bloody tough job—tougher for
her in a way than it was for me, I think. At least I could get out
there in the middle and try and work out my problems. Jude just
had to handle what was going on and hope that it would all be all
right in the end.

She did a mighty job. And after the scare with the pond, the 1997 tour turned out to be a happy one for us all. I found some form, Australia won the Ashes and Judi and the boys thoroughly enjoyed the long and sometimes balmy northern summer days.

Chapter 21

ONE-DAY DRAMAS

A t the start of the 1997–98 season, five of Australia's senior players were summoned to Melbourne to meet the selectors—the Waugh brothers, Shane Warne, Ian Healy and myself. The subject to be discussed was an important one—present and future policy regarding the selection of the Test and one-day teams.

I was first in, and said my piece. 'If you are going to leave me out of the one-dayers, you should leave me out of *all* cricket.' I went on to make the point as strongly as I could: Yes, I had had a bad run with the bat, but I had struggled at all levels—Shield, one-day and Test. During my slump there was a big push for me to be dropped from the one-dayers, and that was of great concern. My belief was always that the leader of Australian cricket—i.e. the captain—should be the leader in all forms of the game. I told them at that meeting: 'I look at it this way—if I'm not good enough to hold a spot in the one-dayers, then I shouldn't be playing the Test matches either.' They told me they had doubts about me as a one-day player, but very much wanted me to captain the Test side.

I was very disappointed. I didn't believe they were right then, and I don't believe now that the principle is right.

So, as Australian captain, I was left out of the one-day team that played against the Cricket Academy side in Adelaide early in the season—a festival game to celebrate ten years of the Academy and also the launch of the new Adelaide Oval lights. It was two months before the start of the 'official' one-day season (i.e. the World Series) and I was bitterly, deeply disappointed.

They gave me no chance. Straightaway everyone knew that I had been 'cut' from the one-day picture. I had come back from England as captain of an Australian side which had retained the Ashes in pretty dashing style. Personally, I had finished off well in England after my long struggle against adversity. But people were still asking me about the future. To leave me out of that game—an absolutely 'nothing' game really—only added fuel to the fire. They could have taken some pressure off me by saying: 'We want you to play this game, although we're honestly not sure about your involvement in the one-day internationals this season. But play this game, and we'll make the decision two months down the track.'

I was told the news in October, the day after I had scored 70 for NSW in beating Queensland in a one-dayer. Trevor Hohns and Steve Bernard, two Australian selectors, called me in and told me I wouldn't be playing in the Adelaide match. I was doubly disappointed. I guess I knew right then that my one-day career was over. I also felt that they were heaping a lot of pressure onto me that I just didn't need at that stage.

My relationship with one-day cricket and the Australian one-day team proved to be a fluctuating and sometimes painful one right through my career. I think it's fair to say that the one-dayers and Mark Taylor never really saw eye-to-eye. I was in and out like a fiddler's elbow—never, it seemed, really secure, because of the perception that existed about me as a batsman. Not until I became Australian captain in 1994 was there any certainty about my selection—and even then I was ultimately dropped cold from the one-day team, and the one-day captaincy.

The one-dayers plagued me throughout my ten years in first-class cricket. Even back in the 1989–90 season when I was rated best batsman in the world under the Deloitte's system, I was only in the 'possibles' when it came to the one-day team, although I did play some matches that year. For all the angst it caused me and others over the seasons, the fact is that my one-day record wasn't too bad. I averaged around 33, with a strike rate of close to 60. But I scored only one 100. I believe that if I had had similar stats, but four or five centuries, I probably would have played some more games. Almost always, it seemed, I was on the edge when it came to one-day cricket.

The pattern started back in the 1990–91 season when my omission from the team at that time was a real jolt to my confidence. Only the previous season I had suddenly jumped from being an up-and-coming player to the top of the world batting lists. One of the best players in the world, they said. Yet without warning early next season, the message was different. Admittedly, when the selectors decided to leave me out of the one-dayers, after the First Test against England in late 1990, I was playing with a broken finger. But the message was clear enough: 'Yes, Mark, you're a good opening batsman, but you're not good enough to play one-day cricket.'

As it turned out for me in the 1990–91 season, chance took me back into the one-day side for the finals against New Zealand—and I ended up winning the Player of the Finals. Allan Border tore a hamstring prior to the deciders and they called me back. I made 41 off forty balls in Sydney, then 71 off ninety-three balls in Melbourne in the second match. At the big Benson & Hedges presentation night at the Sebel Town House in Sydney after I accepted my award, I kicked off by saying: 'Well, it's quite unusual for me to be standing up here receiving a one-day prize.' The press had some fun with that. 'Taylor has dig at selectors', was the theme the next morning. Well, it was pretty gentle, but I guess I did make my point. The fact was that I had been hurt more deeply than I publicly admitted at being dropped from the one-day team.

I always looked on one-day cricket as a break from the harder arena of Test cricket. To me the one-dayers represented a chance to go out there and enjoy yourself a little more. AB and I had very similar philosophies on the one-dayers. We enjoyed playing them—and I can assure you that I did, a great deal—but I never saw them as anywhere near as important as Test matches. Yet, of course, in their own way they are just as important or even more important than the Tests—huge revenue-raisers globally, and absolutely vital to the continued good health of world cricket.

The big day/night games can be very special. The atmosphere at times has been described as 'gladiatorial' and I think that's a fair call. You certainly get that sense out there, under the blazing lights and with a capacity crowd roaring its head off. I'll never forget my first two games as one-day skipper in 1992–93. AB was having trouble again with a hamstring injury, so I got the nod against the West Indies. It was a significant honour—my first call-up to captain the side at any level, but it was all a bit strange. I wasn't really a regular member of the side, but I was Australia's vice-captain. So when AB broke down, all of a sudden I was in—and skipper.

On a nightmare of a wicket in Sydney, we should never really have played. It had rained for four or five days leading up to the game and the wicket was sodden. But they let the crowd in and there was a lot of pressure on the umpires to get a game on. Finally, they settled on a thirty-over game, starting at about five o'clock. We got 101 (I scored nine) and bowled them out for 87 in reply. I took four catches in slips, and ended up winning Man of the Match!

A few days later we played them again in Melbourne, this time at the regulation fifty overs, before 74,450 people. We finished with a fairly modest 198 and they were travelling easily at 2–158. But suddenly the match began to turn; we got a wicket, then another and another. Coming to the last ball they needed five to win with one wicket in hand. Anderson Cummins skied one down the ground and Craig McDermott, running in from long-off, held the catch . . . and we had won an unlikely victory. There was absolute pandemonium as the crowd erupted in a tremendous roar. It was just unbelievable. I can remember just not wanting to go off the ground. On the good days that's what one-day cricket can be like.

I have had plenty of time since to think about the differences between the two games, and my views are pretty clear-cut: yes, you will always get blokes who play one form of the game better than the other. And yes, I was probably one of those. But I don't think the difference is all that great and I have always been of the belief that if you get down to a 50–50 decision between two players, the choice should be to go for continuity. For example, if it was a toss-up between player A and player B for the one-day team, and Player A was in the Test side, I'd go with him.

The widening gap between the personnel of the two sides is very apparent, however. At the time of my departure from Test cricket and just after, the Test top-order was Slater-Taylor-Langer or Slater-Elliott-Langer. Not one of the four was in the one-day side.

Yet I think the two varieties of cricket are feeding off each other more than ever before. Test cricket is, without question, making a comeback on the international scene and the one-day game has played a significant part in that process. I believe that some of the skills one-day cricket has brought in have made the traditional game even better to watch. Fielding, for example, seems to be getting sharper, quicker, better all the time.

And with its determination for a result (and the certainty that that will be achieved in almost every match), one-day cricket has helped change the thinking in the Test arena to quite a degree. There is, without doubt, a greater push for results right across the cricket spectrum and I would suggest that my own record as captain shows that our team pursued an outcome in virtually every match we played. One-day cricket has led to a quickening in the pace of cricket overall, and that is a positive outcome. The other great service that the one-day game has done to the Test program is to help introduce younger people in particular to the traditional game, encouraged by the enjoyment they have had from one-day matches, and by the successes of the Test team. Perhaps there has even been a bit of traffic back the other way, too, as traditionalists accept that 'pyjama cricket' is here to stay and that instead of fighting it they might as well enjoy it.

There was a period when the prophets of doom talked of the pending death of Test cricket. In crowded times, fewer and fewer people would have the time to watch five days of a Test. But people don't have to go for the full five days. They can just go out for a single day and though they mightn't see a result on that day, the chances are they'll still see a lively day's cricket.

There were those who argued that the 'wham-bang' nature of the one-day game would do irreparable harm to the technical side of serious cricket. That hasn't happened either. Generally, good players are good players in both forms of the game, with Mark Waugh a prime example—stepping so easily from one type of game to the other. The starting-point for all players who want to succeed is getting the fundamentals right and developing a basic technique. I tend to think that blokes who set out to be just one-day players will not be great players in either Test or one-day cricket.

If I could turn the clock back ten years and start my career all over again, I would definitely put more time into my one-day play. I look back now and think that it's one area of my game that I could certainly have improved.

I don't believe the decision to drop me from the one-day team in October 1997 came from high-up, as a directive from the ACB. I think it was just the selectors surveying a large base of so many good players and deciding it was time to give some of them a go. If that meant dropping the captain from the one-dayers, well, so be it.

The good news for me was that two days later I went out and scored 100 against Queensland in the opening Sheffield Shield match of the season. I was back in good nick, and starting to bat well.

It was a strange business. The selectors had stuck with me so loyally when I was really struggling. If they were going to drop me they could easily have done it then. But they stuck with me during the tough times, which was great and much appreciated. Frankly, as I have said since, I got a lot more chances than a non-captain would have received during that time. Finally, I came through it. And *then* they dropped me. Strange indeed.

It was the beginning of the 'two-captains policy' in Australian cricket, something with which I have never agreed. I think the majority of astute cricket men believed, before, at that time and since, that having one 'Australian captain' is the best policy.

I can now reveal that the depth of my disappointment and disenchantment with the policy was such that I was ready to resign from the Australian captaincy after the Hobart Test against the New Zealanders that summer. John Fordham and I went as far as working out a letter of resignation. I had scored 100 on a tough wicket in the First Test against the Kiwis, and was brooding over the two-captaincy thing. 'I just don't like it,' I said to John. 'I'm going to stand down.' I would play the three New Zealand Tests as captain, then give the position up. I wasn't retiring. I would continue as a player. I went very close to doing it and had drafted the appropriate letters. In the end I took the advice of a number of people and decided I would hold back for a while. I won't tell you who they were—suffice to say they were people I respected, my wife and best pal Judi among them.

I have never changed my view—that Australian cricket should not have two captains. I've had people trying to convince me that the times are changing and so on. I honestly don't believe times will ever change that much that you chop and change the leadership of a team. I felt very strongly that if the selectors thought I was no longer good enough to play one-day cricket and that Steve Waugh would be as good a captain as myself in the one-day game, then he should be captain of both forms of the game. I would stand down, and play as an opening batsman.

The best cricket teams I played in were truly the best 'teams'. Not necessarily the best eleven individuals—good cricket is about a lot more than individuals. At the centre of any good cricket team, the captain has more say in how things are done than, arguably, in any other sport. A cricket captain runs the show for the full six hours' play each day. The coach doesn't direct the pattern of the game to anything like the same extent as other sports. As captain, you have to run the show—and if you're not in there full-time, it can be a real problem.

The reason why things did eventually work reasonably okay with Steve Waugh and me was because we were both senior cricketers who knew each other well enough to *make* them work. We didn't let personalities get in the way. There was no in-fighting, with Steve trying to take over my job or me getting upset because I wasn't in the one-day side. We made it work. But I regarded the precedent as a dangerous one—and still do. If it happens in another era it might pitch a senior player and a not-so-senior player into the same situation, or two guys who are not mates. And if problems ever develop at that level you can be quite sure it will run right through the team.

NEIL MARKS: *I believe that the ACB's decision to virtually split cricket in two denigrated the No. 1 position in Australian sport—the captaincy of the Australian cricket team. From the very earliest days of the century, with only one or two exceptions, the position of Test captain has been an exalted one. Nothing else in Australian sport has matched it, or even gone close. But the decision of recent seasons to have a 'one-day team' and a 'Test team', with different captains, has changed all that.*

I recall that some years ago the Sydney Morning Herald *reported a survey among soccer-playing youngsters in Sydney. They asked three questions: Who was the Australian soccer captain? Who was the Australian rugby league captain? Who was the Australian cricket captain? Forty-five per cent could name the soccer captain, ninety-five per cent named Wally Lewis as rugby league captain (at a time when that game's profile was about as high as it ever got) and one hundred per cent named Allan Border as captain of the Australian cricket team.*

Every single kid knew the answer to the cricket question—and it's probably been that way since the days of William ('Billy') Murdoch and Joe Darling. But all of a sudden it's different. The 'true' Australian captain (of the Test team) can find himself twiddling his thumbs—a minor figure while the one-dayers are being played. It's not right. If you're Australian captain you're captain across the board in my view. Not to have it that way is to undermine and down-grade something that it is an important institution of Australian life. Someone—I think it was Ray Martin—said that the Australian cricket captain was the second-most important person in Australia, to the Prime Minister. I'll go a bit further and offer another analogy: The Vatican doesn't have one pope for Christmas and Easters and another for ordinary Sundays. I'm not saying the position of Aussie captain is equivalent to that of the Pope—although there's not much in it.

My place in the game had changed. Everyone saw me as the Australian cricket captain—but also as a bloke rated not suitable for the one-dayers. A little later than me that season Ian Healy met the same fate.

Heals was entitled to be disappointed at the way he was treated, given that he was a much-respected and admired member of the team. He had been vice-captain before the England tour but lost his place, with Steve Waugh taking over. There was some irritating talk around that Heals had been dropped because of me, but I'm sure that wasn't the case. I was certainly out of form, but the selectors obviously looked at the whole picture and decided to replace Heals because they didn't see him as the next Australian captain. I was struggling, and if I should have happened to fall on my sword, the next man they wanted to captain Australia was Steve. So they made Steve vice-captain.

I thought it was reasonable policy, but could have been addressed differently. They could have left Heals as vice-captain for England, but let both him and Steve know that Tugger would leapfrog him to the top job in the event that for whatever reason I didn't make it through the series. I think that would have been acceptable—certainly to Heals, who was naturally very disappointed at losing the vice-captaincy.

There was no great drama about the situation to affect the dynamics of the team. However, when I look back on my career as captain I now realise that I wasn't as close to all the players—and couldn't be—as I had been before 1994. That's just the way it is when you are captain. There are times when you have to disappoint even your best mates. It's one cost of leadership.

Australian cricket coped with these changes that summer of 1997–98 and kept battling on. On the Test arena we beat New Zealand 2–0, an expected result against a team ranked a fair way below the top group on the world stage. It was a largely forgettable series. We beat them in Brisbane by 186—with my 112 on a seaming Gabba wicket a good personal start to the international season—and then by an innings and some at the WACA. The Third Test, in Hobart, was drawn, although building to an exciting finish after a plodding five days. New Zealand's last pair Simon Doull and Shayne O'Connor defied sixty-four balls and some vicious leg spinning by Shane Warne to hang on for a draw.

The World Series contest of season 1997–98 took place in the midst of a major pay dispute in Australian cricket.

Revisiting the pay struggle that hit the headlines in 1997–98 and caused some unease among all of us at Australian cricket's top level is to some extent raking over old coals. One of many 'mini-revolutions' that has overtaken cricket in recent years, the drawn-out pay debate certainly caused me more than a little discomfort. I'm not going to labour the details, but the principle fought for was essentially about modernising the pay system, bringing cricket into line with the way things were done in the wider world, and getting a fairer deal for Sheffield Shield players. Much of what went on was misunderstood, and there were things written and said, painting the players as 'greedy bastards', that were disappointing.

The question of pay for players—how it was decided, how fair it was—had been simmering since the late 1980s and probably long before. As far back as 1989, when we were in India for the Nehru Cup, it was all cloak-and-dagger stuff. One player would sidle up to another, and whisper: 'Mate, there's a meeting on in Room so-and-so at 4.30 . . . but don't tell anyone.' It was ridiculous. We'd huddle in a room and everyone would say, 'Keep it quiet, keep the noise down.' We were like twelve-year-old kids trying to sneak a smoke behind the teacher's back.

Anyhow, in 1997, with a viable Players' Association up and running, it all came to a head. Protracted negotiations between the Association representatives and the Board ebbed and flowed for months. In Perth, towards the end of that year when the New Zealanders were here, there was strike talk in the air. As skipper, it worried me greatly. I felt that the last thing cricket needed—or any game for that matter—was a players' strike. It became a real headache for every one of us involved. There were meetings every night. I remember getting out padding up without playing a shot in the Test against the Kiwis as a result, because I was barely concentrating. That particular Test was almost an afterthought, considering the bigger picture at that time. I took the last catch of the game, off Simon Cook, and thought to myself, 'Thank God that's over; now we can get on with more serious things.' It was an unbelievable time. With talk of a looming strike I met with Denis Rogers in Perth in a one-on-one meeting—the chairman of the Board and the captain—and took the Board's offer back to a meeting of the players. They rejected it, believing that although the Board had given some ground things were potentially pretty much as they had always been. We want to change the system, so thanks, but no thanks, was the message. Rogers' offer sounded okay, but the players were rightly determined that things had to be permanently locked in place for generations of future players as well. Denis more or less presumed that because as captain I was conveying the offer, it would be accepted. There were resultant misunderstandings, with Denis concluding that I didn't have the players' support and was off-side with my team. This became public, in a big way. In fact the *only* problem within the Australian team was that we had a problem with the Australian Cricket Board in the way they did things.

There were some bad days. I remember one meeting between the Players' Association and the Board which lasted just forty seconds before they got up and walked out. A strike looked a genuine chance at one stage, but a phone call from Tim May, the Players' Association representative, headed that off, although the threat hung in the air as negotiations continued. This was followed by a cooling-off process—and then real progress to the point where we (the players) signed contracts, in India in early 1998. Continuing squabbling about exactly how SEL Cricket and James Erskine— negotiators for the players—were going to get their money, dragged the thing out to October 1998 when it was finally settled.

Looking back, I see it now as something that was inevitable within the game—the transition from doing something one way to accepting that times and circumstances had changed and that it needed to be done differently. I don't believe there is any lingering, long-term resentment between the Board and the players—although there were times during it when we sure weren't the best of mates. There were things said that hurt both sides. For the summer of 1998–99, the payment pool for players in Australia increased by $1.2 million, with extra money going to Sheffield Shield players and lower-tier ACB players. I was very glad when it was done.

In the World Series the team won the trophy (minus Healy and myself), taking the finals 2–1, after just scraping in ahead of New Zealand and way behind the South Africans who looked clearly the best one-day side in the world at that time. In the finals, however, they unaccountably fell over.

In the second three-Test series, against South Africa, we hung on to win the rubber 1–0 after fighting tooth and nail to dodge defeat in the Third Test, in Adelaide. We dominated in Melbourne, but with Jacques Kallis getting 101 on the final day we couldn't force a win, pinning them at seven-down but unable to take it further. In Sydney, where Warnie bowled superbly in taking 5–75 and 6–34 (the last wicket taken his 300th in Test cricket), we belted them by an innings and 21 runs.

By Adelaide, I knew we were a tired side. We had played a lot of cricket, with the Ashes tour spilling over into a new and crowded home season. We played tired, but showed the necessary grit to keep them at bay. The Proteas always had the upper hand, flaying our bowling for 517 after we had them 7–305 in the first innings.

I then managed something I had never achieved before or since at that level of cricket. I carried my bat, for 169, helping to guide us past the follow-on mark. To be honest, I didn't bat that well. But I hung in and hung in. It wasn't any sort of great innings, but I suppose it was seen as a pretty dogged one. For an opener, I suppose it is a sort of Holy Grail too, to bat right through, and I felt some pride in that.

We saved the match on the last day after they had set us too many to chase—361—with Mark Waugh's 115 not out vital in a day-long struggle as we finished at 7–227. On 107 Mark was involved in an incident which ended up on the front page of newspapers across the country. He was given not out on an appeal for hit-wicket after a ball struck him on the elbow and, in some sort of reflex action which resulted from the blow, his bat broke the wicket. The South Africans were furious, remonstrating angrily with the umpires. And when play ended there was further drama when Hansie Cronje knocked a hole in the door of the umpires' room with a stump as he passed, still seething over what he felt was a wrong call.

After South Africa, there was still no respite. A tough tour to India lay ahead—and one without Glenn McGrath. 'Pidge' was on the sidelines, struggling to overcome problems with strained abdominal muscles, and his absence was a big blow to the team. As he is today, Glenn was one of the premier bowlers of the world in 1998. I felt very strongly that we needed someone to step into his shoes, because I didn't believe we would beat the Indians with spin. Their top batsmen play spin better than anyone in the world. Warnie was ready and prepared to carry the load, but I knew it wouldn't be easy for him and that he would need serious support up the other end. It was up to Mike Kasprowicz and a couple of the other guys who hadn't really had that much cricket to step forward and fill the breach. We were a weary side and it was always going to be a tough campaign.

We lost a lead-up game in Mumbai (Bombay) before the First Test at Chennai (Madras), where I lost a toss I had wanted to win, considering the bare state of the wicket. After keeping them to 257 and then getting ourselves into real trouble, we struggled past them, thanks to Heals (90) and Gavin Robertson (57), and led by 71. We had a sniff. But with the Indians at 2–115 in their second innings there was a critical call. We all went up for an lbw appeal against Sachin Tendulkar when he was on 0. It looked terribly, terribly close, but the umpire gave him the benefit of the doubt. As it turned out it was our last chance.

Tendulkar just smashed us . . . absolutely creamed us for 155 not out. They declared at 4–418 and set us 348 with a day and a bit to go. I got out last ball before stumps to make us three for not many. I went to play a pull shot off Kumble, got a bottom edge onto my thigh pad—and it popped up for a catch in close. Next day we were bowled out for 168 and lost the Test. We had played okay for the first three days but it got away from us.

Before the tour we had tried to persuade the Indian Cricket Board to schedule a Test in Calcutta, at the famous Eden Gardens, one of the great stadiums of the cricket world. The Indian administrators eventually agreed and shifted the Second Test from its original venue at Cuttack to Calcutta. I knew this was almost certainly going to be my last trip to India and I was very keen to play at Eden Gardens. Steve Waugh was the only member of the team who had played there, way back in '87 or so. Well, we got the game—and we got belted, beaten by an innings and 219 runs. The press made the point that in 580 Test matches and 121 years Australia had only three times suffered worse defeats. Their innings of 4–633 was just a free-for-all. Everyone got runs (Laxman 95, Sidhu 97, Dravid 86, Tendulkar 79, Azharuddin 163 not out, Ganguly 65). We made 233 batting first, then 181 in our forlorn second innings chase—and that was that. We got our bums kicked.

At least I had got to play on Eden Gardens! I was impressed. It's not quite an SCG or MCG, but it holds 100,000 people, with a fine playing surface, and a special atmosphere. It is just one of those places you really have to play. I only wish the result had been a little kinder.

It was in Calcutta that an 'incident' in a nightclub put Ricky Ponting onto the front pages—and probably reminded every high-profile professional sportsman across the spectrum that we live in a fishbowl these days. A scuffle after too many drinks got Ricky into the local press and then the Australian media. He was accused of conduct unbecoming to a member of the Australian team. Steve Bernard, the team manager, and I got him in and he was fined $1000. I had a yarn to him afterwards, reinforcing the point that we all had to accept—that we were Australian cricketers twenty-four hours a day and he had to make sure it never happened again. Unfortunately he slipped up again at a Sydney night-spot after a one-day match in early 1999 in another highly publicised alcohol-related incident which brought him a fine, a two-match suspension and uncomfortable appearances on prime-time TV, during which he offered an abject apology. Ricky did the wrong thing, but I really felt for him. He was a young bloke who had made a mistake; just because he was a Test cricketer doesn't mean that he's different from other human beings. If everyone who had had too much to drink in their lifetime had to be paraded on television, it would be a bloody long queue.

I believe we're very, very quick to judge in Australia these days. And there are certain sections of the media which are only looking for these kinds of stories.

The Indian tour had been a tough one but we weren't done with yet. After the Calcutta walloping we held a meeting and vowed to fight back, to salvage some respectability from the tour. At Bangalore we did just that, in a quality performance, despite Tendulkar taking us apart again in the first innings with a magnificent 177. We chased their 424 with 400 and then went out there with our best bowling performance of the tour, knocking them over for 169. Mike Kasprowicz led the way with 5–28. We needed 194 to win, and got them, two-down. I finished on a neat 102 not out, a most satisfying personal conclusion to a tour in which we had been beaten—but had shown fighting qualities, against the odds, at the end.

My close-up look at Sachin Tendulkar during that tour confirmed what I had thought for a long time—that he was the best batsman in the world. Suffice to say that I saw too much of him on that tour—he gave us some terrible beltings. Tendulkar and West Indies' captain Brian Lara are the best two I have seen in cricket's recent times. But I believe that Tendulkar is technically a better player than Lara.

One thing's for sure—they can both maul you! That's the danger with the pair of them—that when they're on song they can shred an attack in double-quick time. No captain wants a batsman to make 100 against his team, but when it's a slow 100, it's not so bad; you can keep the pressure on, hopefully keep picking up wickets at the other end. The difficulty with both Tendulkar and Lara is that when they score runs, they invariably do it at some speed. In full flight, they have everyone under enormous pressure—bowlers, fieldsmen and the captain alike. The speed of their run-gathering is the greatest attribute of both players. It's not so much that they score *big* runs (which they do often enough), but that they score them quickly, applying enormous pressure.

Lara and Tendulkar are similar in build, Sachin the stockier of the two. Both are shortish—and athletic. It's a fact of life in cricket that some of the very greatest of batsmen around the world have been shorter blokes, such as Bradman, Harvey and Border, to name only a few. When it comes to cricket, and batting, small can be lethal— as we found out rather too often on the Indian campaign of 1998. But at least we came away with a victory at Bangalore under our belts.

Buoyed by the win and feeling the time was right, I came out with some fighting words after the game. I made my thoughts on Australia's two-captains policy very clear and also my belief that it had driven a wedge into the game. I spoke my mind on the situation as I saw it as the tour came to its end. I believed there was trouble brewing in Australian cricket.

In fact, as the heat and dust settled on a losing series and a typically testing campaign, I believed I had played my last game as Australian captain. I had pretty much made up my mind that I would stand down. My unease with the two-captains policy was deep-seated and genuine. I decided that I would perhaps play on as an opening batsman in the up-coming Ashes series, if they wanted me. A member of the team, but nothing more.

When ACB chairman Denis Rogers flew to Bangalore before the Third Test, I had told him that my firm inclination was to step down as captain after the match. Denis argued strongly against it. 'That's not what we want to happen,' he said. 'We very much want you to go on as captain. We see you very much as the captain of Australian cricket.' 'I am at the point where I don't think it's the right thing to do,' I told him. 'I really think that when a bloke is in charge as captain he should be in charge overall, and the game should run with that.'

My very public stance on the issue of the two-captains policy after the last Test in India brought me some criticism and perhaps ruffled some feathers. I was accused of being a 'dummy-spitter' and of whingeing—that I was taking a stand only because I was upset at being left out of the one-day side. Well, there was *some* truth in that. Of course I was disappointed at not being in the Australian team, or half of it anyway. But the issue was far bigger than that. It's worth noting, too, I was being repeatedly asked about the issue. After we had won that last Test and the one-day side was poised to take over, I believed it was fair-enough timing to say what I thought. That done, blokes like Ian Healy and me headed for home, no longer part of the equation.

I had told the final press conference in Bangalore: 'I think it's time for everyone to go home and have a think about what we want for Australian cricket next season.' 'What do you mean by that?' they asked me. I responded that there were big issues at hand and the cool of winter was a perfect opportunity for the people at the top of the game to sit down and have a good look at where Australian cricket was heading. I posed the question: Do we still believe in leadership and the captaincy of Australian cricket or do we just pick eleven blokes who we think are going to be best, and chop and change them for the next game, and the next?

To me it was a fundamental question. The place of the national cricket captain in the scheme of things had traditionally been one of some value and importance in the summer life of the nation for a century or more. There had only been thirty-nine of them, after all. To change such a tried and tested system was something that needed a lot of thought and discussion. I didn't believe it had been given anywhere near what it deserved. To change things at the top during a period of considerable success for the Australian game was not something to be taken lightly either. A lot of people did not agree with the two-captains policy: respected ex-players, coaches, administrators and cricket journalists. Their opinions deserved some attention. All those things added up to the reasons why I believed we needed to have a look at the whole thing back home in Australia.

In our talks in Bangalore Denis Rogers revealed to me the Board's plans for a split summer, beginning with the Ashes series and then the one-dayers. So the program from now on would be a Test tour of Pakistan, Tests against England at home and then the World Series Cup. In the uncertainty and tension of world cricket at the time, with the Pakistan bribery allegations and other problems still bubbling, the Board was anxious to maintain stability at the top. Rogers left no doubt that they wanted me to carry on. And thinking over what he had said, I started for the first time to think that the new-look program with the Tests separated from the one-dayers perhaps made it possible for the two-captains concept to function well enough in the short term.

I have no doubt that the state of world cricket was one of the reasons behind the Board's keenness for me to stay on as captain. Controversy raged on a few fronts, and I think the Board saw me as the bloke to try and steer us through. There was the simmering Sri Lankan problem and the match-fixing drama, both of which seemed never-ending. They thought I was the best man to get them through in that I could both play the game and play and understand the politics probably as well as or better than anyone else in the team.

Back home in Australia, the proposed examination of the state of the game took place at a meeting in Melbourne, about a month after the tour. Steve Waugh and I got together with the selection panel and we kicked some ideas around. The selectors were pretty firm in their views—they wanted me to keep going as captain of the Test team and captain of Australian cricket, and for Steve to continue as captain of the one-day team. But it was decided unanimously that there should be closer links between the two, now separate, strands of the game. I was to be briefed and involved in discussions on how things were going within the one-day framework.

The meeting was held in the ACB offices in Melbourne and a crowd of camera crews and journalists were jostling for position outside. 'Was I going to stand down?' 'What was I going to do?' Some people thought I was heavy-handed, forcing the issue too hard for personal reasons. It wasn't that. I was trying to do what I thought was best for Australian cricket. The Melbourne meeting cleared the air and I think all of us walked out of it reasonably happy, with our eyes now lifted to the next challenge, in Pakistan.

I will say publicly now that I found the situation of being in one Australian team and out of the other slightly embarrassing. If I had happened to be a more egotistical type (and I'm not saying that I haven't got an ego), then it would have been even more painful. Suddenly, at a certain time of the cricket season, I became the disappearing man. It was demeaning. I was supposed to be a senior player, a senior figure in Australian cricket, yet I was rated not good enough to play one form of the game. My attitude was quite simple: that I didn't think the captain should be out of the team half the time. Yes, it hurt. I can say that now.

....

Chapter 22

PAKISTAN '98— A TOUR *to* REMEMBER

The 1998 tour of Pakistan, whose rather numbing (and for me, never-to-be-forgotten) highlight begins this book on my life in cricket, was a perfect example of what I mean about the word 'team' as applied to the game of cricket. We flew out without the best spin bowler in the world, Shane Warne—and anyone who knows anything about cricket on the subcontinent realises well enough that spin is king over there. We played only one lead-up game in the tour, at Karachi—a win for us, but no more than a loosen-up against a side way below what we would face in the Tests. That we came back as dominant winners of the series—albeit only by 1–0— was the mark of a terrific team input, with shoulders to the wheel right through the side. We were on top from the first morning of the first day of the first Test, and we never released our grip.

We went into the First Test in Rawalpindi not really knowing what to expect. We had played okay in Karachi, but against moderate opposition, and our key spinner Stuart MacGill seemed to be struggling. As it turned out, we couldn't have played much better. We lost the toss, and early on I dropped a tough catch off Saeed Anwar when he was two and then Heals dropped a toughie off Aamir Sohail when he was two or three. This was not the start we wanted. But by lunch we had them 4–70, grabbing a psychological edge which we never really let go through three Test matches. Saeed Anwar went on to make 100, but we bowled them out for 269 on a good wicket, one for which I had crossed all fingers in the hope of winning the toss. Along the way I took a good catch to get rid of Salim Malik, giving Colin Miller his first Test wicket.

We then went out and smashed them, absolutely demoralising their bowlers after a scratchy start. Wasim Akram bowled really well and got me with one that shifted away late. Justin Langer went for a first-ball duck, and Mark Waugh cheaply. Then we got cracking. Slats made 108, Steve Waugh 157, Darren Lehmann 98 and Ian Healy 82. I was one of the only strugglers. When I fell for 3 the thought occurred to me that I was somewhat out of touch.

Stuart MacGill's effort in that Test reinforced my belief about the team aspects of cricket. 'Magilla' finished up with nine wickets—a wonderful performance. Yet only a short while before he had really been struggling. In a couple of trial games at Maroochydore, he couldn't land them at all. He was bowling almost double-bouncers and our New Zealand opposition hammered him. In the first trial game in Pakistan he was just as bad, hardly landed a ball on a length. We stuck with him and in the Test Stuart continued to battle, still having trouble getting them on the spot. But he kept working at it, kept talking about it, and kept being positive. The team to a man encouraged him throughout and in the end his nine-wicket haul against players renowned for their ability to play spin was a tribute to both his perseverance and some damned good bowling.

We made 513 and bowled them out for 145 the second time around, to win by an innings and 99 runs. We had them nine-down at stumps on the fourth day, and couldn't get the last wicket. Malik was in with Saqlain Mushtaq when bad light brought about an early halt. We were in limbo to an extent—not knowing whether we should go out and have a big night to celebrate a (surely) pending victory. We compromised. We had a few beers in the British Club, but at about 10.30 p.m. I said to the guys: 'C'mon, time to go home.' Next morning we were in no rush to get to the ground. Generally we would be there an hour and a half before the start of play, but on this morning we rolled in at 9.15 a.m. for a 9.55 start. A brief warm-up, a few stretches, twenty minutes of play and we had won the Test, when Glenn McGrath cleaned up Mushtaq lbw. McGrath bowled well in that match, as he always has, and always will. It just seemed that we picked up wickets when we needed them. It was a great start.

Not so great were the events of the next day. Early in the morning Mark Waugh and I were booked on a plane for the forty-five minutes' flight to Lahore to front the Pakistani judicial inquiry into match fixing and to throw any new light, if we could, on the affidavits made by Mark and Shane Warne four years before. After an historic Test match win we were destined for one of the more unpleasant days of our cricketing lives. Rightly or wrongly we had taken a decision not to tell the Australian journalists travelling with the team that we were going. This was a tough call, but entirely to do with reasons of safety and with concerns that we may genuinely have been in some danger. Majid Khan, the former Test captain, head of the Pakistan Cricket Board and a good man who was a driving force behind the inquiry and about getting Pakistani cricket corruption out 'into the open', had told us that he had had death threats. Drop this inquiry or else, he was told. That put the wind up us.

We had a personal and moral obligation to go to Lahore, but also a very real concern about the dark side of what was going on. It was because of that we kept our trip quiet, although as it turned out we shouldn't have bothered. Assurances given to us by the Pakistani authorities that our visit would be strictly confidential soon proved to be a joke. The idea was for Mark and me to slip out of the hotel, fly to Lahore, give our evidence and head straight back to Rawalpindi before anyone knew what was going on.

It half-worked. Travelling with an Australian security man, Reg Dickason, we got to Lahore with no problems. But soon after we landed we found out that one of Justice Malik Mohammad Quayyum's clerks had let all the local media know that Mark Waugh and Mark Taylor were coming to town. It was a violation of a firm agreement, and we were filthy about it. Majid had set up the meeting in the judge's private chambers and there we were met by a small army of journalists and photographers, inside and outside the gates. We were hustled through the crowd, and into the building. Further assurances had been given that the testimony we gave would be strictly confidential. Next day it was on the Internet.

Salim Malik—the man at the centre of the allegations—was present in the judge's chambers. Apparently he had been phoned in Rawalpindi with the news that a couple of Australian players were going to give evidence against him in Lahore and that he'd better go there with his lawyer in case he wanted to cross-examine them. So Malik turned up and was present with his lawyer while I gave my evidence, which was effectively entirely hearsay—relaying what other people had told me. It was a hugely uncomfortable experience. Mark gave his evidence first, while I waited in another room, and was then allowed to stay while I was examined. Malik's lawyer asked me some questions, such as: 'Mark, do you have anything against Salim Malik?' I responded, 'No, Salim never approached me . . . the reason I'm here is because I was begged by the inquiry to come along, and because I have nothing to hide.' The outcome of this long-running scandal remained uncertain well into 1999, although there were signs as I prepared material for this book that it would reach some finality before the next season began.

That day, at least, drew the line on the whole thing from our point of view. Four years earlier, in 1995, Shane Warne, Mark Waugh and Tim May had all sworn affidavits, setting out what had taken place the year before and sent them to Pakistani authorities. From that point onwards there was pressure from over there for our blokes to appear and give face-to-face evidence. My understanding is that in Pakistan, as in our legal system, that sort of direct, spoken evidence carries far more weight than words written on paper. We understood that, and it was why Mark and I went to Lahore, despite our very real concerns about safety and security.

That was a bloody awful day in Lahore. There was drama everywhere. Back in Rawalpindi, the Australian journalists were very upset at being kept in the dark, claiming that our attempt to keep our trip secret was ridiculous and was never going to work. I was never happier to be back in the heart of my team than I was that night, when we attended a function at the Australian High Commission. To have to socialise at a cocktail party, though, shaking hands with all and sundry and trying to put on a happy face, was hard after such a day. I felt as much like doing that as facing Wasim Akram on a greentop.

Back home there was pressure building on me too. In fact it was Groundhog Day again, with my form with the bat being the focus. In a match against a Pakistani Seconds side at Rawalpindi I hit the ball pretty well, but was out for 13. Within a day there were stories appearing back in Australia along the lines of: 'Is Taylor heading into another slump?' I honestly couldn't believe it this time. I had made an unbeaten hundred in the last Test against India, then missed out in one innings of one Test match. Suddenly, I was in bad form and heading into the doldrums. To be fair, I wasn't hitting the ball too well, but to call it a 'slump' after two innings—gee, that was harsh.

Anyhow, in the second innings of the game at Rawalpindi I batted longer than I normally would have, finally declaring when I was 63 not out—and long past the point where there could be a realistic expectation of a result. At the press conference after the game I was asked why I had batted on. I told them the truth: 'Look, for the first time in my life, I made a selfish decision. I felt I needed more of a hit.' From a team point of view I felt it was more important for me to bat for a while and find some touch than it was for us to win the game. I make no apologies. As a matter of fact it was the best thing I ever did! In my next innings, I made 334 not out.

The Test match in Peshawar was preceded by one of those

touring experiences that can make cricket so very special, when you're fortunate enough to play at the highest level. The city of Peshawar sits at the southern end of the Khyber Pass. It is a tough town; the talk is you can buy any sort of drugs and weaponry that you wish there, including fully automatic machine guns. On a day off while we were in Peshawar we were taken on an escorted tour into the Khyber Pass, my second look at this remarkable route through the mountains into Afghanistan, having already gone there in 1994 as well. It is simply extraordinary, barren of just about all greenery with big overlapping spurs. Once a railway wound its way along the floor of the valley below; on the higher peaks, there are many forts.

Our hosts for the day were the men of the Khyber Rifles, who control the pass. There were frequent military checkpoints and soldiers guarding the road at regular intervals as we went by. They took us all the way to a stark high point which overlooks Afghanistan, providing spectacular distant views of a couple of towns across the border. It was an awesome experience to be in this place through which the likes of Alexander the Great and numerous other conquerors had travelled.

There was a disappointing outcome, however, in the over-reaction of some people back home to newspaper photos that appeared from that day of some of the guys posing with a machine-gun battery. It was so strong Steve Bernard felt it necessary to issue a public apology. Apparently some people took offence at Australian cricketers being seen with weapons of war. The fact was that we were in an extremely volatile part of the world, where guns are part of life, carried openly and on sale just about everywhere. To say that it meant that we were in favour of guns is simply ridiculous. I thought it was all over the top. I myself am very much opposed to guns. I certainly don't want to ever own one and I don't believe that ordinary people need them. We only did what any tourist who visits the area would do, but because we were members of the Australian cricket team we had to apologise.

I have already told the story of the Second Test in Peshawar and the triple century I scored. The draw there left us in the box seat to wrap up the series in the Third Test at Karachi, where we had never beaten Pakistan before. We won the toss and built a handy lead in the first innings, with 280 to Pakistan's 252, defying some really good bowling by Wasim Akram who was definitely the pick of their bowlers in the two Tests he played. Batting again, and with about an hour to go on the fourth night, we were close to 350 runs ahead. I was sitting with Steve Waugh. 'What d'you reckon, Tug?' I asked him. 'Should we declare now or bat them out of the game.' Steve and I were pretty much in agreement that we should declare and go for the win. But Geoff Marsh, our coach, was totally against it. He kept grabbing me so I wouldn't put my arms up to declare! I ended up giving in to him. Oh, hell, why not keep going, I thought. I'm allowed to be conservative once or twice in my career.

We batted on, and Gavin Robertson fired in 45 near the end, including twenty off the last over, to put us 418 ahead with a day to play. And if I had held a catch at 3–50 next morning, we may well have won the Test. I dropped Ijaz Ahmed off Glenn McGrath, a sharp chance, low and to the right. But I got both hands to it and should have held it. They would have been 4–50 and we would have been a great chance. But Ijaz and Moin Khan put on 153 and they ground away for the draw through the afternoon, finishing at 5–262. Glenn McGrath and Colin Miller bowled splendidly early on, but our spin attack wasn't so good in that game. Salim Malik was the third of those early wickets to fall, completing a pair for the match. I had never seen our guys so jubilant.

So the Karachi Test dragged on to a draw, ending five overs early with no result possible. We had, however, won the series in Pakistan—without Shane Warne, in front of patriotic crowds and against a darned good cricket team. It was Australia's first series win in Pakistan in thirty-nine years. It meant a lot to us. Victories over there are very hard to come by. We had had the best of it in 1994, but got beaten. This time we had nailed it.

PETER ROEBUCK, Sydney Morning Herald: *Australia's superiority in the series completed in gruelling Karachi brooks no argument. Throughout the campaign they were the strongest side.*

Chapter 23

100 ... AND
ALMOST OUT

My 100th Test match, which coincided with the first match of the Ashes series against England in the summer of 1998–99, was both a deeply felt honour ... and a pain in the butt. My century of Tests came at a favoured haunt, Brisbane's Gabba, where a beautiful wicket waited in the centre. I had come back from the successes of Pakistan really looking forward to the Ashes series and the summer which I felt deep down might well be my last in cricket. But in Brisbane, I wasn't so much a cricketer, I was more a celebrity guest, with never a moment to myself. Mark Taylor Australian Captain had all but disappeared and Mark Taylor Celebrity had taken his place in the wake of the 334, and now the landmark of Test No. 100. In many ways it was a great time, with many of my family and friends in Brisbane for the Test (I left 25 tickets at the gate—five was my previous record!). In other ways it was uncomfortable. For the first time in a Test match I no longer felt what I should have felt: that I was a professional cricketer there to do a job. In fact I was ultimately glad to get the whole thing out of the way and move on to Test No. 101, in Perth.

RON REED, *Daily Telegraph*, Sydney, 20 November 1998: *A funny thing happened to Mark Taylor on the way to his 100th Test match which he celebrates in Brisbane today. He suddenly became the star of the Australian cricket team.*

For all my reservations about my new found 'celebrity' status, the occasion was very special for me—to join a list of other cricketers who had played more than 100 Tests: Allan Border (156), Kapil Dev (131), Sunil Gavaskar (125), Javed Miandad (124), Viv Richards (121), Graham Gooch (118), David Gower (117), Dilip Vengsarkar (116), Desmond Haynes (116), Colin Cowdrey (115), Clive Lloyd (110), Geoff Boycott (109), Gordon Greenidge (108), David Boon (107), Steve Waugh (106), Ian Healy (106), Ian Botham (102) and Courtney Walsh (102).

It was at the end of the match that Channel 9's 'This Is Your Life' crash-tackled me, much to my surprise. It happened at the wind-up to a match which we had seemed destined to win, until the rains came. Tony Greig was firing the questions, 'Mark, you must be disappointed—you played well enough to be 1–nil up,' etc, etc. In fact I was a bit testy. The rain had washed away a win and the week had not been an easy one for me, with just about every waking moment planned for me, enjoyable as it was in many ways. I was doing my best to put it all into words when I felt this tap on my shoulder. Who's this rude bastard, I thought, tapping me on the shoulder while I'm live to air. I tried to ignore him and pressed on. But the bloke kept on trying to get my attention. I spun around—and there was Mike Munro with his red book ...

The worst thing was the way I was dressed. I have always been regarded as a pretty ordinary dresser at the best of times. For the interview with Tony, knowing they only shot waist-up, I had a nice T-shirt on, and felt that I looked quite smart. However, 'This Is Your Life' chose to pan back for a long shot, revealing the Australian captain in nice T-shirt ... rough shorts and a pair of Pakistani sandals. I looked bloody terrible.

During the final day as the rain fell, team manager Steve Bernard had joined me. 'Mate, we have this function on tonight,' he said. 'You're going to have to go along—it's for one of the sponsors.' Last nights of Test matches are traditionally for the 'team'—a chance to relax and reflect. After such a week, I felt I'd had about enough. 'Well, you can tell 'em I won't be there,' I said. 'Mark, it's for CUB,' Steve said. 'You can have a couple of beers.' 'Well, okay,' I said eventually, 'but I'm *not* getting dressed up in team uniform. I'm gonna wear casual gear, and I'm gonna be there for an hour or so and then I'm going out with the guys. I haven't seen them all week, apart from out on the field'. 'Mark, I would suggest that in view of what's happening after the match you will be wearing the team uniform,' said Steve. 'I won't be,' I said. 'You will be,' said Steve. And so it went on: will, won't, will, won't. Meanwhile all the players were winding me up—every one of them (unlike me) being aware of the 'This Is Your Life' scheme. 'Yeah, you tell him, Tubs,' they urged. 'Mate, we're not going to wear the uniform—we'll come along for an hour, then we're going out,' I told him. 'Okay, Mark,' Steve said, having the last word, 'I'll tell them—but I think you *will* be wearing your team outfit.'

Then Mike Munro sprang me with the 'This Is Your Life' shock—and when I went back to the dressing room all the blokes were pissing themselves with laughter. 'What are you going to wear tonight?' asked Steve.

It was a real exercise in deceit. I had kissed Judi and the boys farewell that morning and the plan was that they were coming to the first session, then jumping on a plane and heading back to Sydney. When I got back to the room after the day's play, their gear was of course still there. John Fordham joined me, another conspirator, and I gave him a serious dressing down. Then I started to worry about the show. Who the hell would they trot out?

In the end I enjoyed the experience. They had flown in mates of mine from all over the place, old schoolmates, cricket mates— and even Dave Mason from England. My whole life was paraded before my eyes.

The Ashes series was no great shakes for Mark Taylor, batsman, however. I made 228 runs at 22, a fairly meagre bounty, although I scored some handy runs in the early Tests when we needed them (46 in the first innings in Brisbane, 61 in the first innings in Perth, 59 and 29 in Adelaide). But it was a winning series (3–1) and one in which we generally had the edge from its opening in Brisbane when only the rain thwarted an Aussie win. We had much the best of the first three Tests, including the luckless draw in Brisbane, then comfortable wins in Perth and Adelaide. Then they stole a game from us in Melbourne, outplaying us on the last day, which is some-times all you have to do in Test cricket, and making the most of what, frankly was a pretty poor attitude by us in the last couple of hours. Up until that day at the MCG they hadn't really 'won' a day in the whole series. In Sydney, they fought well, but I felt we were always in front. Winning all five tosses did no harm to the Aussie cause, either.

It was the series in which Stuart MacGill came of age as an international leg-spinner. The second innings in Brisbane was pretty much the giant stride down that track. He got belted to some extent in the first innings but in the second, when we were looking to bowl them out, he got three. Magilla bowled Nasser Hussain with a wrong 'un, and had Mark Ramprakash stumped, advancing down the track. All of a sudden he was really worrying blokes out. We left him out of the Perth Test—a big talking point, but eventually shown to be the right thing to do when the wicket turned out to be a seamer—then he came back in to bowl extremely well in Adelaide and Sydney. He took the quantum leap that bowlers some-times take; he wasn't just getting blokes out who were trying to hit him, he was getting them out because he was bowling too well for them with his mixed bag of tricks.

Darren Gough's hat-trick in Sydney on a wonderful day of Test cricket was a big highlight of the series—and I'm sure not begrudged by any of the Aussies. I felt almost happy for him. Goughie is a lion-hearted performer, a guy with a big ticker who puts in every time he bowls. Compared with Curtly Ambrose at 6ft 10 (2.08m) he's a pocket rocket—short for a fast-bowler at around 5ft 10 (1.78m), but making up for everything else in the effort department. He had a good Ashes series just by sheer hard work.

It was a good-natured series, although never less than hard-fought in the traditional manner. Alec Stewart, the England captain, and I get on well together, and he has a team that is definitely on the improve. They had come to us after a series win against South Africa in England—so our 3–1 result, accurately reflecting the difference between the sides in my view, was a strong effort by the Australian side.

After the Melbourne Test, which we lost in a late photo finish, Steve Waugh copped some flak through a perception held by some in and around the game that he had not shielded his lower-order partners—MacGill and Matt Nicholson—in the late chase for the few runs we needed to win the game . . . and failed to get. Now and then in his career Steve has been called 'selfish', with Ian Chappell nailing him that way a couple of times. Steve is certainly intense and focused to a marked degree, his success rate being the bottom line to the sort of effort he puts in. Once, in earlier years, he was dismissive of players who 'worried about their batting averages'. But a significant switch in approach, from a bloke determined to make every innings mean something to a bloke never, ever going to give his wicket away, coincided with his rise to greatness as a batsman. In the process he transformed himself from a player who got dropped, averaging 37 in 1991, to captain of Australia in 1999, averaging 50. However he went about the Great Transformation, it's bloody hard to be critical of a bloke who has been our best batsman for so long.

On the exciting last day of the Fifth Test in Sydney, with the Poms needing another 183 to reach a target of 287 and us needing eight wickets to win it, I passed what was to be my last personal milestone in big-time cricket. Attempting to square-cut Glenn McGrath, Mark Ramprakash edged a flier to me and it stuck, clean and safe. It was my 157th Test catch, surpassing Allan Border's world-record 156. It is a record of which I am very proud.

When I reflect on those Test catches I took as a slips-field, and all the others, I think back to the little footstool that played its part so many years ago. The long hours I spent as a kid in Wagga throwing a ball against the garage wall in such a way that it might come back and flick off the edge of the stool (or a garbage tin lid) represented my diploma course in preparation for the business of taking slips catches. The great advantage of the primitive practice session I devised was that I never knew when a catch was coming. Most often the ball would miss the edge of the wooden stool. But now and then it would connect and the ball would fly this way or that, with me after it.

The technique taught me the most important lesson of all—to always watch the ball. There is one theory in slips catching that you should watch the edge of the bat. That was never my way. My eyes would be on the ball from the moment it left the bowler's hands. And the good catchers with whom I have discussed the subject, like Bob Simpson, Ian Chappell and Mark Waugh, have all told me that they did or do the same. Mark Waugh, for example, is a brilliant catcher anywhere on the field. And even at bat-pad he'll most often stand there half-turned towards the bowler, watching the ball. He doesn't crouch there staring at the batsman's bat, or pad. Watch the ball—that's the trick. After all, it's the ball you have to catch.

Slips-fielding is an exciting, sometimes nerve-wracking pastime. When the ball is new and flying, it can come at lightning-fast pace. You don't get a lot of time to think about it—and that's what I liked about it. Fielding to the spinners is a different challenge. I have been very lucky in my time to have had the chance to field in slips so often to the bowling of men like Shane Warne and Stuart MacGill, who can really rip the ball past the bat. When leg-spinners of their quality are on, a slips-fielder always feels that he's 100 per cent in the game.

Good slips-fielding to a spin bowler is the toughest challenge.

With the quicks you get a pretty good feel after a ball or two about where to stand and how deep, etc. But finding the right spot for a spinner is not so easy. You've really got to 'read' the wicket and try to judge the pace. For me the toughest prospect of all was fielding in slips to a right-handed batsman off an off-spinner. With off-spinners (to right-handed batsmen) you don't get a lot of chances. If the wicket is slow, the ball won't carry far—and you've got to be up close. When you do get a chance, it's generally low and quick, because the batsman has played the line badly. The best chance is off the big drive, where the ball hasn't spun. A nick then, and the ball will really fly. Or at Perth or Adelaide you might get one that doesn't turn, but skids off and takes the edge, flying low and fast to your left. Those, I think, are the hardest catches.

It's a hero or villain position requiring unflagging concentration. You can stand there all day and not get one. And if you happen to get *two* in a day—then you've had a really big day at first slip. If you're out there all day that can mean ninety overs, 540 balls, six hours, thirty-five degree heat . . . and maybe just one chance. Maybe none. That's the job. And when the chances do come along, then you're expected to catch them. If you don't, people wonder why. In that twinkling of an eye you've established yourself . . . a hero or a villain.

Inevitably I am occasionally asked about this catch, or that. I don't regard any of them as a 'best' catch, but there are certainly ones I remember.

I'll never forget my first one, Desmond Haynes off Allan Border in the second innings at the Fourth Test against the West Indies in 1988–89, at the SCG. Haynes made 143 and batted beautifully, although we had blown them out of the water. The catch was a sitter. The ball hit Ian Healy's gloves and popped up into the air, falling gently for me. But, gee, it felt good. I remember, too, catching Dave Richardson (South Africa) off Warne in the Second Test at Sydney in 1993–94. It was a really fine nick that slipped past Heals, but stuck in my left hand. And Adam Parore off Warne in Brisbane, and Adam Bacher off him again in Melbourne in 1997–98. Both of them were the same—low and quick to the left.

As a slips-fielder, if you catch those you'll know you've done everything right. You're off-balance to an extent and with me, the left was not my preferred side. Your technique has to be exactly right, your hands 'soft'. If you go at it too hard the ball will pop out.

I remember a few off the quicks as well, especially catching Roshan Mahanama in Melbourne off Glenn McGrath in the 1995–96 series. The ball flew off the shoulder of the bat. Not a great catch, but it was my 100th! I was always going to remember that. And Salim Malik in Pakistan in 1998 off Colin Miller, to give him his first Test wicket, a strong deflection wide to my right. And, of course, Mark Ramprakash off Glenn McGrath, in the Fifth Test in 1999 at the SCG—my 157th catch, for the record.

I've had some horror moments in slips too. Back in Adelaide in 1991–92, I put down three in a row—one off Mike Whitney, two off Merv Hughes. It was the last day of the Test and we were trying to bowl them out, and here I was playing butter-fingers in slips. AB was looking at me with that look—and I was thinking, 'Should I get out of here?' And I thought, 'No, I've got to keep going.' I remembered Bob Simpson's words: 'If you drop one, you'll drop three.' Finally I grabbed one that day, Mohammad Azharuddin off Craig McDermott, for 106, with the second new ball. It wasn't a bad catch, either. It swung away late and the nick went low and to my right. I don't remember seeing it into my hands. I just remember thinking, 'God . . . it's stuck!' when I looked down at the ball.

Slips-fielding is like the old saying, 'Love is never having to say you're sorry.' Progressively through my career I made it a habit *not* to say sorry to the bowler when I put one down. I figured there was no-one in the world who hated dropping a catch more than I did, and it wasn't as if I hadn't tried my darndest to hang onto the catch. So why should I say sorry?

For whatever reasons, I believe I was a better slips field at the end of my career than I was at the beginning—notwithstanding that good slips fielding is by its nature much about sharp reflexes. I put it down to the fact that I worked so hard at the 'art' throughout my career—first by myself and with my Dad as a kid, and then under Bob Simpson and Geoff Marsh. Simmo worked me very hard when I was in the State side and the Australian side early on. With his own background he knew maybe more than anyone the advantage of having good slippers. In Australian cricket in recent times we have worked hard at our slips catching. Alongside my 150 catches was Mark Waugh with 100 at second slip. If you've got two blokes at first and second slip who catch eight or nine out of ten, then you're going to win a lot of games.

I enjoyed my years in slips, yarning with the blokes around me, encouraging the bowlers—and doing my darndest to hang onto the one that came my way. I think first slip is a wonderful position. As a cricketer I was certainly no Olympic athlete or Dean Jones or Ross Edwards or Ricky Ponting in the field. I just happened to have good hands and I added to that a lot of hard work over the years. The result was some good catches—and some good memories. For me, being in slips was like opening the batting—they were things that just happened in my career.

My last innings in Test cricket in the Fifth Ashes Test in January, 1999 had a swift and somewhat strange ending. Late on the third day, when we batted for the second time with a lead of 102 (322 to 220), I scratched around like an old hen. I felt knackered and batted that way, just being happy to get off the mark with a two. Two not out overnight, I came to the ground the next day in a far better frame of mind, feeling relaxed and confident. But in the first over from Goughie I got a reasonable ball that decked away and took the edge to be snared behind by Alec Stewart. I hadn't scored another run . . . and that was it for M. Taylor, Test batsman.

The final high-pressure day in Sydney which went our way as we bundled them out for 188, via a spectacular leg-spinning performance by Stuart MacGill of 7–50, giving him twenty-four wickets for the series, was extra special for me, though. With thoughts of retirement in mind, I wore the baggy green cap all day, an important gesture to me; perhaps this would be the last day for me at this place, a neat finish at this grand old ground where I made my Test debut back in 1989, and where the crowds for this Test had been just terrific. To start and finish at 'home' had plenty of appeal. Judi knew better than anyone what was going through my mind, and would not have been surprised if I had announced my retirement in the short speech I made at the end of the day. But that wasn't the way to do it. There remained a little uncertainty at the back of my mind, not that I wanted to drag the thing out when decision-time came. But as I did the victory lap around the ground with the other guys, carrying the new crystal trophy, I gazed up into the stands and thought: 'This will probably be the last time I ever do this.'

JOHN FORDHAM: *I had a strong sense that this was to be a last hurrah for him—that the day would represent something of a final chapter. I watched him through the binoculars. He was so involved . . . up there with his bowlers at the start of each over . . . so obviously savouring the moment.*

From a personal point of view the series was a quietly fading one for me—a pretty accurate snapshot of the reality of a career winding down. I think I probably played as well as anyone in the first three Tests when we had to do well. From then on, I missed out. It seemed that summer the question was increasingly on peoples' lips. Would he play on? John Fordham was keen for me to keep going, knowing that I felt okay in myself and was still performing well enough as a player to warrant my place in the side.

But deep inside, I felt I was losing the edge—and that the fact I had failed to 'finish' off the series was a reflection of that. The reason I didn't make more runs against the Poms was that I was losing the hunger. Without saying it out aloud to anyone I kept thinking to myself along the way in that series: This is my third-last Test, this is my second-last Test, this is my *last* Test . . .

274

With a West Indies tour looming, and international cricket still in some turmoil thanks to the varying dramas which continued to plague it, the ACB was keen for me to keep going. The general view was that the future captaincy of the Australian team came down to a choice between Steve Waugh and Shane Warne, and for me to take the team to the Windies, followed by Steve taking the World Cup side away, would have led to a respectable pause of a few months. Shane would have his chance to get back to peak fitness and the decision-makers would have the opportunity to contemplate all the angles—with the luxury of time on their hands. There is no doubt I forced them into a decision a little sooner than they would liked to have made it.

I can reveal now that the realisation that my career was nearing its end was in fact in my mind from well before the Pakistan tour of 1998, from early May in fact. That month, as I prepared to start a fitness program with Kevin Chevell in Sydney, he asked me a double-barrelled question: 'What are your goals? Are you looking to get back into the one-dayers?'

'Mate, that's not going to happen,' I said. 'I know I'm not going to be part of that again. What I want to do is to get really fit this year—fit enough to get through Pakistan and the Ashes series against England. The way I'm thinking now that will be it for me. I'll give it away then.'

I told Kevin how I felt deep down: 'I feel that I am losing the ambition to tour . . . and the ambition to keep playing. I am keen about this year, though—about hopefully finishing on a good note. To give myself the chance of doing that I want to get as fit as I can—and work from that base.'

The conversation took place on 4 May 1998, my sister Lisa's birthday. For M.A. Taylor, cricketer, it was the beginning of the end. From that day I began the longest sustained period of physical training in my career. My hope was to go out with colours flying high.

Chapter 24

TIME *to* DECLARE

Increasingly through the last home summer of my life as a Test player there was too much of Mark Taylor 'celebrity' and not enough of Mark Taylor 'cricketer'—the malaise that had begun with the crowded days of my 100th Test. I drifted into the role—easing off on the fitness work that Kevin Chevell had put in place for me, starting to get lazy as a player. On reflection it is no surprise at all that I finished the 1998–99 Ashes series badly. The clock was running down.

The people who knew me best knew that I had reached the stage where I didn't really want to keep playing any more. Judi and my Mum and Dad knew what I was thinking. They knew that my hunger for the game had abated. I spoke to Neil 'Harpo' Marks a number of times too. 'What are you really thinking deep down?' he asked me one day. 'I'm thinking about giving it away,' I told him. But I was still playing Shield at that stage, and nothing was certain. Harpo advised me to think a bit more about myself in approaching the final decision and about getting it right for 'me'.

To leave at all was difficult, to leave gracefully and with the timing right harder still. There was pressure from a number of people, the ACB and others, for me to keep going—to the West Indies at least—and I took a pause in my life after the final Ashes Test in Sydney to ponder the future. John Fordham asked me immediately after that last Test what I was going to do. 'I'll probably go to the West Indies,' I said—although without too much conviction. I suppose I was a bit encouraged that way when ACB chief executive Malcolm Speed was quoted in the press as saying about me: 'We'd like him to continue as captain for as long as possible—and that's been the position all along.'

January 1999 was a turbulent month for cricket. Ricky Ponting found himself uncomfortably on the front pages and facing the TV cameras after being involved in a dust-up at a Sydney nightclub following a one-day match. In Melbourne there were stunning revelations when Mark Waugh and Shane Warne gave evidence to the Pakistan Cricket Board's inquiry into match-fixing. The headlines were huge and the two players' testimony quite sensational as allegations against Salim Malik and the bookie named 'John' were made public for the first time.

Meanwhile, an inquiry into all aspects of gambling, match-fixing and bribery involving Australian cricket was under way, conducted by leading QC Rob O'Regan. The breadth of O'Regan's inquiry indicated just how serious the issue was. Among the matters he investigated were:

- an approach made to Dean Jones during the 1992 tour to Sri Lanka;
- allegations of improper conduct in World XI matches in India in 1992;
- an approach made to Allan Border during the 1993 Ashes tour of England;
- an approach made to Ricky Ponting (at Wentworth Park dogs) during the 1997–98 season;
- the two 'suspicious' phone calls I received in Pakistan in 1998.

O'Regan subsequently made a raft of recommendations to the ACB for cricket's future.

On Wednesday 6 January 1999, Judi and I got away from it all with the boys and trekked north to her parents' place up at Halfway Creek, far from Sydney's bustle. I was still debating what to do in my mind. The public presumption seemed to be that I would accede to the Board's wishes and keep playing. 'Jude, if I *am* going to go to the West Indies I'm going to have to get out and do some running up there,' I said before we left. There was no way I could contemplate going to the Windies as some sort of tricked-up 'celebrity captain'. I would only go as a fit and well-prepared player, a batsman determined to pull his weight and do well.

But up there on the far north coast, I didn't do a single thing. I didn't go for one run, I didn't go to the gym . . . I didn't do anything. This was pretty much the final straw—that I wasn't even motivated to run around the block a few times. I talked it over with Judi. 'You know, I just don't want to do it,' I said. 'I honestly just don't want to put in the yards that I know I've got to do if I'm going to the West Indies. I think I should retire . . .'

'If that's what you think, that's what you should do,' she said. I know now deep-down that the decision was locked in place from that point.

We had a week up there, a relaxing time: some golf, some fishing, a few beers, some backyard cricket with two small Taylor boys.

However, soon the rumours started. At a Shield match in Sydney towards the end of January against Tasmania, which was badly affected by rain, I had been buttonholed by journos Phil Wilkins (*Sun-Herald*) and Tony Adams (*Sunday Telegraph*). They asked me about the Ashes series, about my week away . . . what I did up north and so on. And then, 'What about the West Indies, are you still right for that?' I played a straight bat: 'I don't know; I'm still tossing up at this stage,' I told them.

That night I got together with John Fordham over dinner at home at East Ryde. 'I'm having second thoughts about the Caribbean,' I told him. 'I'm getting plenty of reasons from other people why I should go. But I'm no longer sure that Mark Taylor has the reasons there for him to go.'

JOHN FORDHAM: *It was the warning bell, sounding loudly. Mark
had enjoyed his time away from the game . . . the relaxation, the
holiday with the family. I think he was saying to himself: 'How good
this is!' That night, I advised him to sleep on it. I drove home fairly
well convinced that Mark was going to pull the plug on cricket.*

The stories published by the Sydney Sunday papers after my conversations with Wilkins and Adams sparked some speculation that
had reached as far as ACB chiefs Malcolm Speed and Denis Rogers,
who were in Perth for some one-dayers. Their line to the media
was that I hadn't spoken to them, so the presumption was that I
was okay for the tour.

It was in the wake of that Shield match and Saturday night dinner
I had with Fordo that I made my critical call to him, saying that I
had definitely decided to give it away. 'Look, mate, I've changed
my mind. I'm not going to play on,' I told him. 'Geez . . . are you
sure?' he asked. 'Yeah, I am,' I said. 'I don't want to go to the West
Indies as a player and if I don't want to go as a player, there's no
way I should go as captain.'

'Okay . . . well, let's put some wheels in motion,' he said. That
done, I now had to inform the ACB. I first rang Mal Speed and
told him my news. He seemed a bit taken aback, but supportive.
Then I called Denis Rogers, the Board chairman, and he was very
good. 'Obviously I'm disappointed,' he said. 'But I'm not going to
try to talk you out of it—I know you've given it a lot of thought.'
I told him exactly how I felt—that because I didn't really want to
go, the chances were I wouldn't play well over there and that I
certainly didn't want to be there as some sort of 'non-performing'
captain. Denis took it all on board. 'Well, what we've got to do is
to set up the announcement,' he said.

This was the hard bit. Because all the one-dayers happened to
be out of Sydney at that time, in Perth and Adelaide, there was a
dilemma. 'Can you hang on for a week until all the senior cricket
journalists and everyone else are back in Sydney?' Malcolm Speed

asked me. This was something of a nightmare. It was now Wednes-day, 27 January and I hoped to have the whole thing done by the week's end. Instead I had to bite my lip and just keep quiet, under-going a quizzing from some media people when I played a club game for Northern District the next Saturday at Waitara Oval. (I was out for 12 incidentally, slashing at a wide one.) Had I made up my mind, they asked me. Well, I was still thinking about it; I would make an announcement on my future the following Tuesday, I told them. It was true enough, but awkward all the same. For several frustrating days it seemed as if everyone in and around cricket was holding their breath. Would Taylor play on? Or wouldn't he?

Speculation abounded for too many days. When I flew to Laun-ceston on 1 February to attend a function for Sigma Pharmaceu-ticals, with whom I have a business connection, the rumours were that I was heading south for last-minute talks with Denis Rogers about staying on as captain. En route, I gave evidence at the match-fixing inquiry being held in Melbourne.

These last few days represented a frustrating time. Logistics and the way things had fallen were the only reason I delayed doing what I wanted to do. I just wanted to get it over in one dig—to tell the cricket world that, yes, it was over for me, that I wouldn't be playing anymore for Australia, that it had been a truly wonderful experience—and thank you very much for everything. I didn't want any big hoo-ha. I just wanted to cut clean with some dignity, and a few words to set out how I felt about it all.

The other complicating factor was my entirely unexpected naming as 'Australian of the Year'—a wonderful honour which humbled and surprised me in equal proportions. This occurred right in the middle of my trying to give the game away. John Fordham and I sat on the 'secret' for quite a time and worked hard at separating these two pretty emotional moments in my life. While I waited for the opportunity to announce my retirement from cricket, we decided that it could not be allowed to interfere with my Australia Day obligations on 25 and 26 January.

During those two hectic days I shared my intentions only with my family and a few close friends—and with the Prime Minister, John Howard. Monday, 25 January in Brisbane was huge, with a big announcement of the award at the Town Hall, a speech, a press conference and a bundle of radio interviews. Then that night there was a State reception hosted by the Governor at the Sheraton Hotel.

It was before that, in a very traditional Australian way—over a couple of beers—that I told the PM that I was going to retire. 'That doesn't surprise me,' he said, and talked about the importance of timing, how in politics he had always put some value on the principle that you should get out while the going was good . . . before they started calling for your head. I told the PM of my decision in his suite in the Sheraton, where he and his wife Janette had invited John Fordham, Judi and me for pre-dinner drinks. At dinner, I managed to fumble the ball, finishing off my speech with the words: 'Ladies and gentlemen, I am looking forward to my duties as Father of the Year.' I was all speeched-out. There were a few chuckles as I walked off the stage and back at the table I said to Jude: 'I didn't say Father of the Year, did I?' 'Yes, you did,' she said.

The PM has been a great supporter of mine through thick and thin in recent times, although I generated some controversy with a reference to him in a welcome home dinner after the Pakistani tour of 1998. Of the PM, I told a gathering of 600 at Sydney's Wentworth Hotel: 'He is a "cricket tragic"—that's what we call them in the change rooms. He loves the game more than I do.' There was a ripple of reaction to my description of the PM as a 'tragic'. In the *Sydney Morning Herald*, Malcolm Knox wrote: 'Mark Taylor's revelation—that "cricket tragic" is a dressing-room term for a particular type of fan—says much of the ambiguous relationship between performers and audience. Taylor was just being cheeky to a friend, but the term's very existence shows a note of pity, bemusement and even gentle contempt.'

In fact, there was none of any of that in my throwaway line—

and Neil Marks, a former Sheffield Shield player and a man who has devoted his life to the game, put it clearly in perspective when he wrote subsequently in the *Sun-Herald*: 'To be labelled a "cricket tragic" is a term of endearment.' That is exactly the way it was meant. I was thrilled to have the PM and Richie Benaud as special guests at the lunch. Richie was a wonderful supporter of mine in my ten years in Test cricket. I have always regarded him as a great commentator—if not the greatest in the game. When Richie speaks, the players listen.

I digress. The next night, on Australia Day, in a private suite high over Sydney, organised by John Fordham at the Star Casino, I told a group of family and friends of my plans to step down from cricket. It was the end of a hectic day full of functions and commitments. Being unsure exactly when I could make that disclosure public knowledge, I asked them all to keep the news quiet. Very late, there was only my manager and me left—knocking over the last couple of beers, looking over Sydney and coming to terms with the fact that everything was changing . . .

I was gazing out over the lights as Australian of the Year . . . and sitting on a secret. My being named Australian of the Year stirred up all sorts of mixed feelings inside me. At the one time I was humble and proud and a bit overwhelmed by it all, I suppose. I was picked because of what I had achieved overall in my particular field of endeavour, not for being a superb athlete or the best batsman in cricket (although perhaps there was a time in the early '90s when I was that). On reflection, the award was a lot more about the way I played the game—and the way the Australian team played it while I was captain. And the way Australians felt about that. The 334, putting my name up alongside that of the most famous of all Australians, Sir Donald Bradman, helped the cause too.

Yes, I was extremely honoured and very proud—yet in no way did my naming on 26 January make me the best Australian around, by a long shot. I was just one of an army of Australians who had achieved some excellence in so many varied fields in the previous twelve months. And as I said in my acceptance speech in Brisbane, I knew there were a lot of people out there who day-in and day-out worked a hell of a lot harder than I did and achieved great things—yet received no publicity. I thought then of the people who work with the disadvantaged, with drug addicts and alcoholics, giving 100 per cent of themselves to make other lives that little bit better. These fine people get virtually nothing in return—little money, no recognition. These are some of the true Australian heroes, and they were much in my mind during those two days. From the start I always had the award in perspective—although much cherishing the honour, as I always will.

Perhaps I am seen as an 'ordinary' bloke who has achieved something and who has reflected some good and basic values in the way he has gone about his business. I know that the messages I took from my family as a kid growing up were the right ones—and they have stood by me. In the way I tried to conduct myself as cricketer and captain, I suppose part of it was trying to pass on those messages to my own sons, William and Jack. I would think about such things at times when I was out in the middle, playing cricket. As I have written elsewhere, I believe high-profile sports-people have an obligation to conduct themselves the right way, in the wider interest. But sometimes in the heat of battle I would think of my sons. What was the example I wanted to be setting them? I am keen for William and Jack to play some sport in the years ahead. Whether it will be cricket or not, I don't know. That will be up to them. What I do know is that I would like them to be able to look back and say: 'My old man may not have been the best player around, but he played the game the right way. He played it because it was a game and because he enjoyed it, and he played it fairly and with some respect.' For me, the fact that cricket became my livelihood as well as an enjoyment, was an unexpected bonus.

My penultimate document as a player, the retirement letter conveyed to Denis Rogers, pretty-well said it all for me:

1 February, 1999

Dear Denis,

As someone who is immensely proud to have represented his country at cricket and, importantly, to have had the honour of captaining an extremely successful Australian team for the past five years, this is indeed a most difficult letter to write.

Since the Sydney Test early last month, I have had a good deal of time away from the game to review my position as a player and as the Australian Test captain.

And while I have reaped enormous enjoyment and satisfaction from representing my country and sharing in so many memorable Test series victories, I must admit that some personal doubts have emerged these past few weeks concerning whether I would indeed be serving the best interests of Australian cricket and my own best interests by continuing to make myself available for international selection.

When I was appointed Australian captain in 1994, I vowed that when I eventually retired from Test cricket, hopefully, the standing of the Australian team in international cricket would at least be as high as it was when I assumed the leadership from Allan Border.

As well, on a personal basis, it was always my desire to depart the game with a satisfying individual contribution. I believe both goals have been achieved.

As you and your ACB colleagues and the Australian selectors are aware, I have deliberately refrained from making long-term plans concerning my cricket future these past few years; rather, it has come down to a series-to-series decision influenced largely by my own form and how well I was enjoying the game at the time.

And, in considering my future from 1999 onwards, uppermost in my mind has been a strong desire to spend more time at home with my wife Judi and our two sons, William and Jack.

All factors taken into account, as I advised a few days ago, I have decided to retire from international cricket.

This has been a tough decision, but clearly the right one in my view. I am entirely satisfied I have made the correct decision, and for the right reasons.

At this stage, I would like to continue playing for New South Wales, but this will depend on what decisions I eventually make concerning my future business career.

I would be most grateful if you would please convey to your ACB colleagues and the Australian selectors, and the many other people involved in the custodianship of Australian cricket, my great appreciation for their support and encouragement over the years.

I would like to take this opportunity to record the immense enjoyment I have had from the many enduring friendships I've struck playing the game of cricket, from my days as a youngster at Wagga through to the hallowed Test grounds of the world. I will now have more time to enjoy these friendships.

It has been a great honour to have been selected to play cricket for Australia, to have then been appointed the nation's 39th Test captain and to have been associated with performances on the field that have cemented Australia's position as the world's leading Test-playing nation.

To my successor as Test captain and the players who are chosen for the coming West Indies tour, I wish them the same level of success and satisfaction. I will be with them in spirit all the way.

Yours sincerely,
Mark Taylor

Retirement day finally came around—Tuesday, 2 February 1999—and I was delighted when it dawned . . . and when it was done. I had held the duty of Australian cricket captain in the highest possible esteem in the five years of my tenure. Frankly, the split-captaincy arrangement was a significant factor in my mind as I contemplated the future. For me, being half a captain meant that the job was not what it had been. I knew with great clarity that it was time to go.

On the day that I retired my main emotion was: 'Phew! I'm glad it's done.' I felt quite happy, remarkably free. Never was I close to tears or anything like that. I was delighted in fact—that after having had the honour of a wonderful job for five years I was going because I wanted to. I knew I had given it my best and done as good a job as I could have done. With the announcement it seemed that the weight of the world lifted off my shoulders.

The deed was done at Sydney's ritzy Sheraton on the Park Hotel at noon, on a warm Sydney day. I thought about writing out a set 'going away' speech, but discarded the idea. Better, I felt, just to get up there, say what I was thinking, take any questions the media guys might have, then bid them good luck and farewell. Before the press conference I met Denis Rogers and Malcolm Speed privately. 'Is this final . . . or what?' asked Denis with a smile. I told him it was. 'I don't sit here sad,' I told the gathering. 'I sit here quite happy'. 'How would you like to be remembered?' someone asked me. 'As a guy who loved playing,' I answered. 'I always just tried to go out there to enjoy what I was doing.' I was pressed on the question of the next captain, and boxed carefully. 'It's something I want to stay out of, because there are obviously a lot of good candidates,' I said. I told Channel 9 later that Steve Waugh was entitled to favouritism, but I felt that both he and Shane Warne would both make very good captains. It all went very well, and I was genuinely touched by the round of spontaneous applause that came at the end of the conference at the Sheraton. John Fordham and I were ushered out a side door and into a waiting car to be driven to Channel 9 and an interview with Mike Munro for 'A Current Affair'. And that was it. I was no longer Test captain, or a Test cricketer.

MALCOLM CONN, *Australian*, 3 February 1999: *There were occasions when Mark Taylor's timing at the crease was awful. Yesterday, by announcing his retirement, it was impeccable.*

JOHN FORDHAM: *We would have taken out the entire Sydney press corps if we had 'gunned' the car outside the hotel after the conference.*

As we headed away I turned to Mark and said. 'Well, I've got a bloody former Australian captain in the car!' I asked him how he felt. 'I feel all right, mate,' he said.

There was one final disappointment on my last day. Back home at the Taylors there was a birthday party on for Jack, who had turned four on 31 January. As far as I was concerned, I had completed my media commitments for the day, but a couple of newspaper photographers turned up. I asked them to go, and they did—only to come back under instructions from their editor and proceed to take more photos which turned up in the press the next day. I was dirty about that. I had tried to do everything in a fair and even-handed way for the media on that last day. In the end, they had gone a fair way towards spoiling my afternoon.

On Monday, 10 May, the last domino fell, ending my years as a cricketer. After weeks of wondering and pondering I wrote to NSW Cricket Association chief executive Brian Hughes, and rang coach Steve Small to let them know that my career was completely over—and that I would no longer be available for NSW. It was not an easy call. I had loved my years with the Blues, and enjoyed my share of personal and team success. My hope is that the team that continues on into 1999–2000 and beyond can experience some golden years, and the taste of victory, as I did, in 'the Shield'. Records showed that I played exactly 100 first-class matches for NSW, including 85 Sheffield Shield games and scored 6997 runs, with seventeen centuries and thirty-eight half centuries, at an average of 41.40. My runs tally was six short of Alan Kippax's NSW Shield record and my 132 catches a record for the State. It was now official that the end to my career had come on a misty Hobart day back in mid-March, when the fickle Tasmanian weather had finally denied us the chance of taking outright points and thus handing on the Sheffield Shield wooden spoon to Tassie. David Boon had bowed out on the same day. He got a first-ball duck in his last innings and I was skipper of a NSW team which had won the wooden spoon for the first time. It was not exactly a momentous ending for a couple of old Test mates.

In my retirement letter to Brian Hughes I wrote that I was 'entirely satisfied' it was time for me to go, but added: 'It is emotionally difficult to bring to an end what has been a thoroughly enjoyable and satisfying career in NSW cricket. It has been a real pleasure and honour pulling on the blue cap.'

I retired from all levels of the game because my life had moved on, and had to. As I made my announcement I was off to South Africa, for a series of speaking engagements. Since February I had been doing a lot of those, travelling around the country. My involvement with the Olympic movement was revving up. Herb Elliott had made first contact on that, asking me if I could come on board with the ticket-sales program for Sydney 2000. I was delighted to be involved, although the sight of my face on Sydney's buses (360 of them) as part of the promotion was somewhat daunting. As I told the media, I'd never been to an Olympic Games, but as a sports-mad Australian—and someone who had had the thrill of competing before massive home crowds—I feel it is going to be sensational. Being asked to talk to other Australians about the biggest sporting event in our history is a bonus for me.

I valued my other business associations a great deal too—with Fujitsu, BHP, Puma, Ansett and Sigma Pharmaceuticals, enjoying my dealings with good companies, and good people. In mid-May I took the step that I suppose will seem very logical to many people in and around cricket, and certainly does to me. I joined the Channel 9 commentary team, on a three-year contract. Cricket will still be my game, albeit from the other side of the fence.

So, effectively, it was 'on with the first day of the rest of my life' as the winter of 1999 rolled on, and Australia's one-day team was in England, chasing the World Cup.

Reflecting on it all, as far as the game of cricket goes, I wouldn't be changing too much. The question of over-rates needs some attention, though. I noticed in the recent Australia–West Indies series that the speed of the game had slowed again; every day seemed to be forty to forty-five minutes late. On that score I think there's some merit in Ian Chappell's suggestion of penalising captains when the over-rate falls short. He wasn't talking about monetary fines, but rather warnings, culminating in suspension if the slow cricket continued. It's a big call and, as I'm no longer a captain, it's easy for me to say. But I think the idea has much more merit than the other approach of adding on 'penalty' runs for every over not bowled. That, to me, is tampering with the 'pure' game.

Generally, the game is on a good course. I have been delighted with what virtually amounts to a rebirth of Test cricket—with the subcontinent and its enthusiastic supporters playing a strong part in that. Cricket's balance is good now. In Australia I think that people went from not watching the game at all to watching the one-dayers with its air of excitement, white ball, coloured clothing and all the rest. Now, a lot of people have taken the next step— back to the Tests, and in doing that they have seen some wonderful cricket. As I've mentioned before, the first day of my last Test match—in Sydney—was a great example of just what the Test match arena can offer. The SCG was packed to the rafters with 41,000 people and I reckon they all stayed to the very end. The fans that day saw Mark Waugh get 100, Steve Waugh make 90, Australia score 320 runs in eighty-seven overs—and Darren Gough take his hat-trick right at the end of the afternoon. It was one of the best days of Test cricket you could ever ask for.

The end of my career as a player will enable me to re-focus on other things—and especially on the family, on Jude and the boys, and the new Taylor due in October '99.

With the boys, my first and biggest wish is for them to get a good education. Before sport. I always loved sport, as perhaps they will, and it was (and probably always will be) always a fair chunk of my life—but I plugged away at getting a good education too. I tried to find the balance.

What I don't want to happen is for one or other of the boys to come to me when they're thirteen or fourteen years of age and say: 'Righto, Dad, I'm going to do what you did and play cricket for Australia—so I'm going to put school on the backburner.' At that point I'd be pulling them back into line. Education comes first by a fair space on my priority list—though of course if there is to be sport in their lives as there was in mine, I'll obviously encourage them all the way too, as my Mum and Dad did with me.

If the boys choose cricket, there will be extra pressure on them— no doubt. People will expect a lot from them because they happen to be the sons of a former Australian captain. The reality of that of course is that we're not race horses: just because I happened to display a certain affinity for and talent in a particular sport doesn't mean William and Jack will head in that direction. I'll be happy if they do, because I know they'll be playing a great game.

However, sport is only *part* of life. It can't be any sort of totality of life. There is too much else to do. Yes, I made a living out of sport—but I was the exception, not the rule. Way above anything else, sports are there to enjoy—and to help keep people fit and healthy, and ideally to teach a few valuable lessons about how things work in life, too. Involvement in sport can generate great and enduring friendships—and I consider myself immensely fortunate to have played with and against so many terrific cricketers and fine blokes and to have met so many special people along the way. That'll be roughly the message from me when it comes to the junior Taylors. The rest will be up to them.

When, later, they ask me about my own career in cricket, I'll keep it very simple. I'll just tell them that I had the pleasure and good fortune of playing a wonderful game . . . and that I loved it and respected it, and played it the very best I could.

A SPECIAL PARTNERSHIP

eople who know them well will tell you that Mark and Judi Taylor are a 'team'. They do the family shopping together and at home in the new house they planned and watched grow in Sydney's Gladesville the conversation bounces back and forth—funny, gently mocking at times, but always affectionately respectful. Judi and the boys, William and Jack, are Mark's personal team, providing a backdrop with love and support to the glittering career that 'Dad' built for himself in cricket. To preserve the private spaces she felt necessary for their collective life as a family, Judi several years ago took a conscious step back, leaving cricket, the media and the spotlight to Mark. But in conversations for this book, Judi Taylor illuminated with a new and different light aspects of the Taylor life and career in and around cricket. Then Mark gave his view of their relationship and how it developed.

JUDI TAYLOR: I didn't think there was any chance we were going to hit it off when we first met. He had this checked shirt on . . . the worst shirt I'd ever seen. I thought, 'Oh my God.' Then he made a crack about the plastic champagne glass with spots on it I had in my hand. 'You rude bastard,' I thought. At that point we hadn't even been introduced to each other. Then when we were introduced, the first comment he made was: 'Oh, I won't forget your name; it's the same as my mother's, (we're both Judith Ann). I was sitting there thinking, 'Loser!' Anyhow, despite all that, we hit it off pretty well. Remembering the shirt, for his next birthday I bought him a heap of clothes. The geographic separation made it difficult for us, but when I thought about it in later years I believe that was just preparation for what was to eventually follow—when he was off on tours, and I was back home in Sydney.

Cricket had been part of my life by necessity from my early days at home. My Dad and my two brothers were keen fans, and when I was growing up in the country there were only two channels available and only one TV in the house. Right through summer it would be fixed on the ABC, and the cricket. There were days when I thought, 'Not again!' I watched now and then, but never really followed the game.

I remember early on when Mark and I were going out, he took me to the sixtieth anniversary dinner of Northern District club. Sometime during the night Neil Harvey got up and said: 'This boy [Mark] will play for Australia.' 'Naaaah, him?' I thought. Anyhow, he did, and I found myself as a country girl confronting a different lifestyle, in the midst of Test wives and girlfriends where Country Road and Esprit were worn, and you did your tapestry at the cricket.

We were married on 2 April 1989 at Coffs Harbour, and it rained and rained and rained all week. Flooded, in fact. We had to get married on a Sunday, because Mark vowed there was no way he was going to get married on the Saturday, which was April Fool's Day. The rain never looked like stopping. We had planned to drive up to Noosa for our honeymoon, but we couldn't get past Grafton because of the floods. So we ended up honeymooning at Nautilus Resort at Coffs Harbour, followed by a few days up at Bellingen and Dorrigo. Mark loved the place we stayed at in Bellingen; there was a three-hole golf course next door. Rain is supposed to bring good luck to a wedding. Ten years later, we're still here. Three weeks after we were married, Mark headed off on his first Ashes tour.

Ironically, it was another Ashes tour—his last, in 1997—that provided the most difficult period of my life, probably the only time that I got too involved in Mark's cricket. It was just a matter of trying to keep my head above water, and without the support of good friends like Deb and Al Jansson and Jack and Kate Hughes, Neil and Kay Marks and Tracey Bevan, Michael's wife, I doubt I would have made it through. I will be forever grateful to them. The support they gave me was wonderful. That period when Mark was in South Africa and then in England, before his 100 at Edgbaston . . . I don't think he'll ever know how bad things were, how heavy the media focus on him was.

He rang me one night from South Africa at the time of the Second Test and told me he was thinking of standing down. I was thinking, 'Shit!' but I was trying to keep it calm. 'You must do whatever you want to do,' I said. Mark's mum and dad were away, and I didn't know who to talk to. I rang Neil Marks, and told him what Mark had said. 'No, *no!*' said Neil. 'Get a piece of paper!' He then proceeded to give me all these reasons why Mark shouldn't stand down. 'Ring him back this afternoon with some sort of excuse and just run through these things with him.' I did just that.

Mark went through such a stage that he can't even remember talking to me much about it. I can recall one thing he said to me: 'Jude, I'm just sick of being a passenger in the side.' I kept telling him: 'Mark, you are not a passenger—you are the pilot.'

One of the hardest things concerned the fact that William has been able to read since he was three. Because of that, I got to the stage of not getting the newspapers. But it was on radio and TV all the time. The first thing Will would say to me when he got up in the morning was: 'Did Dad get any runs today?' If the answer was no, which it was for a while during that period, William would say: 'I think we need to send Daddy a fax. I think he's going to be sad today.' The logic of a little boy, and the humour in it, probably helped us get through. I think Mark has told the story of the faxes Will sent him, asking him to get some runs, starting with 102 and gradually descending to the point where he asked me one day: 'Should I ask Dad for maybe 20?' Another time he said to me: 'I wish Dad could bowl.' I told him I thought his Dad probably wished that too at the moment.

I got to the stage where I was frightened to turn on the radio or television. I remember going out with the boys to tea one evening with friends, and driving home, I thought I'd just pick up a score on the car radio. 'Taylor's on 16 . . . and he's looking comfortable,' the commentator said. 'That's it,' I said to the boys. 'We'll turn it off and we won't listen to any more.' As we walked into the house the phone was ringing. It was Jack Hughes. 'Jude, he's out,' he said. 'Go and clean your teeth,' I said to the boys. Just then the phone rang again. 'How many times do I have to tell you to go and clean your teeth!' I snapped. Will just looked at me. 'Mum, when Dad gets out you're not supposed to get angry . . . you're supposed to get sad,' he said. I apologised to him. For William, being older and able to grasp what was going on, that was a really tough time.

Generally the media weren't too bad at that time—they didn't hound us too much or anything like that. But I snapped one day. It happened just at the time that Mark scored his 63 against Derbyshire, giving hope that he had turned the corner at last. It was exactly at the same time that the *Daily Telegraph* came out with the 'HE'S OUT!' front page, suggesting wrongly that Mark was going to stand down from the Test team. John Fordham rang to tell me that the story was going to be on the front page next day, and to ask if I knew anything about it. 'No, I don't,' I told him. The *Telegraph* ran with the story anyway the next morning, even though they had been assured it was wrong. The very next day a couple of *Telegraph* reporters turned up on the doorstep. In England Mark had talked about Will's faxes, and how they had helped get him through. They asked me if I would give them a copy of the latest fax, in which I think Will had drawn a picture of cubbyhouse he said he'd like. I just hit the roof! 'Look, we're just trying to make up for this morning's story by putting this in,' they told me. I sent them away. After that a couple of nasty little digs about the Taylors appeared in one of their anonymous sporting columns—one of them about me and the kids being over-confident about Mark playing in the Tests, and booking our tickets for England a month before the First Test. I never intended to go because I thought Mark would be playing. It was more that I wanted to be there in case he *wasn't*.

By the time the Edgbaston Test came around I was too scared to watch Mark bat. I was in bed on the night of his innings when John Fordham rang. 'Jude, he's on 50 . . . I won't say any more,' he said. Up until then every time John used to say Mark was batting well, he'd get out. So we had a rule that he wasn't going to say that any more. I lay there in the dark for quite a time. Finally, I turned the radio on. Mark was on 89. Between then and his 100 I just lay there, barely moving, willing him on. At 100, I flicked the TV on. It was just the sheerest relief. For hours afterwards, the phone just never stopped ringing. Just everybody rang. And cried. Mark couldn't get through on the phone until about nine o'clock the next morning.

Will could picture his cubbyhouse coming. There had been a bet, you see. Tim Jenkins, son of the cricket photographer Viv Jenkins and a close friend of Mark's from high-school days, had put some money on for me, but as it turned out things had got a bit buggered up. My intention was to back Mark to get a century in the first Test, and I put $20 on at 25/1, or so I thought. With a $500 'win' it looked as if Will had his cubbyhouse. The story hit the media and a couple of days later Tim rang me, a bit apologetically. 'Jude, that's not what I put your money on,' he said. He went on to explain that he'd put the $20 on Mark getting most runs overall in the series. So we have it over Tim now. We can show him the picture of the cubbyhouse that William drew and say, 'Oh, well, here's the cubbyhouse that Will couldn't have.'

After Mark got through England in 1997 I sort of relaxed and tried to think of his career from then on as a bonus, and not to worry too much over whether he got runs from then on, or whether he didn't. What happened in Peshawar in 1998 took us completely by surprise. I watched most of the innings on Foxtel, and spoke to Mark at the end of the first night when he was about 112. 'I'll try to get a few more tomorrow,' he said. I didn't think too much about it; I wasn't even thinking he'd get 150 or 200 or anything like that.

I picked the boys up from school the next afternoon and when we got back, Mark was already on 138. From that point on it just seemed to tick over so quickly—the time flew. Will was tremendously impressed when his Dad got to 200, Will being something of a records man, you see. He had the list of records and he was checking them off. He noted Graham Yallop's record of 268 against Pakistan and said: 'Dad can get that.' I let him stay up much later than usual, but once Mark had got to 269 he dropped off to sleep, on the lounge beside me. Before that he had noted Sir Donald Bradman's 334. 'Who's Bradman?' he asked. At six, this was the first time he had heard of Sir Donald—maybe that's the age for all little Australian boys. 'Dad can get 335,' he said after I had explained. 'Will, that's a long way off,' I said.

William was up early the next morning and I think he was actually a bit disappointed that Mark was 'only' 334 and not 335—and even more so when he found out his Dad was going to declare.

It was a hectic and happy day that followed—yet I don't think anything could ever match the elation that came with Mark's 100 at Edgbaston. The feeling of relief was just amazing. The 334 was nice . . . but somehow just not the same.

I think Mark's decision to retire just felt right for both of us. There was no real sadness or emotion attached to it—because although cricket has always been an important part of life for both of us, it has never been the be-all and end-all. I'm sure that helped us through the bad times. I always tended to think that life begins *after* cricket. Since I had the kids, too, my focus in life has changed. Most of my friends and most of my life as well have been outside cricket. Mark's retirement was a change, but not so much of a loss—and he's been able to become more of a 'hands-on' father.

The boys are both left-handed, like Mark (I'm a right-hander), and I guess they'll both play cricket. When I asked him recently what winter sport he was going to play, William told me that he was a summer sportsboy. It won't be easy for them if they do play serious cricket. They'll have to contend with Mark's shadow. It's happening already. At an Under-8s' game this year when Mark came along the boys on the other side were yelling out 'Yahoo, we've beaten Mark Taylor's side'—even though it's not Mark's side. The team is coached by Greg Miller.

People seem to have this idea that we live this glamorous and completely different lifestyle because of cricket. Well, we don't, although cricket has provided some opportunities to travel, and occasional glamour (I've met people like Elton John and Florence Joyner because of cricket). The truth of it, though, is that we're not ones to go out a lot. A good day would be one spent at home with the kids, with maybe a couple of friends or family around for a barbeque . . . not necessarily living the high life.

Mark and I have always done everything together—shopping for the groceries and clothing and so forth. I still find it very unnerving to have people watching us, or following us, or stopping us all the time, although most people are pretty good and polite. It just gets hard sometimes. Before last Christmas when we went out shopping for the kids, we had people coming up to us and saying: 'Oh, it's nice to see you doing normal things.' I just wonder at times like that how people think we live. I don't even have an ironing lady, let alone someone who goes out and does the Christmas shopping!

Really, we haven't changed that much from when we first met over a plastic champagne glass in Coffs Harbour.

MARK TAYLOR: It wasn't exactly love at first sight when Judi Matthews of Corindi and I met for the first time in 1986. In fact I thought she was a bit stuck-up . . . and she thought I was a smart-arse. Now, she's my wife . . . and best mate. Cricket brought us together—the old Tooheys Cup competition in which NSW Shield players were co-opted to country teams. Apart from being pretty handy in the area of finding a future life's partner, the Tooheys Cup treks taught me plenty. I learnt how to hold my alcohol and how to mingle with all different strata of society. We had to play golf with special guests, answer questions on stage before big crowds, do media interviews, mingle with the crowd at sausage sizzles, coach kids and talk to them about cricket. The trips also put a few more dollars in the pocket of a battling uni student. I loved the Tooheys Cup. I got paid, I had a great time and I learnt some social skills which stood me in good stead in later years. Oh, and I also found a wife . . .

Judi and I met in Coffs Harbour on a blind date during one of those matches. Four of us went out together—Judi, her best friend Evelyn, me and a mate of mine. I think it's fair comment that Jude and I didn't hit it off straightaway. When we were introduced she was nursing a plastic champagne glass, sitting there looking very prim and proper. 'Nice plastic glass!' I said. They were the first words I uttered to the girl who was to be my wife. I doubt they'll go down under the heading: 'Great opening lines'. It was only some time later that Judi told me what she thought at that moment—which was roughly: 'Jeez, you rude bastard.'

Then there was the problem of the shirt I was wearing—a present from my sister Tina. Judi gave it something of a bagging.

Things fortunately got better. We went out to dinner at a seafood place in Coffs Harbour, found out that we got on pretty well after all, and kept in touch subsequently. I was living in Sydney, and Judi was at Northern Rivers College of Advanced Education, Lismore, studying for her Bachelor of Business degree, living at the Benelong Motel and working as a receptionist there to help pay her way through college. The relationship that gradually developed was long-distance—definitely geographically difficult. She was up there, and I was travelling around with NSW, playing Shield cricket. Most of our early relationship was conducted through phone calls and letters.

When we started getting serious I recall catching the bus at Hornsby one night, and travelling twelve hours to Ballina. It was a horror trip; I didn't sleep a wink. By 1988 we were together, travelling to England for the enjoyable few months I had with Greenmount. We got engaged over there. I popped the question after coming home from a game of golf one day. I'd had a bad round on a rainy day and I was hoping Judi wouldn't spoil the day further by saying no. I subsequently rang up Judi's father Arnold and asked: 'Can I have your hand in marriage ... er, I mean your daughter's hand?' We were married on 2 April 1989, at St Augustine's in Coffs Harbour. The champagne was drunk out of proper glasses.

Judi and I were married just at the time that things were changing in relation to family and travel arrangements within the Australian team. Once upon a time of course, the tours were 'boys only', with wives and families waiting back home for long months. Then as society changed and travel became so quick and easy, it was logical that partners and families would be there for at least part of the longer tours. For the 1989 Ashes campaign the rules were pretty strict, driven by skipper Allan Border. The tour was four-and-a-half months long and it was agreed that no wives or partners could join the tour full-scale until after four months—i.e. until the cricketing job at hand was under control. However, the arrangement was that wives and families, of course, could be in England, but staying at different hotels, enabling the team to maintain its full focus. The arrangement worked very well. In 1989 Judi stayed with friends up at Bury and when I had a game off, I'd grab a car and duck away for a few days. It was a good system—better than the '93 tour when the rules were more blurred, and no-one was quite sure whether wives could stay at the team hotel, or not. The lines of communication were a bit shaky.

One of the bonuses of being married to Judi Matthews is that she comes from a beautiful part of the world up on the NSW north coast. Her folks have a pub at a place called Corindi Beach and a banana plantation at Halfway Creek, a beautiful little hideaway. There was a wine bar there once—now it's a fruit shop. For a Sydneysider like me it's a terrific escape to go up there to the beautiful beaches and the fishing, away from the cars and the crowds and the phone. More and more I relish those occasional chances. Working the banana plantation was hard yakka, though. It used to take me days to get over a day of cutting and carrying the bananas, and packing them.

As I said at my welcome-home dinner at the Wentworth Hotel after the Ashes tour of 1997, it's Judi who deserves the greatest praise of all for what she put up with through my career. She was the one stuck at home with the kids—not able to experience the 'highs' when I had some success on tour, and having to wear it when I had the 'lows'. I wouldn't have achieved what I did manage to achieve without her.

I was there for the birth of William and Jack and, oh boy, they were tough times. Judi probably reckons so too. William's birth in '92 was a difficult one. Jude had been struggling and they had a monitor on to keep a check on Williams' heart-rate. It kept going up and down and I kept thinking of all the worst possible scenarios. The entire day of 15 May 1992 was one of the worst of my life. But finally, there was a happy ending, with William's healthy appearance at 12.52 a.m., 16 May. Mother and son were okay . . . father was a bit of a worry. Jack's arrival in 1995 was a little easier, although I nearly fainted. Jude believes I'm getting hot flushes already for the next one. Those two days were far tougher than facing any Curtly Ambrose bouncer. The outcomes were just terrific, though, and I consider myself very fortunate to have two such fine sons.

THE DON *and* OTHER GREATS

I first met Sir Donald Bradman on the golf course at Koo-
yonga, one bright morning in the early '90s. It was a chance
encounter—a few words exchanged on the course, then a
further brief chat in the bar of the clubhouse. It meant a
lot to me. For me, as for all of us in cricket, Sir Donald had
always been and still is on a pedestal—unique and almost god-like.

Not long after that he came to the Adelaide Oval a couple of
nights before a Test match, to meet the Australian team and have a
yarn with us. We had dinner together, just the Test team and Sir
Donald. He shared some of his thoughts on the game—it wasn't a
formal 'speech'—and then we asked him some questions. It was all
pretty relaxed, but probably a bit reminiscent of schooldays, with
players shooting up their hands to ask him about this or that, the
sort of thing that any serious cricket fan would love to ask Sir Donald
Bradman—on batting, Bodyline, his own career and all the rest.

It was terrific. And among the many wise words he volunteered,
one thing has always stuck in my mind, something that I have
repeated now and then in speeches I have made since. It was this
simple truth: 'We are all custodians of the game we play.' It's a wonderful sentiment, of course—but for the greatest cricketer of them

all to share it with the group of young Australian players gathered around him that night made us feel very special indeed. I suppose if any one person could say they 'owned' the game it would be Sir Donald—but here he was, just one of us, sharing the pleasure of being a cricketer. 'While you are in the game,' he said, 'do everything you can to make the game better—because it will go on far longer than you can possibly stay in it. Enjoy your time in it, but remember that the game is always going to be bigger than you, and in time, will inevitably surpass you.' That night represented my first real acquaintances with him.

In 1998, when by a twist of fate I scored 334 against Pakistan to equal Sir Donald's Australian Test record from all those years before, the South Australian Cricket Association suggested a get-together between the pair of us. 'Would you like us to try and arrange that?' they asked me. Would I! Sir Donald was apparently enthusiastic too. So it was that two days before the Adelaide Test against England I got the chance to spend some time with him. It was a daunting experience. I wasn't exactly nervous, but I just wondered whether we were going to be able to converse okay for a couple of hours. I even contemplated writing down some questions I could ask him.

I had it all wrong. When I walked into his house it turned out he had a million questions to ask *me*. He wanted to know all about the bribery business involving Mark Waugh and Shane Warne which had just hit the papers. He wanted to know all about the Pakistani players in 1994, and what had actually gone on. He was interested in all the inside information. Though he was more than ninety years of age and physically frail, he was so sharp and on-the-ball mentally. There seemed nothing going on in the game that he hadn't heard of or, in most cases, knew a good bit about.

We sat there in his lounge room, had a cup of tea and talked cricket, and other things. I asked him about Archie Jackson, whose story has always interested me. It had stuck in my mind that someone at the time had declared that Jackson was going to be every bit as good as Bradman. He told me of Jackson's tuberculosis, and how he had been admitted to a sanitarium and advised that he would need at least two years there to have any chance of survival. But Jackson had come out after six months or so, declaring he couldn't stand being in there any longer and just wanted to play his cricket. He died, at twenty-three, not long afterwards.

I asked him about his golf: 'Do you still play?' 'No, I haven't played for twelve or eighteen months,' he said. I used to marvel at those stories of him still playing in his late eighties—and still beating his age.

That day was a wonderful and unique experience for me. It was also a privilege. Sir Donald is a private man, and I understand that absolutely. Because of the demands on him, I don't believe he had any choice but to cut himself off from public life. I know myself since I made my 334 how much more public pressure there has been on me. Sometimes I think: 'God, I can't take it any more—I want to give some time to my kids now.' I have experienced that ever since the innings in Pakistan—a few months. Sir Donald has lived with it for sixty years or more.

I've heard people criticise him. 'Why wouldn't he come to the Invincibles' dinner?' I've heard it asked. For him it would have been the thin edge of the wedge: to go to that dinner or any other would have inevitably led to more pressure and demands on him to go to other occasions. I have no doubt that a certain point in his life Sir Donald Bradman drew a line and said: 'I want my private life back; I want some life to myself.' And who could deny him that, especially as he moved into the twilight years of his long life?

We had our photo taken together that day at his Adelaide home, and he signed it for me. As I left and we made our farewells, he said to me: 'Best of luck in the game.' Then, he paused: 'No, I'll take that back,' he said. 'You don't need any luck to beat those blokes.' On the morning of the match I passed on the message to the other players. Our coach Geoff Marsh had been a bit wary—his initial inclination was to not to tell them. Coaches worry about things like complacency. But I convinced him: 'They're a good enough team to handle a comment like that,' I said. 'What's more, I agree with Sir Donald's sentiments.'

Not long after I had scored my 334, I received a letter from Sir Donald. It's one of my most cherished keepsakes. Essentially he just thanked me for not going past his score. He repeated the sentiment on the day we met. 'Thank you for declaring when you did,' he said. I just told him it was an honour for me to have ended up on the same score—and that with a 600-run total, it had been well and truly time to declare.

'No, you did a great thing for me,' said Sir Donald. 'And thank you for it.'

My life has changed since those remarkable golden hours when I scored my 334. I don't think *I've* changed, but public perception towards me has. I now have a sense of the difficulties confronted by a Sir Donald Bradman, or a Kieren Perkins. Going out to do the simplest thing—a night at the movies, a quiet meal in a restaurant—takes on new dimensions. People stop me to have a chat or to get me to sign something. Most often it's nice, good-natured stuff and I find it hard to say no, even though my inclination is to say: 'Look, I'm sorry, but I'm just having a quiet night out with my family.' But to do that would make me seem big-headed or arrogant. To say I don't care about cricket fans and other people is a million miles from the truth. But I also care about the people I go out with. It's difficult. One result is that I probably don't go out to do the 'normal things' as much as I used to.

I have always enjoyed catching up with the game's past heroes, as I'm sure all the current players do. Sir Donald's idea of 'custodianship'—of the baton being passed on from one generation to another down the years—is a very compelling one. Just as I said about Prime Minister John Howard in a speech in 1997, I am a cricket 'tragic'. I just love the game. People say to me: 'You must get sick of talking about cricket.' Well, I don't. My only dislike really is being *lectured to* about cricket. I have been just so lucky to be able to sit here working on this book and say that I played 100 Test matches for Australia. I have loved cricket from almost as far back as I can remember, although in my early days the thought that I might one day play Test cricket for Australia never even crossed my mind.

The fact that cricket and my place in it have linked me with past heroes adds to my feeling for the game. I can remember my Dad talking about 'Davo' (Alan Davidson) when I was a kid. Now Davo is a mate of mine, and has been for a long time—and I love listening to him talk about cricket. The same with Richie Benaud and Ian Chappell and Rod Marsh. I get to play golf with them, I get to talk cricket with them. Fantastic.

Keith Miller was part of my growing up in cricket. My dad had talked a lot about him, and I had seen black and white footage of him in action. All those years ago I remember Keith coming to a training session for the NSW Under-19s in Melbourne. He was brilliant.

A year or two back, I wrote him a letter inviting him to an Australian team dinner, before a Test in Sydney. I also enlisted the aid of Ian Chappell, who I knew got on well with Keith. 'Chappelli' said he would be delighted to bring him along, if Keith agreed to come. In my letter I said to him: 'Keith, we'd really love to have you along; most of the guys in the team don't know you, but they'd all love to get the chance to spend some time in your company.' He wrote back, politely and apologetically declining. He didn't get around much any more, he said. I was disappointed, although of course I understood. The word 'legend' is over-used, but Keith Miller is one for sure: a great cricketer—batsman, bowler, fieldsman—and such a dashing figure off the cricket field. I feel privileged to have had the chance to talk to him a few times, and I really regretted some of the other players wouldn't get the opportunity that we hoped to set up that night in Sydney, but Keith hasn't been in the best of health in recent years.

In an early scrapbook kept by my father is a column by Bill 'Tiger' O'Reilly, predicting that I had a big future in the game. 'This young man from Wagga has already made a tremendous entry to first-class cricket,' he wrote in March 1986. In the same scrapbook is a serviette signed by the famous old time player 'Stork' Hendry and given to my parents at a dinner in 1986. It reads: 'I have been very impressed with your son's performances and know that he will always be at the top.' Strange how some prophecies work out.

I never met Bill O'Reilly—even though he was up there in the press box at matches in which I played. Bill never went to dressing rooms. And in those earlier days there was a theory abroad in the game that you didn't want to go anywhere near the media anyway, because they were all bastards. Because that feeling existed and because Bill O'Reilly was on the 'other side of the fence' I never got to talk to him. I regret that today. And the wheel has now turned; I'm part of the fourth estate—a commentator myself.

MARK TAYLOR'S WORLD *and* AUSTRALIAN XIs 1989–1999

I ncreasingly in the last year of my career, people asked me my opinion on the 'best' players, the 'best' teams of my time. In sport, such things are always great talking points, triggering endless debate. Most often, I nudged such questions away—preferring to wait until the end when there was a little distance between me and the game, a chance to step back and offer an objective assessment. That time has now come—and from long preliminary lists, and not without considerable difficulty, I have come up with the best World team and the best Australian team of my decade in international cricket. Taking a deep breath, here goes:

MARK TAYLOR'S WORLD XI, 1989–1999
(excluding Australians)

Gordon Greenidge
Desmond Haynes
Brian Lara
Sachin Tendulkar
Viv Richards
Martin Crowe

Jeff Dujon
Wasim Akram
Malcolm Marshall
Anil Kumble
Curtly Ambrose
Saeed Anwar (12th man)

This is a team on entertainment value, and rich in talent—with many champion and near-champion players missing the 'cut'. For example, I have left out the three top wicket-takers in Test cricket history—Sir Richard Hadlee, Kapil Dev and Courtney Walsh, although all were obviously strong contenders. I picked the players who made the greatest impression on me over the years. And what a team it is!

My belief in 'combination' when it comes to opening batsmen back the selection of Gordon Greenidge and Desmond Haynes—although Saeed Anwar could be rated unlucky, and would have been in if I had gone for a left-right balance. Brian Lara and Sachin Tendulkar, who you could juggle either way at 3 and 4, pick themselves—ranking as the two most destructive batsmen of my time. It was with some doubts that I picked Viv Richards—and he would logically be captain of the side. I didn't really see the best of Viv, although I played against him until 1991. But even in his late years he was still the king; he still had an aura about him when he walked out to bat. At 6 I picked Martin Crowe, the best of the Kiwi batsmen by a mile. Richard Hadlee could perhaps be rated unlucky; he was still bowling well when I came on the scene, but probably not *quite* as well as in earlier seasons. The three fast bowlers picked provide a beautiful balance: Akram, left arm quick; Marshall, right arm swinging quick; Ambrose, straight up and down, and lethal. There were so many to choose from: Donald, Malcolm, Dev, Hadlee, Walsh . . .

Kumble got my nod as the team's spinner with his bouncy leg-spin, but it was almost a toss-up. Mushtaq Ahmed has really improved—and especially so after a quiet talk with Shane Warne which led to 'Mushy' cultivating a much more dangerous and sharp-turning 'stock' leg-spinner. The West Indies' Dujon was the best overseas 'keeper' of my time.

It's a side that would win a game or two, I reckon. You will note that there are no English players, a commentary on the last decade I suppose. Jack Russell though is among my four 'unlucky' players, very close to Dujon, and closest to selection of the Englishmen (the other three on my unlucky list: Hadlee, Walsh and Richie Richardson). The batting is tremendously strong, all the way down. Even Curtly, who would bat 11, continues to tell me that he used to open the batting in younger days. Probably the only quality the batting line-up doesn't have is that really solid-type player midstream, apart from Desmond Haynes. It's a batting line-up of tremendous dash. The entertainment value of such a side would never be in question.

MARK TAYLOR'S AUSTRALIAN XI, 1989–1999

Michael Slater
Mark Taylor
David Boon
Allan Border
Mark Waugh
Steve Waugh
Ian Healy
Shane Warne
Merv Hughes
Craig McDermott
Glenn McGrath
Tim May (12th man)

This was a simpler task, with a much smaller pool of players to pick from. But not easy. The two stand-out unlucky players in my view were Paul Reiffel and Dean Jones, fine contributors to the Australian cause during the decade. I put myself in alongside Michael

Slater as opener—one reason being that I would relish the thought of playing again with such a side, and would hate to miss the chance. I was rated good enough to be an Australian opener for the 10 years, so perhaps logic and history can overcome a sense of modesty. Michael Slater, such a dasher, gets my nod over the very different style of Geoff Marsh at the top of the innings. I think from there down the batting top order there is no cause for argument: Boon, Border, M. Waugh, S. Waugh, Healy, Warne.

Glenn McGrath, now one of the world's premier fast bowlers, if not *the* premier fast bowler, picks himself—to open the bowling with Craig McDermott, such a great strike force for Australia over the years. Merv Hughes is *essential* of course—and not just for his entertainment value on tour. Merv was a truly tremendous competitor. I'd have Tim May at 12th man to offer some variety, in case we wanted to play two spinners. To bolster the bowling I'd be going back to Steve Waugh of the earlier '90s when he was more of an all-rounder, to AB—and to Mark Waugh to bowl a few offies if May wasn't in the side.

It is quite a team. I know that as the years pass I will feel increasing pride and pleasure that I got to play with such men.

CAREER STATISTICS

MARK ANTHONY TAYLOR

b. 27 October 1964, Leeton, NSW

Left-hand batsman, right-arm bowler

CAREER IN FIRST-CLASS CRICKET

Debut: 25–28 October 1985
New South Wales v. Tasmania, TCA Ground, Hobart, scoring 12 and 56*

Last match: 11–14 March 1999
New South Wales v. Tasmania, Bellerive Oval, Hobart, scoring 1

BATTING AND FIELDING

season	venue	mat	inn	n.o.	runs	high	100	50	average	catches
1985–86		12	20	1	937	118	2	5	49.31	16
1986	Zimbabwe	2	4	–	46	23	–	–	11.5	2
1986–87		11	20	1	765	186	1	4	40.26	10
1987	Zimbabwe	2	3	–	71	44	–	–	23.66	–
1987–88		10	18	–	459	144	1	2	25.5	16
1988–89		14	26	1	1241	152*	3	7	49.64	22
1989	England	17	30	1	1669	219	3	10	57.55	23
1989–90		12	21	1	1403	199	7	5	70.15	15
1990	New Zealand	1	2	–	9	5	–	–	4.5	2
1990–91		8	14	1	495	183	1	3	38.07	13
1991	West Indies	10	14	–	777	144	3	5	55.5	6
1991	Zimbabwe	2	3	1	86	41	–	–	43	6
1991–92		14	24	1	925	158	2	7	40.21	25
1992	Sri Lanka	4	7	–	161	43	–	–	23	2
1992–93		8	15	1	530	102	2	1	37.85	8
1993	New Zealand	4	6	–	193	82	–	2	32.16	12
1993	England	15	25	2	972	124	3	4	42.26	25
1993–94		10	16	1	763	170	2	4	50.86	15
1994	South Africa	5	10	–	373	75	–	4	37.3	4
1994	Pakistan	4	7	1	111	69	–	1	18.5	4
1994–95		8	15	–	751	150	2	4	50.06	12
1995	West Indies	7	10	1	222	62	–	2	24.66	11
1995	England	1	1	–	61	61	–	1	61	–
1995–96		11	20	1	931	126	2	5	49	24
1996	India	2	4	–	125	41	–	–	31.25	3
1996–97		8	15	–	252	53	–	1	16.8	13
1997	South Africa	5	8	–	186	85	–	1	23.25	3
1997	England	12	19	–	680	129	2	4	35.78	8
1997–98		13	21	2	1021	169*	3	8	53.73	26
1998	India	5	9	1	252	102*	1	1	31.5	6
1998	Pakistan	5	9	2	609	334*	1	3	87	6
1998–99		11	19	–	339	61	–	3	17.84	12
Total		**253**	**435**	**20**	**17415**	**334***	**41**	**97**	**41.96**	**350**

*Note: * indicates 'not out' in this statistics section*

BOWLING

season		overs	runs	wickets	details of wickets
1986–87		3	1	–	
1991–92		2	1	–	
1992–93		3	9	–	
1993	New Zealand	4	15	–	
1993	England	9	31	1	R.P. Davis (Kent), bowled analysis 1–0–4–1
1994	Pakistan	3	11	1	Rashid Latif (Pak.), c Bevan analysis 3–1–11–1
1998	India	1	9		
Total		**25**	**77**	**2**	

Note: All overs were 6-ball

BATTING BY GROUND IN AUSTRALIA

	mat	inn	n.o.	runs	high	100	50	average
TCA Ground, Hobart (1985–86)	2	3	1	90	56*	–	1	45
Newcastle Sports Ground (1985–86)	10	17	–	663	150	1	3	39
Sydney Cricket Ground (1985–86)	49	83	3	3517	186	11	14	43.96
Melbourne Cricket Ground (1985–86)	17	33	1	1273	170	4	6	39.78
WACA Ground, Perth (1985–86)	19	33	2	1170	152*	3	7	37.74
Adelaide Oval (1985–86)	20	37	1	1697	199	4	11	47.14
Brisbane Cricket Ground (1985–86)	19	34	2	1511	164	3	11	47.22
Junction Oval, St Kilda (1986–87)	1	2	–	29	27	–	–	14.5
Devonport Oval (1987–88)	2	3	–	82	72	–	1	27.33
Manuka Oval, Canberra (1989–90)	1	2	–	81	53	–	1	40.5
Bellerive Oval, Hobart (1989–90)	7	12	1	543	123	2	2	49.36
Oakes Oval, Lismore (1991–92)	1	1	–	15	15	–	–	15
Bankstown Oval (1996–97)	1	2	–	68	53	–	1	34
North Sydney Oval (1997–98)	1	2	–	73	50	–	1	36.5
Total	**150**	**264**	**11**	**10812**	**199**	**28**	**59**	**42.73**

Notes: 1. Season in brackets indicates when he first played first-class cricket there
2. Brisbane Cricket Ground is traditionally referred to as 'Woolloongabba'

BATTING BY GROUND IN ENGLAND AND WALES

	mat	inn	n.o.	runs	high	100	50	average
New Road, Worcester	2	4	–	96	40	–	–	24
Athletic Ground, Taunton	2	4	1	173	97	–	2	57.66
Lord's	5	7	–	287	111	1	1	41
Edgbaston, Birmingham	4	8	–	350	129	1	2	43.75
County Ground, Derby	2	4	–	101	63	–	1	25.25
Headingley, Leeds	3	4	–	223	136	1	1	55.75
County Ground, Northampton	1	2	–	97	69	–	1	48.5
County Ground, Southampton	3	5	–	266	109	1	–	53.2
Ashley Down, Bristol	3	4	–	183	141	1	–	45.75
Old Trafford, Manchester	4	8	2	387	124	2	1	64.5
Trent Bridge, Nottingham	4	7	–	459	219	1	1	65.57
Grace Road, Leicester	2	3	–	128	70	–	2	42.66
St Lawrence, Canterbury	2	2	–	92	78	–	1	46
Kennington Oval	5	9	–	401	80	–	4	44.55
The Parks, Oxford	1	1	–	57	57	–	1	57
Durham University	1	2	–	11	10	–	–	5.5
Sophia Gardens, Cardiff	1	1	–	71	71	–	1	71
Total	**45**	**75**	**3**	**3382**	**219**	**8**	**19**	**46.97**

BATTING BY COUNTRY

	mat	inn	n.o.	runs	high	100	50	average
Australia	150	264	11	10812	199	28	59	42.73
Zimbabwe	6	10	1	203	44	–	–	22.55
England and Wales	45	75	3	3382	219	8	19	46.97
New Zealand	5	8	–	202	82	–	2	25.25
West Indies	17	24	1	999	144	3	7	43.43
Sri Lanka	4	7	–	161	43	–	–	23
South Africa	10	18	–	559	85	–	5	31.05
Pakistan	9	16	3	720	334*	1	4	55.38
India	7	13	1	377	102*	1	1	31.41

CENTURIES

1985–86	Sydney	118	New South Wales v. South Australia
	Adelaide	100	New South Wales v. South Australia
1986–87	Sydney	186	New South Wales v. South Australia
1987–88	Sydney	144	New South Wales v. Tasmania
1988–89	Perth	107	New South Wales v. Western Australia[1]
	Perth	152*	New South Wales v. Western Australia[2]
	Sydney	132	New South Wales v. Queensland
1989	Leeds	136	Australia v. England
	Bristol	141	Australians v. Gloucestershire
	Nottingham	219	Australia v. England
1989–90	Adelaide	199	New South Wales v. South Australia
	Brisbane	164	Australia v. Sri Lanka
	Hobart (Bell)	108	Australia v. Sri Lanka
	Melbourne	101	Australia v. Pakistan
	Sydney	101*	Australia v. Pakistan
	Sydney	127	New South Wales v. Queensland[1]
	Sydney	100	New South Wales v. Queensland[2]
1990–91	Sydney	183	New South Wales v. Tasmania
1991	Bassetterre	101	Australians v. WICBC President's XI
	Kingstown	122	Australians v. West Indies Under-23 XI
	St John's	144	Australia v. West Indies
1991–92	Adelaide	100	Australia v. India
	Melbourne	158	New South Wales v. Victoria
1992–93	Sydney	102	New South Wales v. Victoria
	Sydney	101	New South Wales v. West Indians
1993	Manchester	124	Australia v. England
	Lord's	111	Australia v. England
	Manchester	122	Australians v. Lancashire
1993–94	Perth	142*	Australia v. New Zealand
	Melbourne	170	Australia v. South Africa
1994–95	Newcastle	150	New South Wales v. England
	Sydney	113	Australia v. England
1995–96	Melbourne	126	New South Wales v. Victoria
	Hobart (Bell)	123	Australia v. Pakistan
1997	Birmingham	129	Australia v. England
	Southampton	109	Australians v. Hampshire
1997–98	Brisbane	124	New South Wales v. Queensland

	Brisbane	112	Australia v. New Zealand
	Adelaide	169*	Australia v. South Africa
1998	Bangalore	102*	Australia v. India
1998	Peshawar	334*	Australia v. Pakistan

Notes: 1. First innings
  2. Second innings

BATTING FOR NEW SOUTH WALES

opponent	mat	inn	n.o.	runs	high	100	50	average
Tasmania	16	24	1	906	183	2	5	39.39
Victoria	18	34	–	1177	158	3	5	34.61
Western Australia	15	27	1	1032	152*	2	7	39.69
South Australia	16	27	–	1469	199	4	8	54.4
Queensland	20	35	1	1506	132	4	9	44.29
New Zealanders	3	5	–	107	30	–	–	21.4
Zimbabwe	4	7	–	117	44	–	–	16.71
England	2	4	–	232	150	1	–	58
West Indians	2	3	–	232	101	1	1	77.33
Pakistanis	1	2	–	62	62	–	1	31
Sri Lankans	1	2	–	81	53	–	1	40.5
Indians	1	1	–	15	15	–	–	15
Surrey	1	1	–	61	61	–	1	61
Sub-totals:								
Sheffield Shield	85	147	3	6090	199	15	34	42.29
Overseas teams	15	25	–	907	150	2	4	36.28
Total	**100**	**172**	**3**	**6997**	**199**	**17**	**38**	**41.40**

Note: The four matches against Zimbabwe (1986 and 1987) were in Harare and the match against Surrey (1995) was at The Oval. All other matches for New South Wales were in Australia.

BATTING FOR AUSTRALIAN TEAMS (EXCEPT TEST MATCHES)

opponent	mat	inn	n.o.	runs	high	100	50	average
English teams	26	43	2	1737	141	3	11	42.36
West Indian teams	8	8	–	405	122	2	2	50.62
Zimbabwe	2	3	1	86	41	–	–	43
Sri L. Board Pres XI	1	1	–	13	13	–	–	13
NZ Board XI	1	2	–	45	45	–	–	22.5
South African teams	5	9	–	382	85	–	4	42.44
Pakistani teams	3	6	1	101	63*	–	1	20.2
Indian teams	3	5	–	124	57	–	1	24.8
Total	**49**	**77**	**4**	**2893**	**141**	**5**	**19**	**39.63**

Note: Each of these matches was overseas: he never played in tour matches in Australia for Australian XI or Australia A.

SUMMARY OF BATTING IN FIRST-CLASS CRICKET

	mat	inn	n.o.	runs	high	100	50	average
New South Wales: Sheffield Shield	85	147	3	6090	199	15	34	42.49
New South Wales: v. overseas teams	15	25	–	907	150	2	4	36.28
Test matches	104	186	13	7525	334*	19	40	43.49
Australian teams on tour	49	77	4	2893	141	5	19	39.63
Total	**253**	**435**	**20**	**17415**	**334***	**41**	**97**	**41.96**

CAPTAINCY IN FIRST-CLASS CRICKET

	matches	wins	draws	losses
New South Wales: Sheffield Shield	29	11	11	7
New South Wales: v. overseas teams	5	2	2	1
Test matches	50	26	11	13
Australian teams on tour	27	13	11	3
Total	**111**	**52**	**35**	**24**

CAREER IN INTERSTATE LIMITED-OVERS COMPETITIONS

Debut: 5 December, 1985
New South Wales v. Western Australia, Sydney, scoring 13

Last match: 28 February, 1999
New South Wales v. Victoria, Melbourne, scoring 0

BATTING AND FIELDING

season	mat	inn	n.o.	runs	high	50	average	catches
1985–86	3	3	–	83	59	1	27.66	2
1986–87	2	2	–	30	25	–	15	2
1987–88	2	2	–	32	30	–	16	–
1988–89	3	3	–	119	61	1	39.66	3
1989–90	–							
1990–91	4	4	–	51	37	–	12.75	2
1991–92	4	4	–	169	79	2	42.25	2
1992–93	4	4	–	233	84	3	58.25	2
1993–94	2	2	–	73	55	1	36.5	2
1994–95	–							
1995–96	3	3	–	125	70	1	41.66	2
1996–97	–							
1997–98	5	5	–	185	70	2	37	2
1998–99	6	6	–	118	59	1	18.66	5
Total	**38**	**38**	**–**	**1218**	**84**	**12**	**32.05**	**24**

Highest score: 84 v. Western Australia, Perth, 1992–93

Bowling: 2 overs, taking 0–3, v. Victoria, North Sydney, 1991–92.

Note: M.G. Bevan is the only player to score more runs in these competitions for New South Wales, 1274 runs in 33 matches at an average of 60.66.

Captaincy

*Captain in 20 limited-over interstate competition matches,
1992–93 to 1998–99: 15 wins, 4 losses, 1 no result.*

CAREER IN TEST CRICKET

*Debut: 26–30 January 1989
v. West Indies (4th Test), Sydney, scoring 25 and 3*

*Last match: 2–5 January 1999
v. England (5th Test), Sydney, scoring 2 and 2*

BATTING AND FIELDING

season	versus	tests	inn	n.o.	runs	high	100	50	average	catches
1988–89	West Indies	2	4	–	67	36	–	–	16.75	1
1989	England (A)	6	11	1	839	219	2	5	83.9	5
1989–90	New Zealand	1	1	–	9	9	–	–	9	1
1989–90	Sri Lanka	2	4	–	304	164	2	–	76	3
1989–90	Pakistan	3	5	1	390	101*	2	3	97.5	8
1990	New Zealand (A)	1	2	–	9	5	–	–	4.5	2
1990–91	England	5	10	1	213	67*	–	2	23.66	8
1991	West Indies (A)	5	9	–	441	144	1	4	49	3
1991–92	India	5	10	1	422	100	1	3	46.88	7
1992	Sri Lanka (A)	3	6	–	148	43	–	–	24.66	1
1992–93	West Indies[1]	4	8	1	170	46*	–	–	24.28	5
1993	New Zealand (A)	3	4	–	148	82	–	2	37	7
1993	England (A)	6	10	–	428	124	2	1	42.8	11
1993–94	New Zealand	3	4	1	286	142*	1	2	95.33	5
1993–94	South Africa	3	5	–	304	170	1	1	60.8	4
1994	South Africa (A)[2]	2	4	–	97	70	–	1	24.25	2
1994	Pakistan (A)	3	5	1	106	69	–	1	26.5	3
1994–95	England	5	10	–	471	113	1	4	47.1	7
1995	West Indies (A)	4	7	1	153	55	–	1	25.5	10
1995–96	Pakistan	3	5	–	338	123	1	2	67.6	5
1995–96	Sri Lanka	3	5	1	159	96	–	1	39.75	7
1996	India (A)	1	2	–	64	37	–	–	32	–

season	versus	tests	inn	n.o.	runs	high	100	50	average	catches
1996–97	West Indies	5	9	–	153	43	–	–	17	9
1997	South Africa (A)	3	5	–	80	38	–	–	16	3
1997	England (A)	6	10	–	317	129	1	1	31.7	6
1997–98	New Zealand	3	5	1	214	112	1	1	53.5	10
1997–98	South Africa	3	5	1	265	169*	1	1	66.25	8
1998	India (A)	3	6	1	189	102*	1	–	37.8	3
1998	Pakistan (A)	3	5	1	513	334*	1	2	128.25	4
1998–99	England	5	10	–	228	61	–	2	22.8	9
Total		**104**	**186**	**13**	**7525**	**334***	**19**	**40**	**43.49**	**157**

Notes: (A) indicates series played away from Australia
[1] Dropped from 5th Test
[2] Missed 1st Test due to illness

CENTURIES

				Test no.
1989	v. England[1]	136	Leeds (1st Test, 1st innings)	3
		219	Nottingham (5th Test, only innings)	7
1989–90	v. Sri Lanka[1]	164	Brisbane (1st Test, 2nd innings)	10
		108	Hobart, Bellerive (2nd Test, 2nd innings)	11
	v. Pakistan[1]	101	Melbourne (1st Test, 2nd innings)	12
		101*	Sydney (3rd Test, only innings)	14
1991	v. West Indies	144	Antigua, St John's (5th Test, 2nd innings)	25
1991–92	v. India	100	Adelaide (4th Test, 2nd innings)	29
1993	v. England	124	Manchester (1st Test, 1st innings)	41
		111	Lord's (2nd Test, only innings)	42
1993–94	v. New Zealand	142	Perth (1st Test, 2nd innings)	47
	v. South Africa[1] [2]	170	Melbourne (1st Test, only innings)	50
1994–95	v. England	113	Sydney (3rd Test, 2nd innings)	60
1995–96	v. Pakistan	123	Hobart, Bellerive (2nd Test, 2nd innings)	68
1997	v. England	129	Birmingham (1st Test, 2nd innings)	82
1997–98	v. New Zealand	112	Brisbane (1st Test, 1st innings)	88
	v. South Africa	169*	Adelaide (3rd Test, 1st innings)	93
1998	v. India	102*	Bangalore (3rd Test, 2nd innings)	96
1998	v. Pakistan	334*	Peshawar (2nd Test, 1st innings)	98

Notes: [1] indicates century in First Test against that country
[2] Australia's first century v. South Africa since 1966–67.

The highest innings compared:

score	min	balls faced	fours	sixes	how out	team total	result
334*	720	564	32	1	not out	599 (4 wkts, d)	draw
219	554	461	23	–	st Russell b Cook	602 (6 wkts, d)	win
170	495	349	12	–	b Symcox	342 (7 wkts, d)	draw
169*	524	376	21	–	not out	350	draw
164	425	334	17	2	lbw b Ramanayake	375 (6 wkts)	draw

BOWLING

1993 v. New Zealand, Wellington (2nd Test, 2nd innings)	4–2–15–0
1994 v. Pakistan, Rawalpindi (2nd Test, 2nd innings)	3–1–11–1

BATTING AND FIELDING BY OPPONENT

opponent	Tests	inn	n.o.	runs	high	100	50	average	catches
West Indies	20	37	2	984	144	1	5	28.11	28
England	33	61	2	2496	219	6	15	42.3	46
New Zealand	11	16	2	666	142*	2	5	47.57	25
Sri Lanka	8	15	1	611	164	2	1	43.64	11
Pakistan	12	20	3	1347	334*	4	8	79.23	20
India	9	18	2	675	102*	2	3	42.18	10
South Africa	11	19	1	746	170	2	3	41.44	17
Total	**104**	**186**	**13**	**7525**	**334***	**19**	**40**	**43.49**	**157**

BATTING AND FIELDING IN AUSTRALIA, BY GROUND

ground	Tests	inn	n.o.	runs	high	100	50	average	catches
Sydney	11	20	2	676	113	2	2	37.55	18
Adelaide	11	21	1	811	169*	2	5	40.55	15
Perth	9	15	1	490	142*	1	4	35	20
Brisbane	10	18	2	912	164	2	6	57	14
Hobart (Bell)	4	7	1	405	123	2	1	67.5	8
Melbourne	10	19	1	699	170	2	4	38.83	22
Total	**55**	**100**	**8**	**3993**	**170**	**11**	**22**	**43.40**	**97**

BATTING AND FIELDING OVERSEAS

opponent	Tests	inn	n.o.	runs	high	100	50	average	catches
England	18	31	1	1584	219	5	7	52.8	22
New Zealand	4	6	–	157	82	–	2	26.16	9
West Indies	9	16	1	594	144	1	5	39.6	13
Sri Lanka	3	6	–	148	43	–	–	24.66	1
South Africa	5	9	–	177	70	–	1	19.66	5
Pakistan	6	10	2	619	334*	1	3	77.37	7
India	4	8	1	253	102*	1	–	36.14	3
Total	**49**	**86**	**5**	**3532**	**334***	**8**	**18**	**43.60**	**60**

BATTING, BY INNINGS

	innings	n.o.	runs	high	100	50	average
First innings	104	3	4384	334*	9	27	43.4
Second innings	82	10	3141	164	10	13	43.62

BATTING, BY OPENING PARTNER

	innings	n.o.	runs	high	100	50	average
G.R. Marsh	48	3	2262	219	5	17	50.26
D.C. Boon	17	1	631	164	2	2	39.43
M.R.J. Veletta	1	1	101	101*	1	–	–
W.N. Phillips	2	–	18	16	–	–	9
T.M. Moody	6	–	148	43	–	–	24.66
M.J. Slater	78	6	3336	334*	8	18	46.33
M.T.G. Elliott	23	1	852	169*	3	2	38.72
M.L. Hayden	10	–	111	38	–	–	11.1
M.E. Waugh	1	1	66	66*	–	1	–

Notes: 1. Every Test innings was as an opening batsman: this table summarises performances with each opening partner: i.e. he opened the batting with G.R.Marsh in 48 innings, and he scored 2262 runs in those innings. This table does not show opening partnerships, which are shown in a separate table.

2. Summary of opening partners:

	Left- or right-handed batsman	State	Tests as opening partner	from–to
G.R. Marsh	Right	WA	25	1988–89 v. W. Ind.—1991–92 v. Ind.
D.C. Boon	Right	Tas	10	1989–90 v. N.Z.—1993 v. N.Z.
M.R.J. Veletta	Right	WA	1	1989–90 v. Pak.
W.N. Phillips	Right	Vic	1	1991–92 v. Ind.
T.M. Moody	Right	WA	3	1992 v. Sri L.
M.J. Slater	Right	NSW	44	1993 v. Eng.—1998–99 v. Eng.
M.T.G. Elliott	Left	Vic	13½	1996–97 v. W. Ind.—1997–98 v. S. Af.
M.L. Hayden	Left	Qld	6	1996–97 v. W. Ind.—1997 v. S. Af.
M.E. Waugh	Right	NSW	½	1997–98 v. N.Z.

On only one occasion was the second innings opening partner different from the first innings: in 1997-98 v. New Zealand (Hobart, 3rd Test) M.T.G. Elliott opened the batting in the first innings, and M.E. Waugh opened the batting in the second, hence the '½ test' each in the above table.

BATTING, AT 10-TEST INTERVALS

Tests		inn	n.o.	runs	high	100	50	average
After 10th	1989–90 v. Sri L., Bris	18	1	1088	219	3	5	64
After 20th	1990–91 v. Eng., Perth	37	3	1831	219	6	10	53.85
After 30th	1991–92 v. India, Perth	56	4	2694	219	8	17	51.8
After 40th	1993 v. N.Z., Auckland	74	5	3160	219	8	19	45.79
After 50th	1993–94 v. S. Af., Melb	89	6	4044	219	12	22	48.72
After 60th	1994–95 v. Eng., Syd	108	7	4688	219	13	27	46.41
After 70th	1995–96 v. Sri L. Perth	125	8	5439	219	14	33	46.48
After 80th	1997 v. S. Af., Port E	143	9	5756	219	14	33	42.95
After 90th	1997–98 v. N.Z., Hob	160	10	6330	219	16	35	42.2
After 100th	1998–99 v. Eng., Bris	178	13	7343	334*	19	38	44.5

HOW OUT, BY OPPONENT

opponent	bowled	caught behind	c&b	other caught	lbw	stumped	run out	total
West Indies	5	9	1	12	5	–	3	35
England	6	10	3	22	10	4	4	59
New Zealand	2	–	–	6	4	1	1	14

opponent	bowled	caught behind	c&b	other caught	lbw	stumped	run out	total
Sri Lanka	2	3	–	5	4	–	–	14
Pakistan	4	3	1	6	2	1	–	17
India	1	3	–	7	3	1	1	16
South Africa	6	7	–	2	3	–	–	18
Total	**26**	**35**	**5**	**60**	**31**	**7**	**9**	**173**

HOW OUT, BY BOWLERS OBTAINING WICKET MOST TIMES

opponent	no. of times wicket fell to bowlers	no. of different bowlers	most successful bowlers
West Indies	32	7	9 C.E.L. Ambrose, 7 I.R. Bishop, 6 C.A. Walsh
England	55	24	7 D.E. Malcolm, 6 P.M. Such
New Zealand	13	7	4 D.K. Morrison
Sri Lanka	14	9	(no S.L. bowler took wicket more than twice)
Pakistan	17	9	3 Mushtaq Ahmed, 3 Wasim Akram
India	15	11	3 Kapil Dev
South Africa	18	8	4 A.A. Donald
Total	**164**	**75**	

HIGHEST PARTNERSHIPS

329	first wicket with G.R. Marsh	v. England, Nottingham 1989
279	second wicket with J.L. Langer	v. Pakistan, Peshawar 1998
260	first wicket with M.J. Slater	v. England, Lord's 1993
228	first wicket with M.J. Slater	v. Sri Lanka, Perth 1995–96
221	second wicket with D.C. Boon	v. India, Adelaide 1991–92
208	first wicket with M.J. Slater	v. England, Sydney 1994–95
198	first wicket with M.J. Slater	v. New Zealand, Perth 1993–94
194	second wicket with G.S. Blewett	v. England, Birmingham 1997
176	first wicket with M.J. Slater	v. Pakistan, Rawalpindi 1994

SUMMARY OF CENTURY PARTNERSHIPS (40)

First wicket:	17, as below
Second wicket:	13 (7 with D.C. Boon, 4 with J.L. Langer,
	1 with R.T. Ponting, 1 with G.S. Blewett)
Third wicket:	5 (3 with M.E. Waugh, 2 with A.R. Border)
Fourth wicket:	3 (1 with S.R. Waugh, 1 with A.R. Border,
	1 with M.E. Waugh)
Fifth wicket:	1 (with R.T. Ponting)
Sixth wicket:	1 (with I.A. Healy)

SUMMARY OF OPENING PARTNERSHIPS

	partnerships	undefeated	runs	high	100	50	average
G.R. Marsh	48	2	2061	329	4	10	44.8
D.C. Boon	17	1	605	117*	1	4	37.81
M.R.J. Veletta	1	–	33	33	–	–	33
W.N. Phillips	2	–	37	27	–	–	18.5
T.M. Moody	6	–	117	61	–	1	19.5
M.J. Slater	78	2	3837	260	10	15	50.48
M.T.G. Elliott	23	–	721	133	2	4	31.34
M.L. Hayden	10	–	132	35	–	–	13.2
M.E. Waugh	1	–	14	14	–	–	14
Total	**186**	**5**	**7557**	**329**	**17**	**34**	**41.75**

Note: '' in the context of partnerships indicates an unbroken partnership*

CATCHES TAKEN, BY BOWLER

The 157 catches were taken off 27 different bowlers:

51 S.K. Warne
13 C.J. McDermott, G.D. McGrath
11 M.G. Hughes
 9 P.R. Reiffel
 7 T.M. Alderman
 6 B.A. Reid
 5 D.W. Fleming, M.G. Bevan
 4 T.B. A. May, M.S. Kasprowicz, S.C.G. MacGill

3 T.V. Hohns, M.E. Waugh, S.R. Waugh
2 P.R. Sleep, C.G. Rackemann, M.R. Whitney, B.P. Julian
1 A.R. Border, T.M. Moody, G.D. Campbell, G.R.J. Matthews, J. Angel, G.S. Blewett, S.H. Cook, C.R. Miller.

CATCHES TAKEN, BY BATSMEN CAUGHT MOST OFTEN

The 157 catches were taken from 107 different batsmen. Those caught most often:

5 M.A. Atherton (Eng.), G.P. Thorpe (Eng.)
4 M.D. Crowe (N.Z.), R.A. Smith (Eng.)
3 D.J. Richardson (S. Af.), Wasim Akram (Pak.), Salim Malik (Pak.)

SUMMARY OF CAPTAINCY RESULTS

	Tests	wins	draws	losses	series	series wins
v. Pakistan	9	3	4	2	3	2
v. England	16	9	3	4	3	3
v. West Indies	9	5	1	3	2	2
v. Sri Lanka	3	3	–	–	1	1
v. India	4	1	–	3	2	–
v. South Africa	6	3	2	1	2	2
v. New Zealand	3	2	1	–	1	1
in Australia	30	18	7	5	8	8
overseas	20	8	4	8	6	3

DID THE TEST CAPTAINCY AFFECT INDIVIDUAL PERFORMANCE?

	Tests	inn	n.o.	runs	high	100	50	average	catches
Before becoming captain	54	97	6	4275	219	12	24	46.97	73
As captain	50	89	7	3250	334*	7	16	39.63	84

PLAYERS CAPTAINED (35)

50 M.E. Waugh
49 I.A. Healy

46   S.R. Waugh

42   S.K. Warne

40   G.D. McGrath

31   G.S. Blewett

30   M.J. Slater

23   P.R. Reiffel

22   R.T. Ponting

18   D.C. Boon, M.G. Bevan

17   M.T.G. Elliott

14   M.S. Kasprowicz

13   C.J. McDermott

11   J.L. Langer

10   D.W. Fleming, J.N. Gillespie

 8   S.C.G. MacGill

 6   M.L. Hayden, C.R. Miller

 5   T.B.A. May, B.P. Julian, D.S. Lehmann

 4   G.R. Robertson

 3   J. Angel, A.J. Bichel

 2   P.E. McIntyre, S.H. Cook

 1   P.A. Emery, S.G. Law, G.B. Hogg, S. Young, P. Wilson, A.C. Dale, M.J. Nicholson

---

PLAYERS WHO 'TOP–SCORED' FOR AUSTRALIA DURING THE 50 TESTS

The following players played the highest innings in each match:

13   S.R. Waugh

 8   M.A. Taylor

 5   M.J. Slater

 4   G.S. Blewett, I.A. Healy, M.E. Waugh, M.T.G. Elliott

 3   D.C. Boon

 2   M.G. Bevan

 1   M.L. Hayden, R.T. Ponting, J.L. Langer

The following players obtained the best innings bowling figures in each match:

15   G.D. McGrath

 8   S.K. Warne

 6   P.R. Reiffel

 4   C.J. McDermott, M.S. Kasprowicz, S.C.G. MacGill

 2   M.G. Bevan, J.N. Gillespie, G.R. Robertson

 1   M.E. Waugh, S.H. Cook, D.W. Fleming

CAREER IN LIMITED-OVERS INTERNATIONALS

Debut: 26 December, 1989
v. Sri Lanka, Melbourne, scoring 11

Last match: 24 May, 1997
v. England, The Oval, scoring 11

BATTING AND FIELDING

season	venue	mat	inn	n.o.	runs	high	100	50	average	catches
1989–90	Aust.	9	9	–	294	76	–	2	32.66	5
1990	N.Z.	3	3	–	83	56	–	1	27.66	2
1990	U.A.E.	4	3	–	139	60	–	2	46.33	–
1990–91	Aust.	2	2	–	112	71	–	1	56	1
1991	W. Ind.	2	2	–	8	5	–	–	4	1
1992†	Aust.	2	2	–	13	13	–	–	6.5	–
1992	Sri L.	3	3	–	138	94	–	1	46	1
1992–93	Aust.	10	10	–	286	78	–	2	28.6	8
1993	N.Z.	5	5	–	145	78	–	2	29	–
1993	Eng.	3	3	–	162	79	–	2	54	3
1993–94	Aust.	6	6	–	164	81	–	1	27.33	2
1994	S. Af.	5	5	–	117	63	–	1	23.4	1
1994	U.A.E	3	2	1	79	68*	–	1	79	4
1994	Sri L.	3	3	–	53	41	–	–	17.66	3
1994	Pak.	6	6	–	193	56	–	2	32.16	2
1994–95	Aust.	4	3	–	108	57	–	1	36	1
1995	N.Z.	4	4	–	165	97	–	1	41.25	5
1995	W. Ind.	5	5	–	152	66	–	1	30.4	3
1995–96	Aust.	10	10	–	423	90	–	4	42.3	5
1996†	Ind & Pak	7	7	–	193	74	–	2	27.57	1
1996	Ind.	5	5	–	302	105	1	1	60.4	2
1996–97	Aust.	8	8	–	143	29	–	–	17.87	6
1997	S. Af.	2	2	–	24	17	–	–	12	–
1997	Eng.	2	2	–	18	11	–	–	9	–
Total		**113**	**110**	**1**	**3514**	**105**	**1**	**28**	**32.23**	**56**

Notes: 1. † *indicates World Cup*
2. *Highest score: 105 v. India, Bangalore, 1996*
3. *No bowling in limited-over internationals*
4. *'U.A.E.' = Sharjah in the United Arab Emirates.*
5. *The International Cricket Conference did not recognise matches v. 'Australia A' in 1994–95 as official, and they are excluded.*
6. *In one match (v. India at Dunedin, 1995) he batted at no. 7, scoring 0, in all other innings he opened the batting.*

BATTING, BY OPPONENT

	mat	inn	n.o.	runs	high	100	50	average
Sri Lanka	17	17	1	733	94	–	6	45.81
Pakistan	18	18	–	622	76	–	6	34.55
India	9	9	–	336	105	1	3	37.33
New Zealand	15	14	–	567	97	–	6	40.5
Bangladesh	1	–						
West Indies	23	23	–	485	66	–	2	21.08
England	8	8	–	243	79	–	3	30.37
South Africa	18	18	–	443	63	–	2	24.61
Zimbabwe	3	2	–	79	45	–	–	39.5
Kenya	1	1	–	6	6	–	–	6

HIGHEST PARTNERSHIPS

189	first wicket with M.E. Waugh	v. Sri Lanka, Perth 1995–96
154	first wicket with T.M. Moody	v. Pakistan, Brisbane 1989–90
147	second wicket with M.E. Waugh	v. New Zealand, Auckland 1995
135	first wicket with M.E. Waugh	v. Sri Lanka, Sydney 1995–96
133*	second wicket with M.E. Waugh	v. Sri Lanka, Sharjah 1994

SUMMARY OF CENTURY PARTNERSHIPS (20)

First wicket:	9 (3 with M.E. Waugh, 2 with T.M. Moody, 2 with M.J. Slater, 1 with G.R. Marsh, 1 with D.C. Boon)
Second wicket:	8 (4 with M.E. Waugh, 3 with D.M. Jones, 1 with R.T. Ponting)
Third wicket:	2 (1 with D.C. Boon, 1 with M.E. Waugh)
Fourth wicket:	1 (with S.G. Law)

CAPTAINCY, BY OPPONENT

opponent	matches	wins	tie	losses
West Indies (1992–93)	17	9	–	8
Pakistan (1992–93)	10	5	1	4
New Zealand (1993)	7	5	–	2
England (1993)	5	2	–	3
Sri Lanka (1994)	9	5	–	4
India (1994)	6	1	–	5
South Africa (1994)	9	5	–	4
Zimbabwe (1994–95)	3	3	–	–
Kenya (1996)	1	1	–	–
Total	**67**	**36**	**1**	**30**

Note: First season captained against each opponent is shown in brackets

CAPTAINCY, BY VENUE

	matches	wins	tie	losses
in Australia	27	16	1	10
in New Zealand	6	4	–	2
in England	3	1	–	2
in U.A.E.	3	2	–	1
in Sri Lanka	3	1	–	2
in Pakistan	7	5	–	2
in West Indies	5	1	–	4
in India	11	5	–	6
in South Africa	2	1	–	1

MARK TAYLOR COMPARED

Comparative statistics as at 10 April 1999

Most first-class runs for New South Wales:

runs		mat	100	average	from	to
8005	A.F. Kippax	87	32	67.26	1918–19	1935–36
6997	M.A. Taylor	100	17	41.40	1985–86	1998–99
6848	M.E. Waugh	84	23	56.59	1985–86	1998–99
6773	J. Dyson	94	14	44.27	1975–76	1988–89
6612	K.D. Walters	103	19	41.85	1962–63	1980–81
6419	W. Bardsley	83	20	53.04	1903–04	1925–26
6308	M.G. Bevan	74	25	61.84	1990–91	1998–99
6266	G.R.J. Matthews	135	9	37.98	1982–83	1997–98
5998	R.B. McCosker	79	19	48.76	1973–74	1983–84
5823	V.T. Trumper	73	15	51.08	1894–95	1913–14
5813	D.G. Bradman	41	21	98.53	1927–28	1933–34

Most Sheffield Shield runs for New South Wales:

runs		mat	100	average	from	to
6096	A.F. Kippax	61	23	70.88	1919–20	1935–36
6090	M.A. Taylor	85	15	42.29	1985–86	1998–99
5664	M.E. Waugh	69	21	54.99	1985–86	1998–99
5648	J. Dyson	82	11	42.15	1975–76	1988–89
5602	K.D. Walters	91	17	39.17	1962–63	1980–81
5567	G.R.J. Matthews	116	8	37.11	1982–83	1997–98
5369	M.G. Bevan	64	21	60.32	1990–91	1998–99
5280	R.B. McCosker	70	17	48.44	1973–74	1983–84
5208	S.R. Waugh	67	16	51.56	1984–85	1998–99

Most first–class catches for New South Wales:

132　M.A. Taylor, in 100 matches (1985–86—1998–99)

118　G.R.J. Matthews, in 135 matches (1982–83—1997–98)

106 R. Benaud, in 86 matches (1948–49—1963–64)
105 R.B. McCosker, in 79 matches (1973–74—1983–84)
102 R.B. Simpson, in 67 matches (1952–53—1977–78)

Most first–class catches in a season for New South Wales:
21 M.A. Taylor, in 12 matches (1988–89)
20 R.B. McCosker, in 13 matches (1982–83)
19 J. Dyson, in 9 matches (1984–85)

TEST CRICKET

Highest individual scores:

375	B.C. Lara	West Indies v. England, St John's	1994
365*	G.S. Sobers	West Indies v. Pakistan, Kingston	1958
364	L. Hutton	England v. Australia, The Oval	1938
340	S.T. Jayasuriya	Sri Lanka v. India, Colombo (Prem)	1997
337	Hanif Mohammad	Pakistan v. West Indies, Bridgetown	1958
336*	W.R. Hammond	England v. New Zealand, Auckland	1933
334*	M.A. Taylor	Australia v. Pakistan, Peshawar	1998
334	D.G. Bradman	Australia v. England, Leeds	1930

Highest scores by a Test captain:

334*	M.A. Taylor	Australia v. Pakistan, Peshawar	1998
333	G.A. Gooch	England v. India, Lord's	1990
311	R.B. Simpson	Australia v. England, Manchester	1964

Highest individual scores in Pakistan:

334*	M.A. Taylor	Australia v. Pakistan, Peshawar	1998
280	Javed Miandad	Pakistan v. India, Hyderabad	1982–83
257*	Wasim Akram	Pakistan v. Zimbabwe, Sheikhupura	1996
235	G.S. Chappell	Australia v. Pakistan, Faisalabad	1980

Most runs in a Test:

456 (333, 123)	G.A. Gooch	Eng. v. India, Lord's	1990
426 (334*, 92)	M.A. Taylor	Aust. v. Pak., Peshawar	1998
380 (247*, 133)	G.S. Chappell	Aust. v. N.Z., Wellington	1974

Most runs in a Test series:

runs		Tests	innings	average		
974	D.G. Bradman	5	7	139.14	Aust. v. Eng.	1930
905	W.R. Hammond	5	9	113.12	Eng. v. Aust.	1928–29
839	M.A. Taylor	6	11	83.9	Aust. v. Eng.	1989
834	R.N. Harvey	5	9	92.66	Aust. v. S. Af.	1952–53
829	I.V.A. Richards	4	7	118.42	W. Ind. v. Eng.	1976
827	C.L. Walcott	5	10	82.7	W. Ind. v. Aust.	1955
824	G.S. Sobers	5	8	137.33	W. Ind. v. Pak.	1958
810	D.G. Bradman	5	9	90	Aust. v. Eng.	1936–37
806	D.G. Bradman	5	5	201.5	Aust. v. S. Af.	1931–32

Most runs for Australia:

runs		Tests	inn	n.o.	high	100	average	from	to
11174	A.R. Border	156	265	44	205	27	50.56	1978–79	1994
7622	S.R. Waugh	115	185	35	200	19	50.81	1985–86	1999
7525	M.A. Taylor	104	186	13	334*	19	43.49	1988–89	1998–99
7422	D.C. Boon	107	190	20	200	21	43.66	1984–85	1995–96
7110	G.S. Chappell	87	151	19	247*	24	53.86	1970–71	1983–84
6996	D.G. Bradman	52	80	10	334	29	99.94	1928–29	1948
6149	R.N. Harvey	79	137	10	205	21	48.42	1947–48	1962–63

Most runs for Australia v. England:

runs		Tests	inn	100	average	from	to
5028	D.G. Bradman	37	63	19	89.78	1928–29	1948
3548	A.R. Border	47	82	8	56.31	1978–79	1993
2660	C. Hill	41	76	4	35.46	1896	1911–12
2619	G.S. Chappell	35	65	9	45.94	1970–71	1982–83
2574	S.R. Waugh	37	60	7	58.5	1986–87	1998–99
2496	M.A. Taylor	33	61	6	42.3	1989	1998–99

Most hundreds for Australia in England (no. of Tests in brackets):

11   D.G. Bradman (19)

 5   W. Bardsley (21), A.R. Border (25), M.A. Taylor (18), S.R. Waugh (18)

Most catches:

157 (world record)	M.A. Taylor, in 104 Tests (1988–89—1998–99)
156	A.R. Border, in 156 Tests (1978–79—1994)
122	G.S. Chappell, in 87 Tests (1970–71—1983–84)
122	I.V.A. Richards (W. Ind.), in 121 Tests (1974–75—1991)
120	M.C. Cowdrey (Eng.), in 114 Tests (1954–55—1974–75)
120	I.T. Botham (Eng.), in 102 Tests (1977—1992)
110	R.B. Simpson, in 62 Tests (1957–58—1978)
110	W.R. Hammond (Eng.), in 85 Tests (1927–28—1947)

100 Test appearances for Australia:

		v. Eng.	v. S. Af.	v. W. Ind.	v. N. Z.	v. Ind.	v. Pak.	v. Sri L.
156	A.R. Border	47	6	31	23	20	22	7
115	S.R. Waugh	37	10	24	17	8	14	5
115	I.A. Healy	33	12	28	11	9	14	8
107	D.C. Boon	31	6	22	17	11	11	9
104	M.A. Taylor	33	11	20	11	9	12	8

Most appearances as captain for Australia:

		wins	draws	tie	losses	from	to
93	A.R. Border	32	22	1	38	1984–85	1994
50	M.A. Taylor	26	11	–	13	1994	1998–99
48	G.S. Chappell	21	14	–	13	1975–76	1983
39	R.B. Simpson	12	15	–	12	1963–64	1978
30	I.M. Chappell	15	5	–	10	1970–71	1975

Carrying bat through innings for Australia (9 batsmen, 11 instances):

J.E. Barrett 67* out of 176 v. England at Lord's, 1890

W.W. Armstrong 159* out of 309 v. South Africa at Johannesburg, 1902

W. Bardsley 193* out of 383 v. England at Lord's, 1926

W.M. Woodfull 30* out of 66 v. England at Brisbane, 1928–29

W.M. Woodfull 73* out of 193 v. England at Adelaide, 1932–33

W.A. Brown 206* out of 422 v. England at Lord's, 1938

W.M. Lawry 49* out of 107 v. India at Delhi, 1969

W.M. Lawry 60* out of 116 v. England at Sydney, 1970–71

I.R. Redpath 159* out of 346 v. New Zealand at Auckland, 1974

D.C. Boon 58* out of 103 v. New Zealand at Auckland, 1986

M.A. Taylor 169* out of 350 v. South Africa at Adelaide, 1997–98

Highest opening partnerships:

382   R.B. Simpson and W.M. Lawry v. West Indies, Bridgetown 1965

329   G.R. Marsh and M.A. Taylor v. England, Nottingham 1989

260   M.A. Taylor and M.J. Slater v. England, Lord's 1993

Australians batting through complete Test day(3):

R.B. Simpson and W.M. Lawry v. West Indies, Bridgetown 1965 1st day

G.R. Marsh and M.A. Taylor v. England, Nottingham 1989 1st day

S.R. Waugh and G.S. Blewett v. South Africa, Johannesburg 1997 4th day

Index